# MOUNTAIN BIKING

# Park City & Beyond

## GREGG BROMKA

Off-Road PUBLICATIONS
Salt Lake City, Utah

www.offroadpub.com

Mountain biking has inherent risks and dangers. Hazards, whether cited in this book or not, can present themselves at any time and under a variety of circumstances and might occur where they did not exist previously. Every rider must use his/her best judgement to determine where, when, and under what circumstance to ride a particular route to ensure his/her safety, the safety of others, and to minimize environmental impacts.

All routes presented in this book were deemed open to bicycles at the time of publication; *however,* access privileges, management policies, land status, and signage may change without notice. Trails may be rerouted, altered, or closed, thus making the descriptions in this book inaccurate. In the event that a trail crosses private property, the land owner makes no claim that the trail or any portion of his/her property is free of hazards. Trespassing is a serious offense that is punishable by law. Obtain expressed permission from land owners to cross private property. That said, *Ride At Your Own Risk!*

Cover photo: Deer Valley Resort

Back cover photos:
Top: Deer Valley Resort
Left: Eagle Trail
Right: Mid Mountain Trail

Cover design by Off-Road Publications

Copyright © 2006 by Gregg Bromka/Off-Road Publications
All rights reserved.

No part of this book may be reproduced in any form or by any electronic or mechanical means, including information storage and retrieval systems, without permission in writing from the publisher, except by a reviewer, who may quote brief passages.

All text, maps, illustrations, and photographs by Gregg Bromka/Off-Road Publications.
Map shaded relief by *All Topo Maps: Utah,* by IGage, www.igage.com

First edition, first printing 2006
5 4 3 2 1
Printed in the United States of America

Comments, corrections, and suggestions are welcome and should be sent to the author c/o Off-Road Publications.

Published by
Off-Road Publications
3009 S 2000 East
SLC UT 84109
www.offroadpub.com

ISBN: 0-9624374-7-6
Library of Congress Catalog Card Number: 2005906415

# Table of Contents

Acknowledgments iv
Area of Coverage Map v
Ride Location Maps vi
Ride Guide (Rides Rated According to Difficulty) viii
Map Symbols xi

## Introduction
About this Guide 1
Visitor Information 5
Mountain Trails Foundation 5
Trail Description Format 5

## Stuff You Should Know
Trail Etiquette 9
Policies, Rules, and Regulations 11
Planning Your Ride 13

## What's In a Name?
Mining Moguls to Ski Moguls 19

## Park City Rides
1. Mormon Trail 25
2. Great Western Trail 28
3. Glenwild 33
4. McLeod Creek-Willow Creek Trails 38
5. Round Valley-Rail Trail 42
6. Union Pacific Rail Trail 46
7. Lost Prospector-Rail Trail 50
8. Solamere 55
9. Deer Crest 59
10. Deer Valley Resort 63
11. Tour des Suds 72
12. Town Loop 78
13. Sweeney's Switchbacks 82
14. Park City Mountain Resort 85
15. Spiro Trail 95
16. Beyond Spiro 99
17. Shadow Lake 105
18. The Canyons Resort 109
19. Mid Mountain Trail (North) 115
20. Mid Mountain Trail (Middle) 121
21. Mid Mountain Trail (South) 126
22. Mid Mountain Trail (the "Full Monty") 130
23. Mid Mountain Trail-Wasatch Crest 137
24. Park City to Salt Lake City 142
25. Park City to Provo 148

## Kamas Rides

| | | |
|---|---|---|
| 26. | Hoyt Peak | 157 |
| 27. | Upper Setting Road | 160 |
| 28. | Shingle Creek | 163 |
| 29. | Trial Lake | 166 |
| 30. | Beaver Creek Trail | 169 |
| 31. | Soapstone Basin | 173 |

## Heber Rides

| | | |
|---|---|---|
| 32. | Bench Creek Trail | 179 |
| 33. | Little South Fork Trail | 184 |
| 34. | Mill Hollow-Duchesne Ridge | 188 |
| 35. | Dock Flat | 191 |
| 36. | Willow Creek North Trail | 194 |
| 37. | Racetrack Peak | 197 |
| 38. | Strawberry Narrows Trail | 201 |
| 39. | Strawberry Peak | 206 |
| 40. | Bald Knoll-Windy Pass | 209 |
| 41. | South Fork Deer Creek Trail | 212 |
| 42. | Ridge Trail 157 | 216 |
| 43. | Dutch Hollow | 221 |

## Appendix

| | |
|---|---|
| Sources of Additional Information | 227 |
| About the Author | 228 |

## Acknowledgments

Hats off, rather helmets off, to the people of Park City–everyone: locals, who built the first trails (sometimes without permission) two decades ago and laid the foundation; land owners, who either turned their heads or gave a nod of approval; bike shops, who held grassroots races, adopted trails, and kept the passion alive; Deer Valley Resort, Park City Mountain Resort, and The Canyons Resort for turning their ski mountains into fat-tire playgrounds, Jan Wilking (Bicycle Utah) and the Park City Chamber for spearheading a movement to promote trails; Snyderville Basin Special Recreation District, who proved that government works for the people, and Mountain Trails Foundation for being liaison, fund raiser, trail builder, promoter, and peace keeper amidst it all.

A round of applause goes to Wasatch Mountain State Park for giving local riders trail building privileges and then adopting those trails into the Dutch Hollow Trail System. Continued applause goes to the Wasatch-

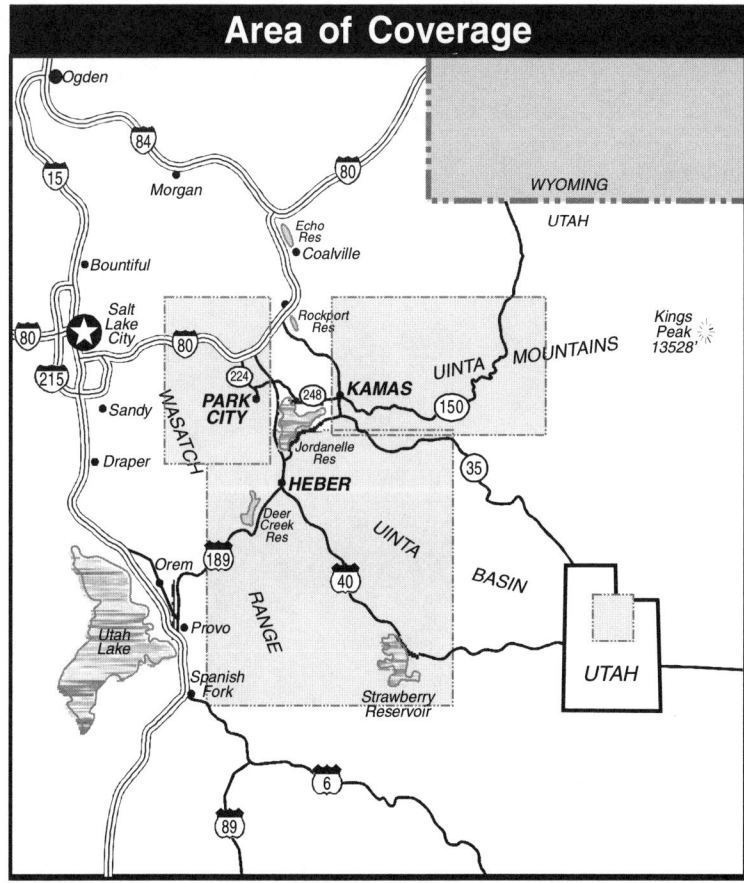

Cache National Forest (Kamas Ranger District) and Uinta National Forests (Heber and Pleasant Grove Ranger Districts) for keeping trails open to mountain bikes.

Thanks to Rob Matlak for editing; to Vince Desimone, Craig Williams, and Cindi Schwandt for proof-reading; and to Troy Duffin for all-around trail knowledge, trail construction, and a "take-the-bull-by-the-horns" leadership of the Mountain Trails Foundation.

High fives go my biker buddies who accompanied me on numerous rides, divulged cherished trail secrets, and patiently stopped for my photographic needs.

A technical thanks to Mark Silver and John Zobell (iGage)for complimentary use of *All Topo Maps: Utah*, which was used to generate the shaded relief profiles of the trail maps.

Lastly, and always, hugs and kisses to my wife, Tricia, for her undying support of my two-wheeled obsession, and to my daughters Joanna and Kelly, who, little do they know it, will be kick-ass mountain bikers some day.

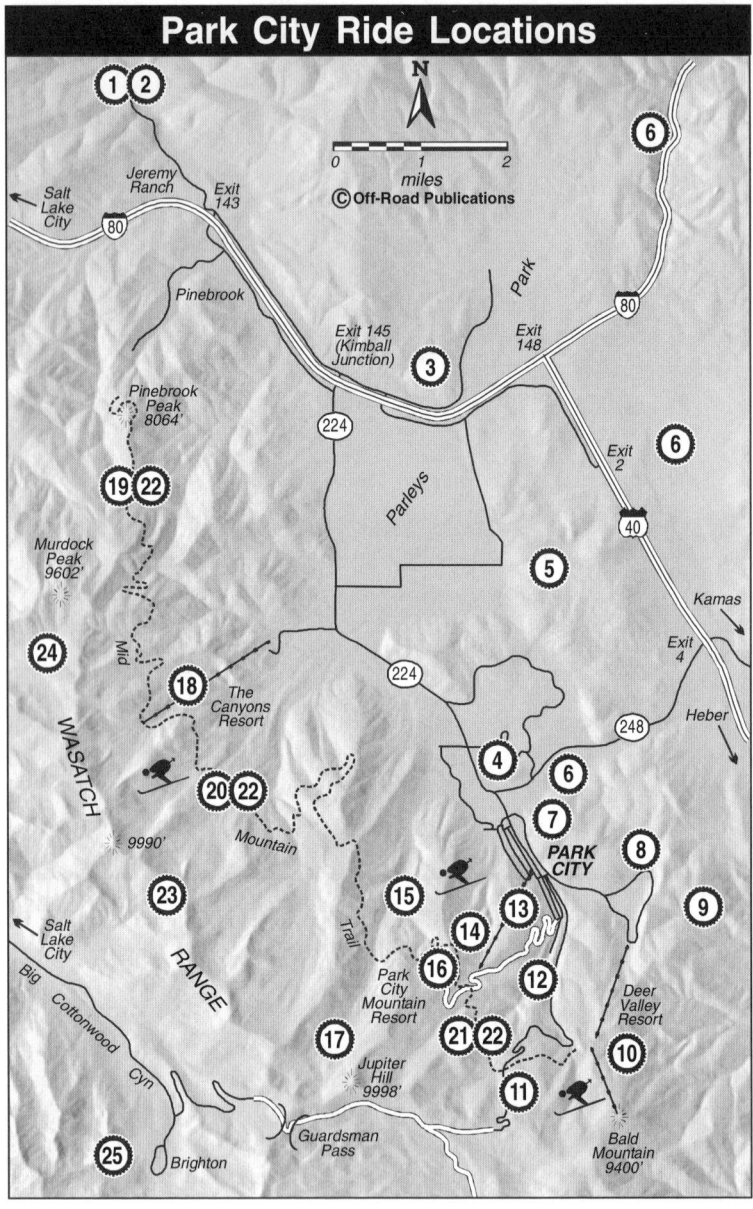

# Kamas Ride Locations

# Heber Ride Locations

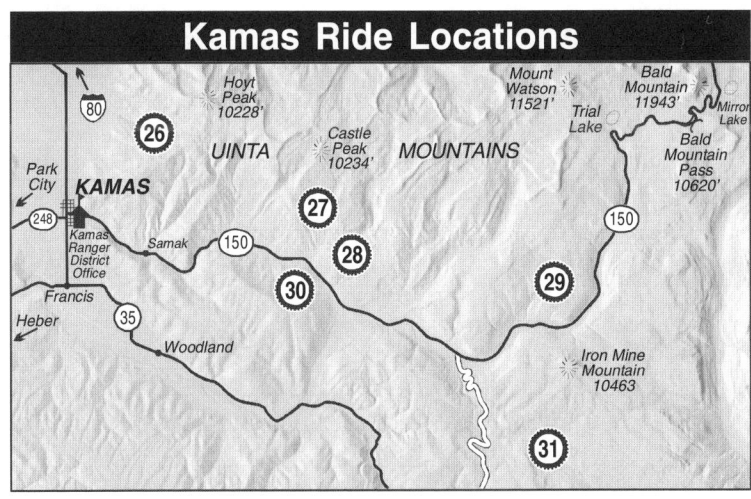

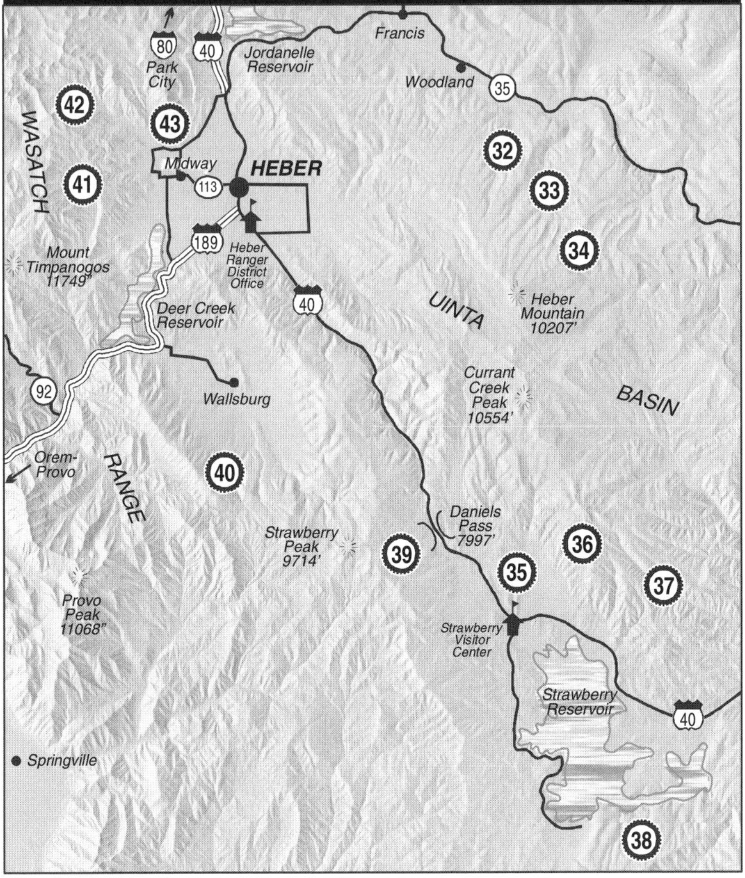

# Ride Guide
## Park City Rides

| Trail Name | Length (miles) | Type | Tread ST | Tread DT | Tread DR | Tread BP | Tread PV | Phys Diff | Tech Diff | Gain (feet) |
|---|---|---|---|---|---|---|---|---|---|---|
| Union Pacific Rail Trail | 26.6 | Out & Back | | | | ● | | E-S | 1-2 | 1300 |
| McLeod Creek - Willow Creek | 8.4 | Loop | | | | ● | | E | 1-2 | 360 |
| Deer Valley Resort | 50+ | ALL | ● | ● | | | | E+-X | 3-5+ | -2500 |
| The Canyons Resort | 14+ | ALL | ● | ● | | | | M-S | 2+-4+ | 200+ |
| Lost Prospector | 6.9 | Loop | ● | | | ● | ● | M | 1-3+ | 600 |
| Park City Mountain Resort | 30+ | ALL | ● | ● | | | | E+-M+ | 2-4+ | -1200 |
| MMT (South) | 9.9 | Loop | ● | ● | | | | M | 2-4 | 900 |
| Glenwild | 8.4 | Loop | ● | | ● | | | M | 2-3+ | 1000 |
| Round Valley | 14.2 | Loop | ● | ● | | ● | | M | 1-3+ | 720 |
| Mormon Trail | 9.0 | One-Way | ● | | | | | M | 2-5 | 1400 |
| MMT (North) | 7.4 | One-Way | ● | | | | | M | 2-3+ | 400 |
| Town Loop | 6.8 | Loop | ● | ● | | ● | ● | M | 1-4+ | 1000 |
| Spiro Trail | 7.2 | Loop | ● | ● | | | | M+ | 2-3+ | 1400 |
| Solamere | 7.5 | Loop | ● | | | | ● | M+ | 2+-4+ | 830 |
| Deer Crest | 9.7 | Loop | ● | | | | ● | M+ | 3-4+ | 1800 |
| Beyond Spiro | 15.6 | Loop | ● | ● | | | ● | M+ | 2-4+ | 2000 |
| Sweeney's Switchbacks | 5.9 | Loop | ● | ● | | | | S | 2-4+ | 1400 |
| Tour des Suds | 6.4 | Out & Back | ● | ● | | ● | ● | S | 1-4 | 2050 |
| Shadow Lake | 14.7 | Loop | ● | ● | | | | S | 2-3+ | 2400 |
| MMT (Middle) | 20.2 | Out & Back | ● | ● | | | | S | 2-3+ | 2300 |
| MMT (Full Monty) | 28-32 | Out & Back/One-Way | ● | ● | | | | S | 2-3+ | 2500+ |
| Park City-Salt Lake City | 29.0 | Out & Back | ● | ● | | | ● | S | 3-5 | 3250 |
| MMT-Wasatch Crest | 29.2 | Loop | ● | ● | | | | S+ | 2+-5 | 3800 |
| Great Western Trail | 19.4 | Loop | ● | | ● | | ● | S+ | 2+-4+ | 3000 |
| Park City-Provo | 47.5 | Out & Back | ● | ● | | ● | ● | Death March | 2-5 | 7500 |

**Type:**
- ↔ One-Way
- → Out & Back
- ↻ Loop

**Tread:**
- ST: Singletrack
- DT: Doubletrack
- DR: Dirt Road
- BP: Bike Path
- PV: Paved Road

**Physical Difficulty:**
- E: Easy
- M: Moderate
- S: Strenuous
- X: Extreme
- ☠ Death March

**Technical Difficulty:**
1: Smooth dirt & gravel roads
2: Smooth trails, washboard dirt roads.
3: Variably choppy trails & dirt roads
4: Rough, rutted, rocky trails & dirt roads.
5: Extremely rough trails & roads--caution!

# Rated According to Difficulty
## Park City Rides

| Highlights | Tr # | pg |
|---|---|---|
| Old RR turned to smooth rec. path. Out-&-back from PC is easy or go the distance one-way. | 6 | 46 |
| Paved & gravel paths along creeks and past historic farm. Great for kids and flatlanders. | 4 | 38 |
| Two lifts net you 2,500 vert. Easy cruising to "wicked" DH runs. So many trails, so little time. | 10 | 63 |
| Gondola to Red Pine Lodge. Ride MMT out-&-back, Crest loop, or descend great STs. | 18 | 109 |
| Great intro to ST riding. Good views of town. Finish on mellow Rail Trail. Lots of options. | 7 | 50 |
| Town Lift gains 1,200 vert. DH runs, cross-country trails, or hill climbs; plus family activities. | 14 | 85 |
| The mellow side of MMT links to spirited Little Chief & John's '99. Sweet, forested STs. | 21 | 126 |
| Great early-late season ride. Fun STs; add on Cobblestone Loop for more ST. | 3 | 33 |
| Scenic tour on bike paths and sagebrush STs. Best early-late season. Explore new trails. | 5 | 42 |
| Historic trail now ST. Water crossings and man-made structures are tricky. Great descent. | 1 | 25 |
| Canyons Resort to Pinebrook when completed. Must ride gondola or climb to get to it. | 19 | 115 |
| Lunchtime loop from town. Starts easy, gets tough. Dicey STs require honed skills. | 12 | 78 |
| One of many ways to ride classic "up" trail. Master this and move on to endless options. | 15 | 105 |
| Contrived trails around ritzy development on quality STs. Good views. | 8 | 55 |
| Spin Cycle and more through ritzy Deer Crest! Killer race course. | 9 | 59 |
| 2nd of many ways to ride classic "up" trail. Add on or subtract side routes--it's the PC way. | 16 | 99 |
| Short course that can kick your butt. Switchbacks 'o plenty. Beginners loath, experts love. | 13 | 82 |
| Classic climb that's always a guessing game. Race day is a kick; w/ picnic & lots of suds. | 11 | 72 |
| 3rd way of many to ride Spiro. Climb to alpine lake w/ awesome ST descent. | 17 | 105 |
| Classic ride between PCMR & Canyons. Loop it on Farm Trail for full effect. | 20 | 121 |
| IMBA Epic! Cornerstone of PC trails. Go Full Monty or make smaller loops. Many optons. | 23 | 130 |
| Ride over the Wasatch Range on killer STs. Big climb nets bigger descent. Utah top 10. | 24 | 142 |
| Cross country epic on MMT and Wasatch Crest. Killer views and trails. Lunch @ Red Pine. | 22 | 137 |
| Backcountry adventure on 3,000-mile trail. Climbs pack a punch. Remote--don't bonk! | 2 | 28 |
| Go big! Follow Great Western Trail across entire mountain range. Be fit, be prepared, or die! | 25 | 148 |

# Ride Guide

## Kamas Rides

| Trail Name | Length (miles) | Type | Tread ST | Tread DT | Tread DR | Tread BP | Tread PV | Phys Diff | Tech Diff | Gain (feet) |
|---|---|---|---|---|---|---|---|---|---|---|
| Beaver Creek Trail | 18.8 | ↔ | ● | ● | | | | E-M | 2-3+ | 1100 |
| Shingle Creek Trail | 5.0 | ↔ | ● | | | | | M | 2-5 | 460 |
| Soapstone Basin | 15.4 | ↻ | | ● | ● | | | M | 2-4 | 1400 |
| Upper Setting Road | 14.0 | ↔ | | ● | ● | | | M+ | 2+-4 | 2260 |
| Trial Lake | 17.0 | ↻ | | ● | ● | | ● | M+ | 2-4+ | 1750 |
| Hoyt Peak | 22.6 | ↻ | | ● | ● | | ● | S+ | 2-4+ | 3500 |

## Heber Rides

| Trail Name | Length (miles) | Type | Tread ST | Tread DT | Tread DR | Tread BP | Tread PV | Phys Diff | Tech Diff | Gain (feet) |
|---|---|---|---|---|---|---|---|---|---|---|
| Willow Creek North | 8.8 | ↻ | ● | ● | ● | | | E+ | 2-4 | 650 |
| Dutch Hollow | <17 | ALL | ● | ● | | | | E-S | 2-4+ | <1000 |
| Dock Flat | 12.6 | ↻ | | ● | ● | | ● | M | 2-3 | 900 |
| Mill Hollow-Duchesne Ridge | 12.1 | ↻ | | ● | ● | | | M | 2-3+ | 1450 |
| South Fork Deer Creek | 6.4 | ↻ | ● | | | | | M | 2-3+ | 1150 |
| Strawberry Peak | 16.5 | ↻ | | ● | ● | | | M | 2-3+ | 1750 |
| Bench Creek | 18 | ↻ | ● | ● | | | ● | S | 3-5 | 2400 |
| Ridge Trail 157 | 12.3 | → | ● | ● | | | | S | 3-4+ | 2100 |
| Strawberry Narrows | 21.4 | ↻ | ● | ● | | | ● | S | 2-5 | 2400 |
| Little South Fork | 22.6 | ↻ | ● | ● | ● | | ● | S | 3-5 | 2800 |
| Racetrack Peak | 30.4 | ↻ | | ● | ● | | ● | S | 2-3+ | 4000 |
| Bald Knoll | 22.0 | ↻ | ● | ● | | | ● | S+ | 3-5 | 3500 |

**Type:**
- ↔ One-Way
- → Out & Back
- ↻ Loop

**Tread:**
- ST: Singletrack
- DT: Doubletrack
- DR: Dirt Road
- BP: Bike Path
- PV: Paved Road

**Physical Difficulty:**
- E: Easy
- M: Moderate
- S: Strenuous
- X: Extreme
- ☠ Death March

**Technical Difficulty:**
1. Smooth dirt & gravel roads
2. Smooth trails, washboard dirt roads.
3. Variably choppy trails & dirt roads
4. Rough, rutted, rocky trails & dirt roads.
5. Extremely rough trails & roads--caution!

# Rated According to Difficulty

## Kamas Rides

| Highlights | Tr # | pg |
|---|---|---|
| Easiest ride in the book. Great for families--take a picnic. Many trailheads. ATVs on part. | 30 | 169 |
| Only ST in Uintas that's worth a damn, but damn those water bars. Short, hard climbs. | 28 | 163 |
| Loop around alpine basin w/ option to stunning viewpoint. Tough climb then easy cruising. | 31 | 173 |
| Steady climb on smooth and choppy DT. Options to alpine lake or "wicked" ST descent. | 27 | 160 |
| Scenic tour of mountains, lakes, & rivers. Nasty climb, then easy. Fast highway descent. | 2 | 166 |
| Mother of hillclimbs. Huge view of Wasatch "back" from top. Fast, jackhammer descent. | 26 | 157 |

## Heber Rides

| Highlights | Tr # | pg |
|---|---|---|
| Uintas best kept secret. Easy cruise, short climb, blazing descent, 7 water crossings. | 36 | 194 |
| New trail system in WMSP. Easy to hard, short to long, smooth to technical. Spring & fall. | 43 | 221 |
| Tour around Strawberry countryside. One hard climb. Good grub at Daniels Summit Café. | 35 | 191 |
| Reservoir to ridge loop. Steady climb, rolling DT, secret ST return. High elev = cool climes. | 34 | 188 |
| Sweet American Fork ST. Good climb, fun descent. Add-on more trails nearby. | 41 | 212 |
| Tour of Strawberry Ridge w/ 360° view from peak of Wasatch and Uintas. Good cruising. | 39 | 206 |
| Locals' favorite about to go mainstream. Challenging backcountry STs. Worth the drive. | 32 | 179 |
| American Fork classic ST. Buffed & rugged trails. Great descent at end. Killer views. | 42 | 216 |
| Seldom-used ST that begs to be ridden. Ride loop on dirt roads or out-&-back on ST only. | 38 | 201 |
| Big climb on roads nets killer descent on ST. Shuttles are for wimps! Agony hill-Ugh! | 33 | 184 |
| Dirt road tour to remote areas. Wicked climb on "back nine," then blazing descent. | 37 | 197 |
| Explore GWT to remote areas. Rugged trails. Amazing views of S. Wasatch Range. | 40 | 209 |

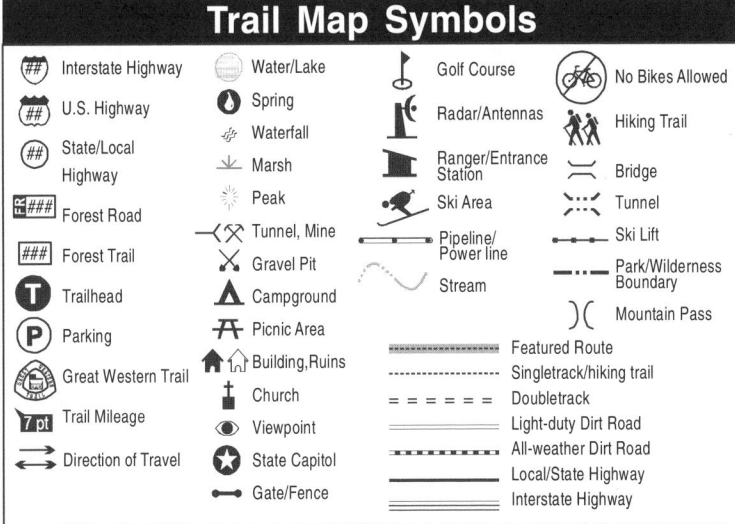

## Trail Map Symbols

# INTRODUCTION

# Introduction 1

## About This Guide

Let's get one thing straight: mountain biking in Park City is difficult, not so much physically—although Park City has it's fair share of tough rides—but navigationally. Open up the *Park City Trail Map*, by Mountain Trails Foundation, and you'll see a dumbfounding spider's web of trails. With nearly 350 miles of designated mountain biking routes within a 5-mile radius of town—more trails are on the drawing board—Park City could very well have the greatest density of trails per square mile of any resort town in the nation! That's something to brag about. But the abundance of trails also means innumerable choices, choices that inevitably leave riders asking, "Where do I start?" and "Where do I go?" This book answers both questions.

*Mountain Biking Park City & Beyond* attempts the impossible by unraveling Park City's tangle of trails and presenting logical routes of varying length, difficulty, and attraction. It's not the final word because any given trail can be ridden differently. For instance, if you ask 10 people how they ride Spiro Trail, then you'll likely get 10 different answers. If you make your way to the "Five-way junction" at Park City Mountain Resort, then you'll have to choose between five different options. To say Park City has 25 rides, cut and dry, is not only misleading but laughable.

To fully grasp the concept of mountain biking in Park City, you must look beyond the simplicity of the Table of Contents to the complexity of the chapters themselves. Riding in Park City is all about options: linking together trail segments, adding more trails, or subtracting others. That's why nearly every chapter has options, options, options, which provide endless opportunities to customize your ride. Stick to the 25 Park City routes in this book and you'll go home happy, but if you add a twist to your favorite route or explore a previously passed trail, you'll become caught up in the never-ending world of mountain biking bliss that is Park City.

But wait, there's more. Park City is a singletrack lover's dream come true, that's for sure. But if the day arrives when you tire of Park City's trails (heaven forbid), or if you simply long for the solitude of a backcountry retreat, then head to the mountainlands surrounding Kamas and Heber. Hundreds of miles of exceptional mountain biking routes lead through the Wasatch-Cache National Forest, Uinta National Forest, and Wasatch Mountain State Park. Here's a summary of what you'll find in all three locations.

### Park City:
The word is out: Mid Mountain Trail (MMT) is the place. Dedicated as an IMBA Epic Ride in 2004, the Mid Mountain Trail has proven to be the most significant trail-building project in Park City's mountain biking his-

<< Joe descends Eagle Trail—and likes it!

Mid Mountain Trail is now the cornerstone of Park City's trails network.

tory. At the time of publication, MMT was just a few miles short of fulfilling its 30-mile-long quest to link together Deer Valley Resort, Park City Mountain Resort, The Canyons Resort, and Pinebrook near I-80. MMT is not just a ride of attrition. Since it intersects dozens of trails along the way and can be reached by chairlifts at all three resorts, MMT can be ridden in a variety of ways, so everyone can enjoy it.

All three of Park City's ski resorts, Deer Valley Resort, Park City Mountain Resort, and The Canyons Resort, have opened their doors to mountain biking, and each offers a refreshing twist on the lift-served mountain biking theme. Deer Valley's ever-expanding trail system is a freerider's haunt that runs from the top of Bald Mountain to the base at Snow Park Lodge. Park City Mountain Resort's Town Lift takes you from Park Avenue to middle-mountain elevations where you can freewheel back to the base or pursue an endless array of cross-country trails. The Canyons Resort's gondola puts you right on the Mid Mountain Trail, where you can explore in both directions or link to other downhill runs at the resort.

Spin Cycle lives! The corkscrew, amusement park-style trail of old Telemark Park has been revived but relocated to the exclusive Deer Crest subdivision. It's as thrilling as ever. Link Spin Cycle with neighboring trails and you have the making of one helluva race course. Speaking of racing, Park City plays host to local and national mountain biking events for cross-country and downhill racers and is the site of the new Endurance 100 Race.

Hang with the locals on an evening group ride and get the inside scoop on trails.

North of town and tucked away in East Canyon, the Mormon Trail follows a historic pioneer trail, and a nearby ridge-top singletrack traces part of the 3,000-mile Great Western Trail.

Although always at the mercy of "progress," the contrived trails of Solamere, Glenwild, and Sun Peak developments appear destined to withstand the test of time and offer spring and fall jaunts on quality singletracks when higher routes are snow-bound. Round Valley and Lost Prospector, also excellent early and late season rides, offer tasty singletracks for those who don't want to scale entire mountains. Short on time? Take a lunchtime ride on Sweeney's Switchbacks or Town Loop; both leaving right out the back door of town.

But if you're jonesing for rides that epitomize the original concept of "mountain" biking, then test your mettle against two trans-Wasatch epics: Park City to Salt Lake City and Park City to Provo. Whoa!

### Kamas:
The Mirror Lake Highway out of Kamas, a designated Scenic Byway, provides access to a half dozen rides in the western Uinta Mountains. Families and first-time bikers will enjoy the tame Beaver Creek Trail, which has been extended to nine miles long. Across the highway, Shingle Creek Trail is the only true singletrack in the region. Soapstone Basin remains an all-time favorite where doubletracks circle a vast alpine meadow; an optional spur takes you to a jaw-dropping view of deep canyons and some of the state's tallest peaks.

Road ride anyone?

Like to climb? Upper Setting Road and the Trial Lake loop rise from the lush valley floor to pristine alpine lakes for which the Uinta Mountains are famous. But the granddaddy of hill climbs is the burly grind to Hoyt Peak. Reward for your effort is a magnificent view of the Wasatch Range's "backside" and a descent that seems endless.

### Heber:

Only a stone's throw from Park City, Heber is a nexus of mountain biking for those wanting to escape the high-zoot trails of Park City. Heber's trails are both close enough for day trips and far enough away for a weekend camping vacation.

Are you a singletrack purist who would go to the ends of the earth for a choice one-laner? There's no need to my friend because all you have to do is drive as far as Wasatch Mountain State Park's new Dutch Hollow Trail System. Located only minutes from Heber, Dutch Hollow boasts nearly 20 miles of trails and doubletracks designated for mountain bikes that range from tame to technical. Its low elevation is prime for early and late-season riding.

If you're a Wasatch Range mountain biking veteran, then you likely know about the network of excellent singletracks in American Fork Canyon. With access from Heber, you can put a new twist on two classics: Ridge Trail 157 and South Fork Deer Creek Trail.

Woodland pales in comparison to the nation's big name mountain bike destinations, (in fact you might miss it if you blink while driving through), but its Bench Creek and Little South Fork Trails are classic backcountry adventures you'll never forget. And Willow Creek North and Strawberry Narrows Trails are secluded, seldom-traveled trails just begging to be tickled by knobby tires.

If singletrack is not your forte and you would rather spin on dirt roads, then try the mellow Dock Flat Loop, the moderately challenging Strawberry Peak loop, or the burly Racetrack Peak loop.

## Visitor Information

Everyone knows Park City is home to the Sundance Film Festival, but the list of other activities and events that give Park City its pulsating beat would constitute a small book in itself: sports and recreation, arts, dance, music, film, theater, dining, nightlife, and much more. The Park City Chamber of Commerce and Visitor's Bureau is your one-stop-shopping source for all things Park City: (800) 453-1360, (435) 649-6100, www.parkcityinfo.com

## Mountain Trails Foundation

Mountain Trails Foundation (MTF) is a non-profit organization in Park City whose mission is "to promote and preserve trail access for all non-motorized users." Their mission includes 1) Education of the public on matters relating to land use planning and conservation practices in the use and improvement of land, particularly with respect to multi-use trails and trail systems. 2) The physical improvement of trail systems through signage, trail construction and maintenance operations on trails. 3)Facilitating the acquisition and administration of trail easements by public agencies or in some cases the acquisition of trail easements directly for the use and benefit of the public.

In short, MTF is largely responsible for maintaining access to the trails you ride. MTF produces the *Park City Trail Map,* which is an indispensable supplement to this guidebook and the most up-to-date source of trail information. For more information on MTF, visit their web site: www.mountaintrails.org.

## Trail Description Format

Trail descriptions have been developed to provide you with all the necessary information to make your bike ride safe and enjoyable. Here's how each trail chapter is laid out:

### Just the Facts:
This data provides the ride's bare-bones specifications that detective Joe Friday of the television series *Dragnet* would want to know. For some bikers, this is all that is needed.

**Location** is the proximity of the trail from the nearest town or city.

**Length** is the total miles to complete the route.

**Type** is the route's layout. *Out-and-back:* You ride from the trailhead to a distant location and return by retracing your tracks. Mileage is for the entire round trip. *Loop:* You ride from the trailhead to a distant location(s) and return to the trailhead via a different route or a continuation of the same route. You always move forward across new terrain. *One-way:* You ride from the trailhead to a distant location, where the ride ends. You'll need to arrange a vehicle shuttle to return to the starting point.

**Tread** is the route's surface, and the miles of each kind of tread for the entire route is given. *Singletrack* is a narrow one lane dirt path, i.e., a maintained or unmaintained trail or game path. *Doubletrack* is an unimproved dirt road consisting of dual parallel lanes, usually separated by a raised berm of dirt or grass, i.e., a "jeep" road. High clearance or four-wheel-drive may be required. *Light-duty dirt roads* and *all-weather gravel roads* are generally suitable for passenger cars when dry, but may require four-wheel-drive when wet. *Paved road* is any secondary, primary, or interstate roadway.

**Physically:** Physical difficulty is the amount of exertion required to complete the ride. These ratings are subjective and are relative to other rides in this guidebook only and may differ significantly from those of rides in other locations or other books. *Easy-Easy+:* up to 10 miles and/or less than 1,000 feet of elevation gain. These rides are geared for bikers who are new to the sport or new to the area, ride infrequently, and possess basic off-road riding skills. *Moderate-moderate+:* 10-20 miles and/or 1,000-2,000 feet of elevation gain. These rides are geared for bikers who ride periodically, possess good off-road riding skills, and are game for a small adventure. *Strenuous-strenuous+:* 20-30 miles and/or 2,000-3,000 feet of elevation gain. These rides are geared for strong bikers who ride on a regular basis, are acclimated to high elevations, and possess advanced bike handling skill. Typically, these rides *go places! Extreme:* over 30 miles and/or more than 3,000 feet of elevation gain. These routes are reserved for elite bikers who have indefatigable fitness and razor sharp skills.

**Technically:** Technical difficulty is the measure of bike-handling skill needed, or the probability that a rider will have to touch down a foot ("dab") or dismount and walk part of a trail. Technical difficulty is based on, but not limited to, sand, gravel, loose or embedded rocks, ruts, fallen trees or limbs, unusually steep ascents or descents, water bars, water crossings, and cow pies. *Tech 1-1+:* smooth dirt roads with light sand, gravel, or washboards. *Tech 2-2+:* lightly rutted or rocky dirt roads and doubletracks or mostly smooth singletracks. *Tech 3-3+:* variably rough, rocky, and rutted doubletracks and singletracks that require you to keep your eye on the trail and watch your front wheel—a typical singletrack. *Tech 4-4+:* very rough, rocky, and rutted doubletracks and singletracks with persistent obstacles that warrant your full attention. Dismounting and walking or hike-a-biking may be required. *Tech 5-5+:* extremely rough trail conditions or severe gradients that can result in dire consequences if you try to ride a section and fail. Hike-a-biking for extended periods is not uncommon.

**Gain** is the total amount of climbing (in feet) required to complete a ride. On out-and-back rides, you'll have to re-climb every hill you descend, and gain reflects this total elevation.

**Why Should U Ride This Trail** sets the tone of a ride and gives you a glimpse into the ride's inner soul. Each ride is unique, and this section should help you decide is a given ride appeals to you.

### Details:

This section presents the turn-by-turn narrative necessary to complete the ride without getting in over your head or lost, heaven forbid. Although a painstaking attempt has been made to accurately describe every route, the narratives are not exhaustive. Part of the fun of mountain biking is following and finding the route, and every biker must assume responsibility for paying attention to his/her surroundings and for having a general sense of direction. Miles set in bold type (**mX.X**) in the trail description correspond to miles noted on the trail maps. Even if your bike computer differs from the mileages listed, you'll still be able to cross-reference the description to the trail map to determine your whereabouts and to guage your progress.

### Know Before You Go:

This lists notes, precautions, and unusual hazards that pertain to the trail along with any fees, regulations, and restrictions.

### Maps & More Information:

This section lists the standard USGS (United States Geological Survey) 1:24,000 scale (7.5 minute) topographic quadrangle(s) that cover the entire trail, plus sources to contact for additional information.

### Trailhead Access:

This provides directions for driving to the trailhead from the closest town or major roadway.

### Trail Maps & Elevation Graphs:

Trail maps were computer generated using USGS topographic maps as a base. The described route is highlighted with gray shading to distinguish it from other trails and roads. Mileages inside little black boxes correspond to those set in bold type (**mX.X**) in the "Details" category. The elevation graph shows the route's change in elevation, distance, and tread surfaces, and notes key landmarks or locations.The shaded relief aspect of the maps was generated by *All Topo Maps: Utah*, version 7.0 by **iGage**. This software package of digitized topographic maps can be purchased at most major outdoor retailers or by contacting iGage: 1545 S 1100 East, Salt Lake City UT 84105, www.igage.com, (801) 412-0011.

# STUFF YOU SHOULD KNOW

## Trail Etiquette

Webster defines *etiquette* as "... the forms [and] manners established by convention as acceptable or required for social relations ..." Etiquette, therefore, applies to both tea parties and mountain biking, and riding responsibly is a subject that cannot be overemphasized. Your every action has an impact on the trail, on the environment, and on how you are perceived by others.

The "Rules of the Trail" by the International Mountain Bike Association (IMBA) provides a simple guideline to riding right. Although it may seem lengthy, it boils down to basic common sense: *Expect and respect* others, and *be kind* to the dirt beneath your tires. Keep trails open by setting a good example of environmentally sound and socially responsible off-road cycling.

**1. Ride on Open Trails Only:** *Respect* trail and road closures (ask if uncertain); avoid trespassing on private land; obtain permits or other authorization as may be required. Federal and state wilderness areas are closed to cycling. The way you ride will influence trail management decisions and policies.

Only You Can Prevent . . . Trail Closures!

**2. Leave No Trace:** Be sensitive to the dirt beneath you. Recognize different types of soils and trail construction; practice low-impact cycling. Wet and muddy trails are more vulnerable to damage. When the trailbed is soft, consider other riding options. This also means staying on existing trails and not creating new ones. Don't cut switchbacks. Be sure to pack out at least as much as you pack in.

**3. Control Your Bicycle**: Inattention for even a second can cause problems. Obey all bicycle speed regulations and recommendations.

**4. Always Yield the Trail:** Let your fellow trail users know you're coming. A friendly greeting or bell is considerate and works well; don't startle others. Show your respect when passing by slowing to a walking pace or even stopping. Anticipate trail users around corners or in blind spots. Yielding means slow down, establish communication, be prepared to stop if necessary, and pass safely.

<< Enough said!

# 10 Mountain Biking Park City & Beyond

Give horses lots of room by stepping off the trail and waiting for them to pass.

**5. Never scare animals:** All animals are startled by an unannounced approach, a sudden movement, or a loud noise. This can be dangerous for you, others, and the animals. Give animals extra room and time to adjust to you. When passing horses, use special care and follow directions from the horseback riders (ask if uncertain). Running cattle and disturbing wildlife is a serious offense. Leave gates as you found them or as marked.

**6. Plan ahead:** Know your equipment, your ability, and the area in which you are riding—and prepare accordingly. Be self-sufficient at all times, keep your equipment in good repair, and carry necessary supplies for changes in weather or other conditions. A well-executed trip is a satisfaction to you and not a burden to others. Always wear a helmet and appropriate safety gear.

Granted, this may seem like a lot to remember when your sole objective is to pedal through the woods for a while. If anything, remember this one point every time you ride: Just because you *can* doesn't mean you *should!*

Riding skillfully is *cool*. Riding recklessly is *lame*.

## Policies, Rules, & Regulations

**Park City:** Mountain biking in Park City is unique because all lands surrounding town are privately owned, up to the Wasatch Crest where public National Forest lands begin. Through the concerted efforts of trail advocacy groups, local and regional government agencies, private landowners, businesses, and individuals, public recreational access on these private lands has been granted to a large extent; however, trail access privileges may change or be denied without notice. You are considered a guest when on private property. Stay on trails posted open to recreational uses, obey all signs restricting travel, and do not trespass. The *Park City Trails Map,* by Mountain Trails Foundation, is your best source for current trail information.

**United States Forest Service:** The Wasatch-Cache and Uinta National Forests maintain an open policy toward mountain bike use. Bicycles are allowed on all roads and on trails that are posted open to bicycles. Be aware that trails and roads may not be constructed or maintained specifically for bicycles and that you may encounter motor vehicles on some routes.

**Wilderness Areas:** Mountain bikes are *not* allowed in state and federal wilderness areas. Pertaining to the area of coverage in this guidebook, this includes the High Uintas and Mount Timpanogos Wildernesses.

Play by the rules and everyone is happy.

Just because you can doesn't mean you should.

**Mill Creek Canyon:** Although Mill Creek Canyon is on the Salt Lake side of the Wasatch Range, one trail in this book ventures into Mill Creek Canyon—Park City to Salt Lake City. *Recreational Use Fee:* A fee is charged per vehicle upon exiting Mill Creek Canyon ($2.25 per vehicle). Bicyclists and pedestrians who do not drive up Mill Creek Canyon are not charged the fee, currently. Contact the Public Lands Information Center at REI for additional information: (801) 466-6411.

*Odd-Even Day Trail Access Policy:* Mountain bikes are allowed on upper Mill Creek Canyon trails on *even-numbered* calender days. Mountain bikes are not allowed on upper Mill Creek Canyon trails on *odd-numbered* calender days. Upper Mill Creek Canyon trails are defined as Big Water, Little Water, and Upper Mill Creek/Great Western Trail. This regulation does not apply to Mill Creek Pipeline or Wasatch Crest Trails.

*Leash Policy:* Dogs must be leashed on all trails in Mill Creek Canyon on even-numbered calender days. Dogs may be off leash on all trails on odd-numbered calender days. Your pet must be under control at all times.

Detours, closures, get used to it—it's Park City.

**American Fork Canyon/Alpine Scenic Highway:** The Uinta National Forest has implemented a recreational use fee for UT 92/Alpine Scenic Highway between American Fork Canyon and Provo Canyon and for the Cascade Springs area. Vehicles must pay a fee when entering the area: $3 per vehicle for a three-day pass.

**Mirror Lake Scenic Byway:** The Wasatch-Cache National Forest has implemented a recreational use fee for UT 150/Mirror Lake Scenic Byway. Vehicles must pay a fee if they stop and park along the road or at any recreational site. The fee is $3.00 per day per vehicle or $6.00

# Stuff You Should Know 13

Know where you can and can not ride.

per week per vehicle and is payable at self-serve stations or at the Kamas Ranger District Office (50 East Center St., Kamas UT 84036, (435) 783-4338).

**Ski Areas:** Each of Park City's three ski areas, Deer Valley Resort, Park City Mountain Resort, and The Canyons Resort, are privately owned. Mountain bike use is allowed but restrictions may apply. Check with each resort for specific policies and obey all signs restricting travel. Be alert to activity on slopes above you. Maintenance operations and heavy machinery may be present at any time.

**Watershed Areas:** Bicycles are not restricted from any canyons that provide culinary water to the Wasatch Front; however, domestic animals (pets, horses, and grazing animals) are not allowed in Big Cottonwood and Little Cottonwood Canyons, and Mountain Dell Canyon, except by special permit. Domestic animals are currently allowed in Mill Creek Canyon.

## Planning Your Ride

The trails in the Park City, Kamas, and Heber areas range from short jaunts just out of town to remote backcountry treks. While it is reasonable to adjust your preparedness for each ride, never underestimate your need for water and food, the prospect of rapidly changing weather, and the possibility of having to address a mechanical or health-related problem.

## Water and Food:
Water and food are essential to life, and the lack of either one can turn the most blissful ride into an agonizing nightmare. Play it safe and overestimate your consumption of both; the added weight is trivial. Remember the cyclists' axiom: Eat before you feel hungry, drink before you feel thirsty. Consume food and water at regular intervals, rather than one large binge midway through the ride.

## Tools and Repair Equipment:
Some people ride with just the shirt on their back, others seem to pack a complete hardware store. Learn the basic on-trail repair techniques, or ride with someone who has. Don't wait for a mishap on the trail to realize how little you know about your bike. Carry the "basic tool kit" at least, which can be stuffed easily into a small under-the-saddle pack:
- Tire levers
- Patch kit
- Spare tube
- Frame-mount pump or compressed air cartridge

**Now consider these extras:**
- Multi-purpose tool
- Chain tool
- Crescent wrench, pliers, or vise grips
- Flat head and/or Phillips screwdrivers
- Hex and socket wrenches
- Spoke wrench
- Duct tape
- Pocket knife

**Still more stuff:**

Spare brake and derailleur cables, chain lube, sunscreen, lip balm, water purification tablets, toilet paper, and zipper-top bags for left over snacks. And don't forget money, in case you need a bribe for a lift.

*A word of advice:* It's reasonable to share the load if you ride with a group, but stay close together or regroup often. It does little good for the lead rider to be carrying the pump and patch kit if another rider is a mile behind with a flat. If you ride solo, you may have to carry the whole works.

**Accessories & Emergency Gear:**
- Lock
- Cyclometer
- Camera
- Waterproof jacket
- Waterproof matches or lighter
- Compass and map
- Flashlight or headlamp
- Plastic whistle
- Emergency blanket

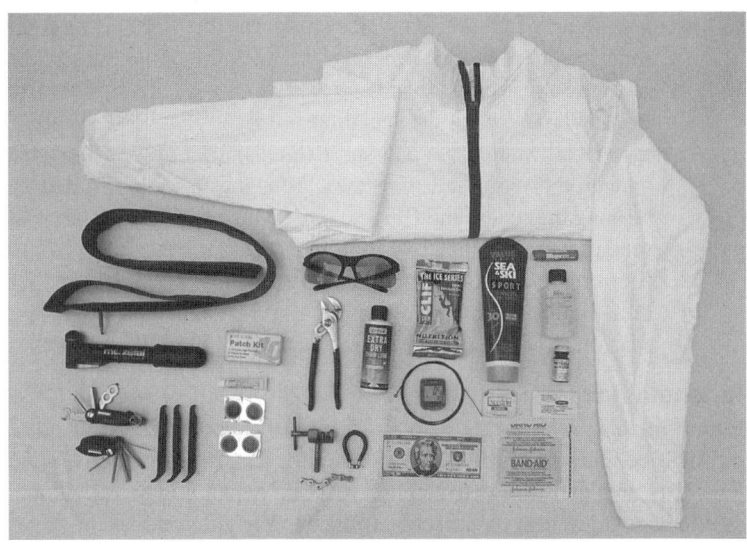

Left: the essentials (spare tube, pump, multi-tool, tire levers, patch kit); middle: more stuff (energy bar, sunscreen, chain tool, pliers, spoke wrench, spare cable, first aid, water purification tablets, lip balm, money); top: lightweight waterproof/breathable jacket.

- First aid kit
- Cell phone

**Clothing:**

Clothing is a personal matter and varies from no fashion to high zoot. Regardless, consider function as well as style.

- Helmet: Today's helmets are incredibly lightweight, well ventilated, and utterly vogue. Like the American Express Card, "don't leave home without it."
- Padded bicycling shorts and gloves: Whether skin-tight lycra or cargo style, padded bike shorts cushion the bumps and prevent chaffing and blistering where you need it most.
- Shirt: Synthetic materials are preferred over cotton because they wick moisture away from your skin and dry quickly.
- Shoes: Lightweight hiking boots or mountain biking shoes provide support both in the pedals and on the trail.
- Extra layers: Layering is the key to maintaining a comfortable body temperature and preventing excessive perspiration while exercising, especially in cool or damp weather. Wear layers of synthetic materials next to the skin and a nylon or breathable-weatherproof shell on the outside. Cotton sweat pants and sweaters are poor choices, especially for rainy weather.

- Rainwear: Afternoon thunderstorms during the summer are common in the Wasatch Range and Uinta Mountains, even if the morning sky is cloud free. Pack along lightweight rainwear or at least a garbage bag—just cut three holes for your head and arms.
- Eye wear: Sunglasses and sport shields are highly fashionable and protect your sensitive eyes from the sun's harmful rays, passing branches, and flying debris. Make sure glasses are fastened securely with a retention strap.
- Sunscreen: Sunscreen is a must because the greater Park City area is considered high elevation. Exposed skin can burn in less than one hour. Use a sunscreen with a minimum SPF of 30.

## Potential Hazards:

Health-related problems can result from lack of preparedness, inadequate physical conditioning, and plain misfortune. Weather conditions in the Park City area can vary between the extremes depending on the season: sweltering valley heat to cool moist forests to frigid wind-swept ridges and peaks. Plan for current and forecasted weather conditions.

**Lightning:** During the summer, afternoon thunderstorms are common and they can be violent. Don't be fooled by the morning's cerulean sky. If lightning is proximal and strikes are frequent, get off ridges quickly. Seek shelter at lower elevations in valleys, between boulders in rocky slopes, or in heavily forested areas. Avoid shallow caves, open meadows, lone trees, or isolated tree clusters. Separate yourself from your bike. Then get low: sit or lie down.

The best protection against being caught in a thunderstorm is to start your ride early and complete it by midafternoon. Always carry some form of rainwear.

**Hypothermia:** The lowering of the body's core temperature is not just a winter-related health concern. Frigid mountain rains and the lack of food and water can attenuate the onset of hypothermia. Symptoms include feeling deep cold, numbness, shivering, poor coordination, slowing of pace, and slurred speech. Advanced symptoms include blueness in the skin, fingers, or lips; severe fatigue; irrationality and disorientation; and decreased shivering followed by stiffening of muscles.

Treat a hypothermic victim by seeking shelter and warmth. Replace wet clothes with dry clothing, or cover the victim with wind-proof materials. Encourage the victim to ingest food and warm fluids or to move at a slow and steady pace to raise body temperature.

**Heat exhaustion:** *Hyper*thermia (raised body temperature) is caused by exposure to hot environments and overexertion. Blood vessels in the skin become so dilated to promote internal cooling that blood to the brain and other vital organs is reduced to inadequate levels. Symptoms include nausea, dizziness, mild confusion, headache, slight temperature elevation, and dehydration. Cool the victim by seeking shade or by wetting the victim and fanning vigorously, and encourage drinking cool fluids.

**Altitude sickness:** Park City rests at 7,000 feet above sea level, and trails rise to over 10,000 feet. Ascending to these high elevations without acclimating may produce headaches, fatigue, loss of appetite, drowsiness, and apathy. (It's about the same feeling as a hangover.) Treatment includes rest, adequate consumption of fluids and food, and pain relievers. If you're visiting from low elevations, proceed slowly at first or allow an extra day to adjust to the new environment.

**Bad Water:** Water does not have to be visually polluted to be bad. Mine wastes, bacteria and viruses, or *Giardia lamblia* can pollute water. Giardia, which is introduced to surface waters from animal and human waste, causes intestinal distress, cramps, and loss of appetite. Symptoms can last for weeks if not treated medically. Avoid all surface waters and carry plenty of water with you; otherwise, treat the water by boiling it for 10-15 minutes, purifing it through a filtration device, or disinfecting it with chemicals (Potable Aqua, Globaline, or iodine). Keep in mind that boiling or disinfecting water does not rid it of mineral toxins from mining waste.

**Hunting Season:** Big-game hunting season in Utah runs from early September through the end of October. Fortunately for mountain bikers, hunting is not allowed on most of the lands surrounding Park City; however, much of the Uinta Mountains is prime deer and elk habitat. Avoid the opening and closing days of hunting season, stay on main dirt roads, forfeit remote singletracks, and wear brightly colored clothing. Contact the Utah Division of Wildlife Resources for more information: (801) 538-4700, www.wildlife.utah.gov.

# WHAT'S IN A NAME?

## Mining Moguls to Ski Moguls

Before its current name was coined, Park City went by several names, including "Upper Kimballs," "Upper Parleys," and "Parleys Park City." But according to John W. Van Cott's *Utah Place Names*, pioneer resident George Snyder just didn't like the latter and shortened it to Park City in 1872 to refer to the beautiful mountain valley in which the town resides. Despite all the name changes endured by Park City in its earliest years, its residents, who call themselves Parkites, should be thankful their town was not called "Connorsville."

In 1869, Colonel Patrick E. Connor was dispatched to Utah to keep watch over territorial governor and L.D.S. president Brigham Young and to ensure that the Mormons stayed true to the Union during the Civil War. Connor and his men were California mining veterans with gold and silver in their veins. From Camp Douglas above Salt Lake City, Connor kept one eye on Brigham Young (he purportedly had one cannon permanently sighted on Young's Beehive House) and one eye on the nearby mountains, and Connor's men prospected for ore during their routine expeditions.

The old miners hospital at City Park.

Connor's soldiers discovered copper in the Oquirrh Mountains, which were eventually developed into the world's largest excavation—Kennecott's Bingham Canyon Copper Mine. They also struck silver in the Wasatch Mountains at a sawmill called Alta. Over Guardsman Pass and on a peak between present-day Park City and Heber, three soldiers marked an ore strike with a red handkerchief on a stick. The mountain and mine were called the Flagstaff, and thus laid the foundation for the future mining town.

In the blink of an eye, gentile prospectors (i.e., non-Mormons) flocked to northern Utah, prod-

<< Park City welcomes mountain bikers, too.

> **What's in a Name?**
>
> Parleys Park City was named after Parley P. Pratt, a Mormon pioneer who ran a toll road from Salt Lake City up Parleys Canyon (I-80 today) to the valley at the top, which was then named, not suprisingly, Parleys Park.

The historic Silver King Mine.

ding and poking the mountains religiously in hopes of striking pay dirt. Ironically, Brigham Young proclaimed, "there is no happiness in gold." Tell that to the 23 millionaires the mines of Park City produced. George Hearst, father of newspaper magnate William Randolf Hearst, simply topped off his established wealth by reaping millions from the burgeoning Ontario Mine. Thomas Kearns, on the other hand, had the rags to riches experience every prospector dreamed of emulating.

Kearns lived the life of a "bindlestiff," says Larry Warren in *Park City: Mountain of Treasure*, riding the rails from town to town and job to job. While laboring in the Ontario Mine, his foreman David Keith pointed him toward some unclaimed land called Mayflower, which Kearns proceeded to prospect in his spare time. After toiling in the dirt for six years, he struck it rich. Kearns, along with partners Keith and Albion Emery, consolidated their workings into the gigantic Silver King Coalition Mining Co. Kearns and Keith later moved to Salt Lake City, and purchased the *Salt Lake Tribune*. Later in time, a Salt Lake business center, a Park City boulevard, and an entire town in the west Salt Lake valley came to bear Kearns' name.

Upon his death, Emery's wife, Susanna Bradford inherited stock in the Silver King worth $100,000,000, and Susanna became know as the Silver Queen. Truly, she lived a life fit for a queen, with lavish residences in Salt Lake City, New York City, and Paris, but in 1942, when she died, she was pennyless.

The story of Solon Spiro is one of the most heart-breaking in the mining circle. The nephew of a pioneer merchant, Solon labored away in his uncle's store, bought stock in other mines, prospected profitably, and eventually formed his own mining company. But his workings produced little ore and his main shaft was constantly flooded, so Spiro drove a tunnel three miles long, and so straight you could see daylight from its end, to drain the water. After burrowing into the mountain and with little ore to show for his effort, Spiro succumbed to defeat and sold his claim to his competitor, the Silver King, at a bargain price. Adding

> **What's in a Name?**
>
> Heber City was named for Heber C. Kimball, who was instrumental in converting people to the Mormon faith in England. Kimball Junction, Exit 145 on I-80, also bears his name.

Mural of life in the mines located along the Poison Creek Trail.

the greatest insult to injury, the Silver King tunneled just 40 feet farther in Spiro's old mine and struck a giant body of ore, one that Solon had predicted was there all along.

The miners of Park City were a colorful spectrum of European and Asian descent, who brought with them their diverse cultures and religions. Although the ethnic communities were close knit, as on "Swede Alley," baseball proved to be a unifying force, and some miners were hired not for their underground skills but for their prowess on the ball field. By the end of the 19th century and with a population of over 6,000, Park City was one of the wealthiest mining camps in the nation, and one of the wildest. Whiskey flowed in the town's 27 saloons like rivulets of snowmelt on a warm spring day. Park City was a hedonistic island amidst a sea of pious agrarians. Still, a symbiosis existed between Park City and the neighboring Mormon hamlets of Heber and Kamas. After all, you can't grow crops on mine tailings and you can't milk an ore cart.

Amidst the heyday, there was also tragedy. In 1898, an overzealous cook sparked a fire that burned all of Main Street and much of Park Avenue to the ground in four short hours. But before the smoke cleared, the united residents were already rebuilding their beloved town, and Park City literally rose from the ashes.

Nary a week went by when news of a miner's death didn't blemish the pages of the local *Park*

> **What's in a Name?**
> First settled by Mormon pioneers in 1857, Kamas was named after an edible bulb called *camassia quamash*, which was a staple for Native Americans who inhabited the region.

**22** Mountain Biking Park City & Beyond

Explosives cache near the Judge Mine in Daly Canyon.

*Record,* and mountain life at 7,000 feet kept the undertaker busy. In 1902, a powder magazine exploded deep in the Daly-West Mine, killing 34 miners and going down on record as Park City's most catastrophic mining accident.

Like the many western mining camps of the time, Park City fell victim to fluctuating silver prices, and during the early 20$^{th}$ century, recession and then the Great Depression did more than temper the mining industry. Soon, the rail lines that once hauled ore out of Park City were hauling its residents out.

During that same time, however, Americans were amusing themselves with "longboard snowshoes," also known as "skis," and Parkites found pleasure in ski touring over the same mountains they mined. The Norwegians took the sport to the air, literally, and a jump was built on the old Creole mine dump just above town. Winter carnivals spurred competitions, and professional "ski riders" took flight from nearby Ecker Hill in 1931, with the legendary Alf Engen setting a world record.

> **What's in a Name?**
>
> Located a few miles southeast of Kamas, the town of Samak is Kamas spelled in reverse to distinguish it from its neighbor.

Park City loves a parade.

World War II lifted the mining industry temporarily but killed the ski jumping tournaments. After the war, Park City slipped into a deep slumber and even earned itself a spot in a guidebook to ghost towns, documents Larry Warren. The town continued to dabble in skiing, with a small t-bar operation on the mine slopes of Deer Valley; however, it wasn't until 1963 when Treasure Mountains Resort (now Park City Mountain Resort) opened that Park City realized the true motherlode lay on top of the mountains, not under them. The light powder that fell on the Wasatch glittered like silver, and Park City entered a new era of prosperity.

Although the fledgling resort struggled in its early years—a gondola broke down as much as it ran and a "lift" took skiers underground through the old dark, dank mine tunnels—Park City flourished as a resort town. Today, with three world-class resorts under its belt, including Park City Mountain Resort, Deer Valley Resort, and The Canyons Resort, Park City handily rivals high-zoot resorts like Aspen, Colorado. But not even Aspen can boast of having hosted alpine ski events in the Winter Olympic Games, as did Park City in 2002.

> **What's in a Name?**
>
> What do you call the town's "public, open square with benches, trees, and playgrounds?" What else than the palindrome, Park City City Park!

# PARK CITY RIDES

## Mormon Pioneer Trail

### JUST THE FACTS

**Location:** 13 miles northwest of Park City; 4 miles north of Jeremy Ranch
**Length:** 9 miles, out-and-back
**Tread:** All singletrack
**Physically:** Moderate (steady climb with rocky creek crossings)
**Technically:** 2-5 (smooth trail with rocky creek crossings; a few man-made ramps require adept skill.)
**Gain:** 1,400 feet
**In a nutshell:** Little Emigration Canyon to Big Mountain Pass and back

### WHY SHOULD U RIDE THIS TRAIL?

Ride in the shadow of the Mormon Pioneers when they emigrated to Utah in 1847. Little Emigration Canyon was the culminating ascent from where Brigham Young first gazed upon the distant Salt Lake Valley and surmised it to be the right place for his settlement of Zion. Today, this well-worn path is nicely suited for mountain bikes. The grade is gentle overall, except for the last quarter mile, and the trail is a blend of smooth dirt and rocky creek crossings. The trail receives little maintenance, and downed timber has been an issue in the past. Nowadays fallen trees present opportunities for anonymous individuals to build rough-cut ramps, boardwalks, and elevated bridges a la "freeride style." Whereas the pioneers were on a one-way mission, yours is two-way, and the return flight is one of the sweetest downhills around.

### Details

Cross the footbridge over East Canyon Creek, and weave through the thickets to a fence, where you must climb over a small set of stairs. As you enter the canyon, you are reminded of those who ventured this way nearly 150 years ago because trail posts note that this was the historic route of the Mormon Trail, the Pony Express, and the California Trail. Can you imagine the hardships endured by the first pioneers as they hauled their lives' possessions in weighty handcarts through the brambles and along the cobble creek up to Big Mountain Pass? It's unfathomable. The trip is quite different today on a lightweight bicycle with cushy full suspension.

You'll cross the cottonwood and aspen-shaded creek many times, and it's tricky to steer across the chunky cobbles. Your feet will get wet during spring when the creek is flowing, but by midsummer it dries up altogether (tech 3-4+). The trail is smooth packed dirt, however, where it follows the stream's bank (tech 2). Still, you need to anticipate a few steep berms that require bursts of power and good balance. Nearly a mile and a half up the canyon, you come to a wooden ramp built over a fallen tree. Rev up the rpms and don't balk, or you might tumble. This little stunt is a

<< Sweet Park City singletrack

**26**    Mountain Biking Park City & Beyond

If you twitch you'll pitch.

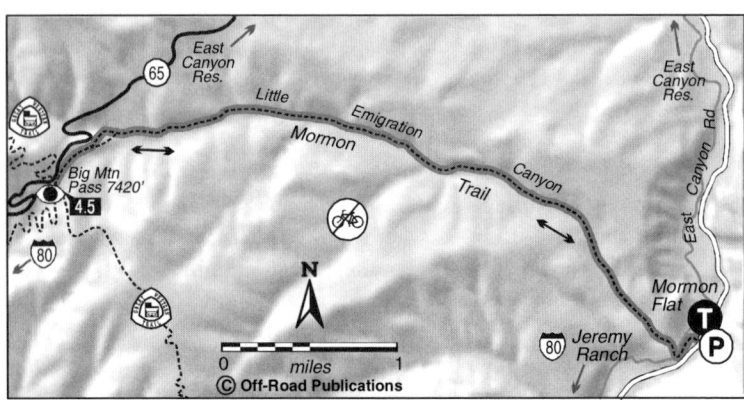

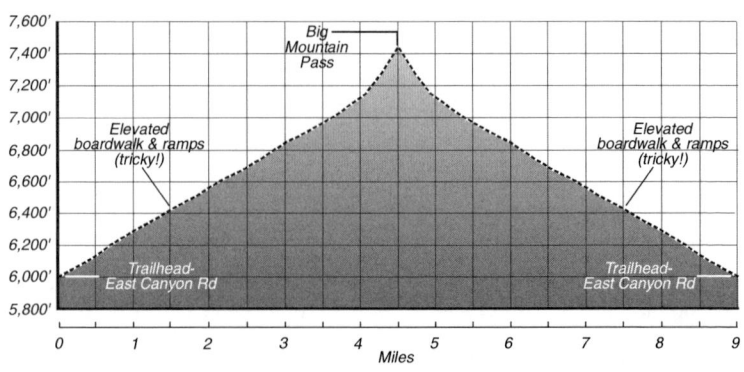

prelude to a trickier maneuver farther up the trail, where a raised, angled boardwalk bridges the stream. Falter there and you'll plunge head first into the drink. If you can master these obstacles, then you'll make easy work of yet another ramp over a fallen tree farther on.

Skirt a beaver pond, venture from woods to meadows and back, and then enter a large clearing at the head of the canyon. The trail splits for a few hundred yards; the right fork is a tad easier. After the paths merge, pump with full force in your granny gear to make the final pitch to the top; it's a real bruiser.

Read the interpretive plaque about the Mormon Pioneers at the parking area at Big Mountain Pass (**m4.5**), and enjoy the combined view of towering peaks, deep canyons, and a distant saline valley. You can even spot Kennecott's Bingham Copper Mine, the world's largest open pit mine, on the faraway Oquirrh Mountains.

Now, hunker down for the thrilling return descent that the Mormon Pioneers were compelled to pass up. It's fast and furious because gravity takes hold quickly. In fact, some freeriders enjoy the ride "free" of the climb by shuttling to the top by way of the East Canyon Highway. Keep your speed in check, and keep your eyes forward in anticipation of changes in the trail and, most importantly, other bikers and hikers coming up the path. Pass with caution and consideration. Do you dare to catch air off the ramps on the way down?

### Know Before You Go

- This route is popular with hikers, so yield the trail courteously.
- The canyon is surrounded by private property, so stay on the main trail.
- All man-made structures on the trail can be unstable, so use caution.
- There is an outhouse at the trailhead and at the trail's summit, but there are no water taps.

### Maps & More Information

- USGS 1:24,000: Big Dutch Hollow and Mountain Dell, Utah.

### Trailhead Access

From I-80, take Exit 143 for Jeremy Ranch, located 2.4 miles west of Kimball Junction and 14 miles east of Salt Lake City. Go left onto Rasmussen Road then right onto Jeremy Ranch Road. Pass the golf course clubhouse and go down to the intersection with Daybreaker Drive. Fork left onto the graveled East Canyon Road, which is suitable for passenger cars, and continue 4.1 miles to the signed trailhead for "Mormon Flat, Little Emigration Canyon."

## Great Western Trail

### JUST THE FACTS

**Location:** 4 miles north of Jeremy Ranch (see "Option" for other trailhead)
**Length:** 19.4 miles, loop
**Tread:** 0.1 mile paved road, 4.3 miles dirt road, 15 miles singletrack
**Physically:** Strenuous (steady climb up Mormon Trail; many short, stiff climbs on Great Western Trail)
**Technically:** $2^+$-$4^+$ (a blend of smooth and rugged trails)
**Gain:** 3,000 feet
**In a nutshell:** Mormon Pioneer Trail-GWT-Moose Hollow-East Canyon Road

### WHY SHOULD U RIDE THIS TRAIL

*Get away from the contrived trails that pass through ritzy neighborhoods, slip into the wilds, and explore a part of the 3,000-mile-long Great Western Trail (GWT) sitting right in your own backyard. Although the mileage falls shy of true epic proportions, the elevation you'll gain, the variety of trails you'll ride, and the canyons and mountains you'll conquer will suggest otherwise. You'll embark with a pleasant climb on the Mormon Trail and then continue on the more arduous and adventurous Great Western Trail, which follows the crest of the Wasatch Range from Big Mountain Pass to Parley's Summit. The hardships endured and rewards reaped along the GWT flip-flop like the moods of Jekyll and Hyde. The loop concludes with a spirited descent to Jeremy Ranch and with rolling miles on East Canyon Road.*

### Details

Cross the footbridge over East Canyon Creek, and weave through the thickets to a fence, where you must climb over a small set of stairs. As you enter the canyon, trail markers remind you of those who ventured this way nearly 150 years ago, for this was the historic route of the Mormon Trail, the Pony Express, and the California Trail. The path is smooth-rolling, by and large, when following the stream's bank (tech $2^+$); however, it's rough and choppy when crossing the creek, which you must do many times (tech $3^+$-$4^+$). You'll get your toes wet during spring, but the creek dries up by midsummer. Regardless, you must attack each crossing with confidence in order to stay upright.

About a mile and a half up the trail, you'll come to makeshift wooden ramps covering downed trees and to a rickety boardwalk bridging the stream (tech 4-5). Falter on the narrow boardwalk, and you'll land headfirst in the drink. Skirt a beaver pond, venture from woods to meadows and back, and then enter a large clearing at the head of the canyon. The trail splits for a few hundred yards; the right fork is a tad easier. After the paths merge, pump with full force in your granny gear to make the final pitch to the top; it's a real bruiser, and it sets the tone for the rest of the ride.

Read the interpretive plaque about the Mormon Pioneers at the Big Mountain Pass parking lot (**m4.5**), and enjoy the combined view of towering peaks, deep canyons, and a distant saline valley. You can even spot Kennecott's Bingham Copper Mine, the world's largest open pit mine, on the faraway Oquirrh Mountains.

Feeling fresh? You better because the upcoming Great Western Trail packs a wallop. Go around the steel gate and tackle a climb that stings like a knockout punch. Coast a bit, and then climb again. A series of exciting descents (tech 3+) take you to a broad meadow at the head of Dry Hollow, which is decked with plump yellow mule-ear wildflowers in early summer.

Dropping off Bald Mountain on the Great Western Trail with the Mill Creek ridge in background.

Don't bother trying to ride the upcoming hill. It's so steep and the tread is so hammered that you'll be wise to save your energy (tech 5); and you'll need all you can muster for the short, rugged climb to the top of Bald Mountain (**m8.1**). Take a well deserved break on Bald Mountain and admire the sights of the Mill Creek ridge to the south, the Salt Lake Valley and Oquirrh Mountains to the west, Mountain Dell Reservoir far below, and Parley's Park and the distant Uinta Mountains to the east.

Still feeling fresh? If not, then you might be in trouble because the remainder of the GWT takes a less-than-direct course to Parley's Summit, and there is still a lot of elevation to gain. Sections of the trail are nasty, like the ensuing drop off of Bald Mountain (tech 4+), but some are so sweet they will replace any grimace with a mile-wide grin. Watch for a junction about 1.6 miles south of Bald Mountain and atop a short, tough climb. Stay straight/south, aiming toward the Mill Creek ridge, and drop down a steep hill on loose rocks. Don't take the faint trail forking right/west, affectionately called "Baby Head Ridge," because it drops precipitously toward Mountain Dell over loose, chunky rocks the size of a newborn's noggin (tech 5). Tackle a drawn-out mile-long climb; then relish flat, smooth, silky tread as the route swings east and arrives at the Qwest relay towers (**m11.8**).

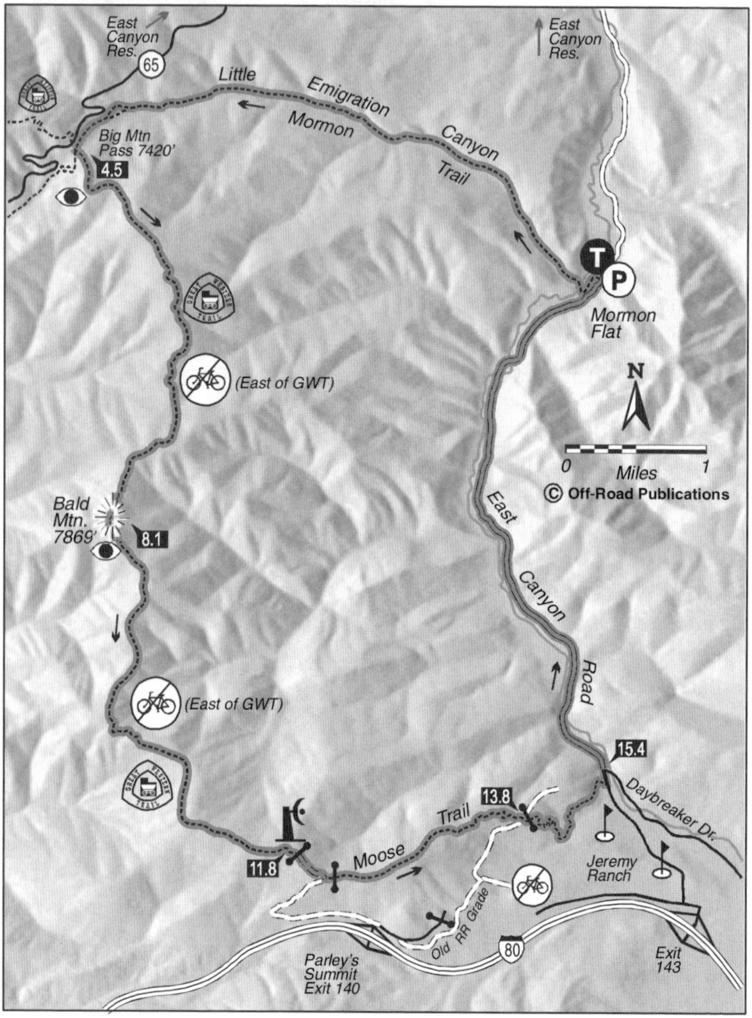

30  Mountain Biking Park City & Beyond

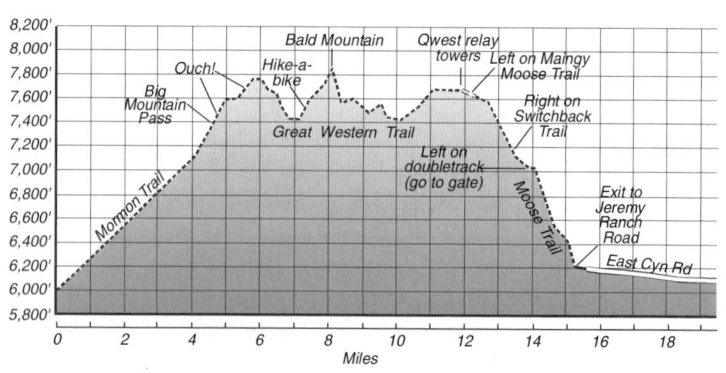

Little Dell Reservoir is merely a puddle when viewed from the top of Bald Mountain.

Head down the dirt service road for 0.3 mile to where it bends right, and fork left onto a trail at a rickety steel gate. Moose Trail is an old doubletrack that has healed over into a fast-paced singletrack (tech 3). Whoa! Fork right onto Switchback Trail while descending, and exit to a wide doubletrack. Take the track left to a gate and pick up Moose Trail again (**m13.8**). A quick drop dumps you out at the entrance gate to the private Moose Hollow Community at the corner of North Cove Road and Saddle Back Road. Cross the road at the gate to resume on Moose Trail. This last section of singletrack (tech 3) curves across sagebrush hills and behind custom homes before it exits to Jeremy Ranch Road. Go left to the dirt East Canyon Road (**m15.4**), and wind down with 4 miles of easy cruising alongside East Canyon Creek back to the trailhead (tech 2).

**Option:** Parley's Summit Trailhead
Salt Lakers can cut short the drive to the trailhead and log a few extra miles of singletrack by starting this loop from Parley's Summit on I-80. Park on the north side of the highway and pedal up the paved frontage road *exactly* 0.3 mile, and fork right on a faint, unsigned trail dropping from the road's edge. (You missed the trail if you top out on the road at a

private gate.) This secret trail briefly parallels the highway then slips into the aspens on what was the original railroad grade up Parley's Canyon. Parts of the path are still coated with the original cinders. Watch carefully for an unsigned doubletrack forking left 1.1 miles from your car and just past a zone of very lush foliage. (If you reach a gate next to a house, you missed it, and the "no trespassing" sign will confirm it.) Pedal up the doubletrack, pass the junction with Switchback Trail, and pick up Moose Trail at the gate (**m13.8** in the description above).

Upon making the loop described above to the Qwest relay towers, you can take Moose and Switchback Trails down to the doubletrack and then retrace your tracks on the old railroad grade, or you can simply descend on the Qwest access road to I-80 at Parley's Summit. Be forewarned: portions of the latter are steep and deeply rutted (tech 4).

### Know Before You Go

- Do not underestimate this ride; it's long and arduous, so be prepared with sufficient water and food.
- Mormon Pioneer Trail is popular with hikers, so yield the trail.
- The GWT is rugged and remote and is no place to bonk or get stuck in foul weather.
- Much of the GWT is bound by private property, so stay on the trail.
- There are outhouses at the Mormon Flats trailhead and at Big Mountain Pass, but there are no water taps.

### Maps & More Information

- USGS 1:24,000: Big Dutch Hollow and Mountain Dell, Utah
- Public Lands Information Center (at REI, Salt Lake): (801) 466-6411
- Wasatch-Cache National Forest (Salt Lake Ranger District): (801) 943-1794
- *Mountain Biking Utah's Wasatch Front,* by Gregg Bromka (Off-Road Publications): Available at your favorite bike shop or book store.

### Trailhead Access

From I-80, take exit 143 for Jeremy Ranch, which is 2.4 miles west of Kimball Junction and 14 miles east of Salt Lake City. Go left on Rasmussen Road then right on Jeremy Ranch Road. Pass the clubhouse and go down to the intersection with Daybreaker Drive. Fork left on the graveled East Canyon Road (suitable for passenger cars), and continue 4.1 miles to the signed trailhead for "Mormon Flat, Little Emigration Canyon." Salt Lakers can start from Parley's Summit, Exit 140 on I-80. (See "Option" above.)

# 3 Glenwild

## Just the Facts

| | |
|---|---|
| Location: | 7.3 miles north of Park City |
| Length: | 8.5 mile, loop |
| Tread: | 8.4 miles singletrack. 0.1 mile |
| Physically: | Moderate (Stealth is moderate, moderately easy.) |
| Technically: | 2-3+ (Stealth and Blackhawk switchbacks; the rest is buf... |
| Gain: | 1,000 feet |
| In a nutshell: | Stealth-Glenwild Loop-Blackhawk |

## Why Should U Ride This Trail

The Glenwild Loop exemplifies the new age of Park City, where recreational trails have become an integral part of a new development's master plan. Open space is plentiful at Glenwild, so its trails are more naturally tied to the land than the somewhat contrived trails around other developments. The loop's double-climb, double-descent profile, moderate difficulty rating, and generous amounts of buffed trails make it well-suited for riders of every level from strong beginners with a solid fitness base, to everyday mountain bike bums looking for quality singletrack, to pro racers wanting to log sprint intervals. Regardless of who you are, Glenwild is loads of fun. Since the loop is low and exposed by Park City standards, riders flock to it during spring and remain loyal to it through autumn. And being located only 20 minutes from Salt Lake City, valley bikers will find that Glenwild is easier to access than many Wasatch Front rides.

### Details

This loop can be ridden in either direction, but clockwise seems to be the norm. Counterclockwise is a tad harder. So go with the flow, or be a rebel and go against the grain. It's a free world, right?

Go to the vehicle bridge over the creek, and fork left onto Stealth Trail. The smooth dirt path follows the meandering stream then veers away from it, rising up the sagebrush hills. Parts of Stealth can get choppy from exposed rocks in the tread, especially at the tightly carved switchbacks (tech 3+). When you hit the rough stuff, either pump hard on the pedals or dismount quickly and you'll be cruising again. Pass the 24/7-Jeremy Ranch Connector Trail (**m1.7,** see "Option" below), and keep chugging up Stealth. Join with a dirt road and pedal up it 0.1 mile; then fork left on Glenwild Loop Trail. (Glenwild Loop Trail also forks right from the road [see "Option"].) Climb around more tight turns, cross a road, and top out at Kimball Knoll (**m2.8**).

You've paid your first set of dues, so it's time for a return on your investment. Bank down a dozen switchbacks (tech 3) over the next mile and cross a road next to a gate. Now, kick in the afterburners and jet across the meadows on baby-butt smooth singletrack, passing Cobble-

You'll score buttery smooth trail on Glenwild Loop's "back nine."

stone Loop along the way (see "Option"). Giant slalom skiers will appreciate the sweeping turns and free-flowing nature of this segment. Lean into the turns and have faith in your knobbies. Cross paved Glenwild Drive to continue on Glenwild Loop Trail (**m5.3**). The trail veers into the sage hills for the second climb of the day, which is smoother and easier than Stealth (tech 2-3). Top out next to the Glenwild guard station, stay straight/left at the junction with Glenwild Loop Trail, and round a left-hand switchback (see "Option"). Do the same farther down the trail where Blackhawk Trail forks right and crosses the road. Descend around switchbacks to the edge of the meandering creek, and roll along the stream's bank back to the trailhead.

**Option:** 24/7-Jeremy Ranch Connector
Need to get from Glenwild to East Canyon or vice versa? If so, then 24/7-Jeremy is the way—and it's all singletrack. The trail branches from Stealth Trail about 1.7 miles up and runs 4.7 miles to its western trailhead behind Jeremy Ranch at the three-way intersection of Jeremy Ranch Road, Daybreaker Drive, and East Canyon Road. From Stealth, the trail first undulates near the 6,700-foot mark to Red Hawk Road. Beyond Red Hawk Road, the trail curves through some hollows for about one-half mile, stay-

East Canyon
N
0
Miles
0.5
© Off-Road Publications
Cobblestone Loop
Redhawk
Cobblestone
24/7-Jeremy Connector
Glenwild
Loop
Glenwild
Drive
5.3
2.8
Stealth
1.7
Kimball 7138'
Road
Loop
Ranch
Glenwild
Loop
Guard station
Glenwild
Black-hawk
80
Stealth
Blackhawk
Bitner
Kimball Junction Exit 145
Bitner Road
80
224
Park City

7,400'
7,200'
7,000'
6,800'
6,600'
6,400'
6,200'
6,000'
Kimball Knoll
Junction w/ Glenwild Loop Trail
Junction w/ 24/7-Jeremy Trail
Stealth Trail
Glenwild
Cross paved road near gate
Junction w/ Cobblestone Loop
Loop
Cross Glenwild Drive
Trail
Pass guard station
Blackhawk Tr.
0
1
2
3
4
5
6
7
8
Miles

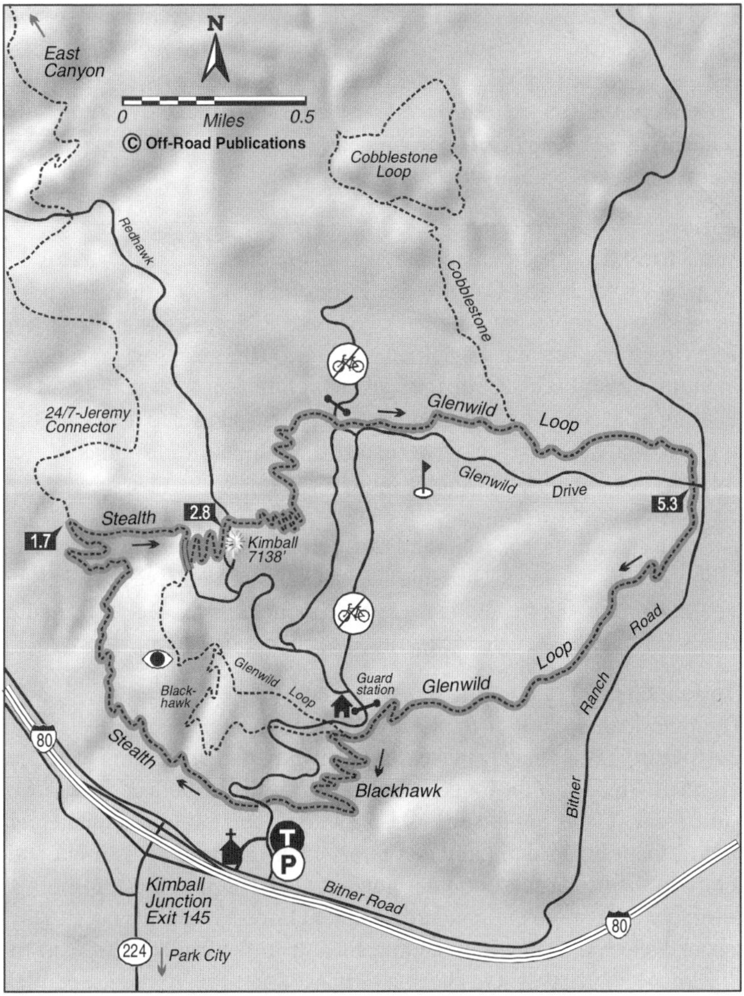

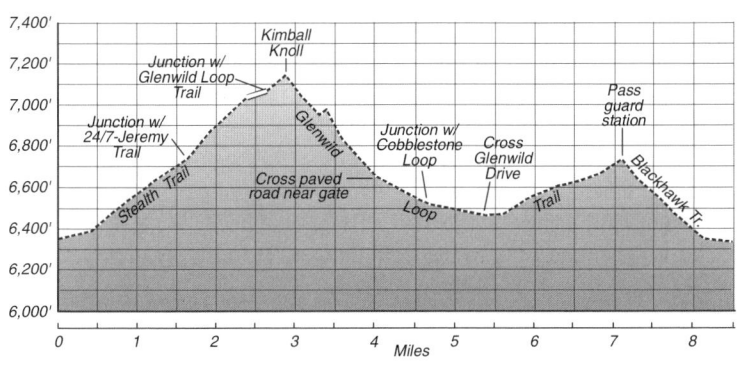

ing at roughly the same elevation, then descends nearly 500 feet over the last 1.5 miles to the western trailhead on Daybreaker Drive. When ridden eastward from the Daybreaker Drive trailhead, the first 1.5 miles is a steady, moderately strenuous climb. The rest of the way to Stealth rises and falls gradually. Be alert to hikers and runners, especially one mad mack who claimed he could out run any mountain biker "24/7."

**Option:** Cobblestone Loop
Add 3.6 miles, 450 vertical feet, and about one-half hour to the Glenwild Loop by exploring the Cobblestone Loop. Built in 2003, this "lollipop-shaped" route delves into the backwoods of Parley's Park and is a fun little circuit on excellent singletrack (tech 2-3). The stem part of the lollipop, or out-and-back section, is a gradual climb across sage hills. After crossing a paved road, the trail enters a wooded hollow and intersects the loop portion. Counterclockwise seems to be the norm. Portions of the trail are pocked with small cobbles (thus the trail's name), but the choppy tread is no match for today's smooth-riding full-suspension bikes. Climb again on the loop's backside and descend along the side of a wooded hollow to close the loop. The return leg to Glenwild Loop is a long wavering glide on smooth tread. Plans exist for more trails to take off from the loop's far side, so keep your ears tuned for future developments.

**Option:** Glenwild Loop Trail
The mile-long section of the Glenwild Loop Trail between Blackhawk and Stealth Trails officially makes the Glenwild Loop a loop. Huh? Though it's often skipped for the longer climb on Stealth Trail, both get you to the same place. That's not to say that Glenwild Loop Trail is not an integral part of the trail system. On the contrary. You can use it to bail out and return to the trailhead after climbing Stealth Trail, or you can eke out a few more miles from the standard Glenwild Loop by taking it *back* to the top of Stealth and then descending Stealth to the trailhead instead of Blackhawk. Whatever! Go check it out next time. The grades are gentle, and the view of the ski jumps at the Utah Olympic Park is pretty keen.

**Option:** Upper Blackhawk Trail
Upper Blackhawk Trail often gets snubbed for the longer Stealth Trail when riding the Glenwild Loop. Upper Blackhawk is generally considered a downhill-only route because the grade is pretty steep and the trail is rough in spots. Try this next time: Ride the standard loop, but when you pass the guard station atop the second climb, fork right on Glenwild Loop Trail as if heading back to upper Stealth. Cross the paved road and fork left on upper Blackhawk for a wild little descent (tech 3-4). After crossing back over the road, stay to the right and you'll finish off the ride in the usual fashion on lower Blackhawk Trail.

# Glenwild Loop

Check out the ski jumps at the Utah Olympic Park from Glenwild.

## ! Know Before You Go

- These trails are popular with hikers and runners, horses are allowed on the loop's back/north side, so ride cautiously and yield the right of way to others. Step off the trail to let horses pass.
- All paved roads are private; there is no public access to the Glenwild community.
- The Spring Creek Trailhead has an outhouse, water tap, and picnic area.

## ? Maps & More Information

- USGS 1:24,000: Park City West, Utah (trails are not shown).
- *Park City Trail Map,* by Mountain Trails Foundation.

## Trailhead Access

From Park City, drive north to Kimball Junction at I-80 (Exit 145) and turn right onto Bittner Road (north frontage road). Turn left onto Glenwild Drive in 0.4 mile and park at the Spring Creek Trailhead.

## 4
# McLeod Creek-Willow Creek Trails

**JUST THE FACTS**

| | |
|---|---|
| **Location:** | North end of Park City |
| **Length:** | 8.4 miles, figure-eight loop (3.5 miles for short loop) |
| **Tread:** | 3.4 miles paved paths, 5 miles dirt and gravel paths |
| **Physically:** | Easy (gradual climb from the halfway point back to the starting point.) |
| **Technically:** | 1-2 (wide paved and dirt trails; be alert to other trail users) |
| **Gain:** | 360 feet |
| **In a nutshell:** | McLeod Creek-Willow Creek-McLeod Creek-McPolin Farm Trail-McLeod Creek |

### WHY SHOULD U RIDE THIS TRAIL?

*This little jaunt is ideal for families with children, first time riders, or anyone looking for easy miles, scenic views, and friendly trails. You might make new friends on this ride, too, because the trail is a magnet for riders and hikers seeking fresh air and happy faces, especially on warm, sunny weekends. The McLeod Creek Trail follows a willow-lined stream through neighborhoods and then across open spaces. Willow Creek Trail makes a loop on dirt trails through Willow Creek Estates. On the return, the paved McPolin Farm Trail passes a historic ranch, where cattle graze in broad pastures. Throughout the entire route, the lofty Wasatch Range creates a postcard-perfect backdrop.*

### Details

Pick up the paved McLeod Creek Trail near the west entrance to the Dan's Foods parking lot. Ride behind condominiums and cross Saddle View Way. After crossing Holiday Ranch Loop, you'll pedal alongside the creek where tall brush provides a pleasant buffer from the intrusions of civilization. Beyond the Meadows Drive crossing, the trail becomes a wide dirt lane running alongside the highway. The Canyons Resort is dead in your sights. Pass the tunnel under the highway, which leads to the McPolin Farm Trail (**m1.6**), and follow the trail as it bends north around Quarry Mountain. (You'll go through the tunnel on the return. If you are riding the short loop, then go through the tunnel now and pick up the description below at **m6.5**.)

McLeod Creek gushes at your side and flows through a canopy of willows and cottonwoods. Cross a long footbridge, jog left then right through farm fields, and come to Old Ranch Road (**m3.1/4.9**). Cross the road, and head north on Willow Creek Trail/East 224 Connector Trail, which passes the custom homes of Willow Creek Estates. Cross Split Rail Lane about 1 mile from Old Ranch Road, and loop back south on the continued Willow Creek Trail. (You can add on several miles by riding out and back on Swaner Nature Trail/East 224 Connector.) It's all uphill from here, so pace yourself. Fortunately the hills are nearly imperceptible. Exit Willow Creek Trail to Split Rail Lane, and follow the bike lane back to

Willow Creek Tr.
Old Ranch Road
Old Ranch Road
3.1/4.9
224
N
0 miles 0.5
© Off-Road Publications
7-11
White Pine Canyon Rd
Quarry Mtn 7416'
McLeod Creek Tr.
1.6/6.5
McPolin Farm
Farm Trail
Meadows Dr.
Payday Dr.
Holiday Ranch Loop
Dans Foods
Kearns Blvd.
Park Ave
Iron Mountain 9018'

(Hills not as steep as they appear!)
Dans Foods parking lot
Tunnel to Farm Trail
Cross Old Ranch Road
Cross Old Ranch Road
Tunnel to Farm Trail
Dans Foods parking lot
McLeod Creek Trail
Willow Creek Trail
McLeod Creek Trail
Farm Trail
7,000'
6,900'
6,800'
6,700'
6,600'
6,500'
6,400'
6,300'
6,200'
6,100'
6,000'
0 1 2 3 4 5 6 7 8
Miles

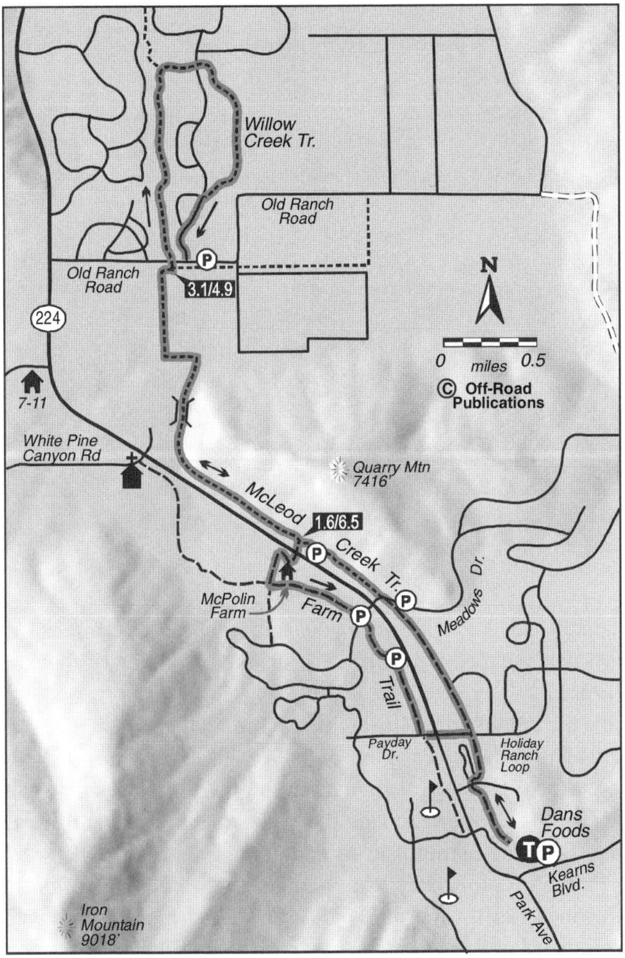

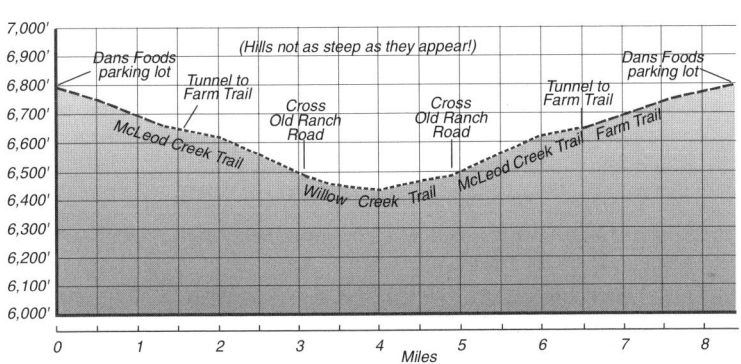

Nick and Steve cross McLeod Creek on route to Willow Creek Trail.

Old Ranch Road. As you retrace your tracks on McLeod Creek Trail, the scenery's new perspective will add freshness to your legs if they are starting to tire.

Take the tunnel under the highway (**m6.5**), and zigzag right then left around McPolin Farm. Turn left on the paved Farm Trail, and enjoy the picture-perfect scene of cattle grazing in grassy pastures set against the Wasatch Range. (You can add another mile, round trip, by turning right on the Farm Trail and taking it to its end at the intersection of UT 224 and White Pine Canyon Road.) Ride parallel to the highway after crossing Allen Springs Drive (alternate parking); then cross the highway at the intersection of Payday Drive (west) and Holiday Ranch Loop (east). Retrace your tracks on McLeod Creek Trail to the Dan's Foods parking lot.

### ❗ Know Before You Go

- This route is not a race course, so leave your heart rate monitor behind and enjoy a slower pace.
- Ride in single file on the right side of the trails and be alert to oncoming trail users, especially hikers and children.
- There is an outhouse and picnic table at McPolin Farm.
- While on paved trails, watch out at crossroads for pylons that restrict vehicles from the trails.
- Do not drink the stream water, as it may be contaminated with bacteria from wildlife and livestock.

McLeod Creek-Willow Creek Trails   41

The Farm Trail is fun for the whole family.

### ? Maps & More Information

- USGS 1:24,000: Park City West, Utah (trails are not shown).
- *Park City Trail Map,* by Mountain Trails Foundation.

### Trailhead Access

Park at and embark from the Dan's Foods parking lot, located behind the Olympic Visitor Information Center on the northeast corner of Park Avenue (UT 224) and Kearns Boulevard (UT 248). Heed any parking restrictions. Alternate parking areas are located on the north side of UT 224 across from McPolin Farm, on both sides of UT 224 at the intersection with Meadows Drive, and on Old Ranch Road near the entrance to Willow Creek Estates.

## 5
## Round Valley-Rail Trail

### Just the Facts

| | |
|---|---|
| **Location:** | Ride from town, or drive 6.5 miles to west trailhead or 2.5 miles to east trailhead |
| **Length:** | 14.2 miles, loop (Round Valley Trail, proper, is 5.6 miles one-way) |
| **Tread:** | 1.5 miles paved roads sidewalks, 4.1 miles paved paths, 3 miles dirt and gravel paths, 5.6 miles singletrack |
| **Physically:** | Moderate (two steady switchbacking climbs and lots of cruising) |
| **Technically:** | 1-3+ (gravel on bike paths; smooth and choppy singletracks) |
| **Gain:** | 720 feet |
| **In a nutshell:** | McLeod Creek-Round Valley-Rail Trail |

### Why Should U Ride This Trail

*Ski and mountain bike in the same day? That's an oxymoron in Park City, right? Wrong. In April and under the right conditions, you can hit the slopes and then the dirt, and Round Valley is the place. Good sun exposure and low elevations, by Park City standards, mean that Round Valley is one of the first Park City trails to melt out after winter, so it's ideal for preseason conditioning. Round Valley's singletracks are loads of fun, combining moderate climbs, countless switchbacks, and fast straightaways. Paved and dirt paths are linked together to complete the loop. They offer plenty of sightseeing as they follow willow-lined streams, pass farm fields and open spaces, and trace an old railroad grade.*

### Details

You can start from many places in Park City, but the Union Pacific Rail Trail trailhead is most central. From the trailhead, go right on Bonanza Drive then left on Kearns Boulevard (UT 248), following the sidewalks along the way. Cut across the Dan's Foods parking lot to its west side, and pick up the paved McLeod Creek Trail near the Silver Creek Medical Center. The paved trail passes behind some condos and homes, then follows a willow-lined creek to Meadows Drive. Cross the road and continue on the wide gravel path alongside UT 224 (tech 2), passing the historic McPolin Farm, which sits across the highway. The trail bends around Quarry Mountain and crosses open spaces and farm fields before it turns east and follows alongside Old Ranch Road. Go past the entrance station for Quarry Mountain Ranch, staying on dirt trail for another 0.8 mile, and then exit to Old Ranch Road. Take the road around a ninety-degree left bend to reach Round Valley's western trailhead (**m5.8**).

Take the trail to the right (left is an equestrian trail), and make an immediate left turn to begin the first of Round Valley's two climbs. The trail zigzags up the sage and brush hills, rising moderately on packed dirt and choppy rocks (tech 3). With each passing turn, the valley recedes below and the looming Wasatch Crest grows more impressive. Cross a doubletrack at the top of the climb 1.5 miles from the trailhead. (This

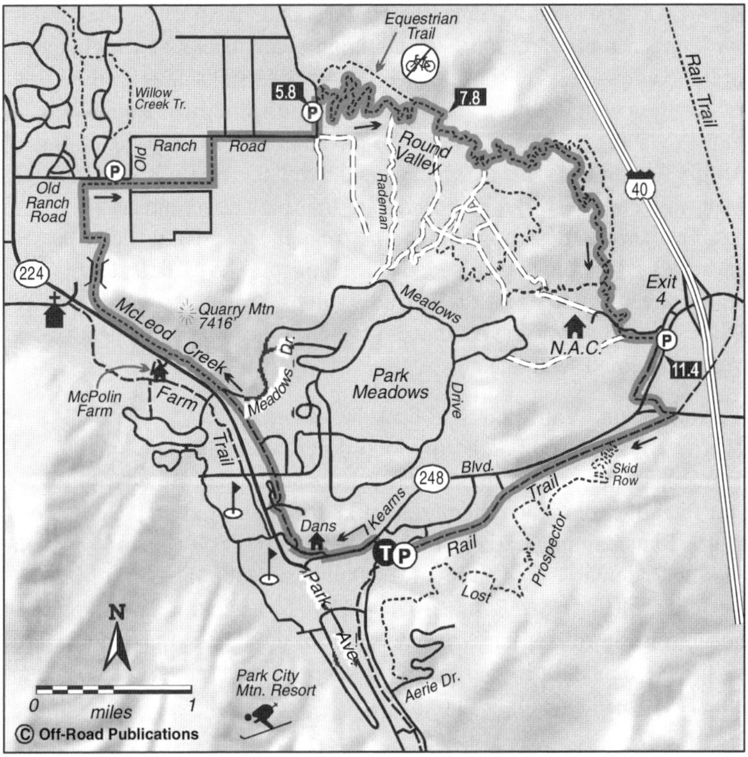

# Round Valley-Rail Trail

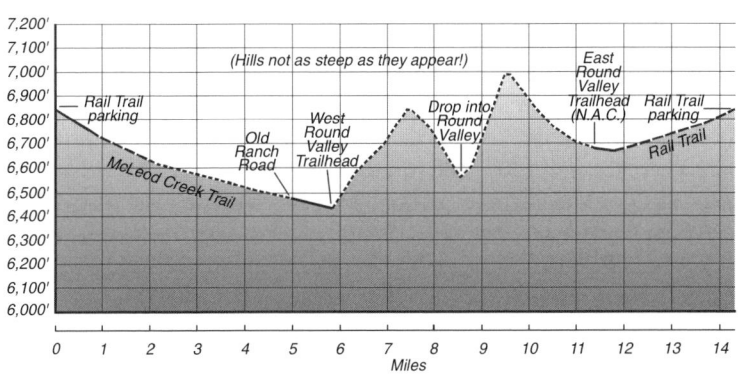

track is a cutoff to the Park Meadows subdivision via Rademan Ridge Trail, which in turn links to Rossman and Sandstone Crest Trails on Quarry Mountain.)

Descend along a buried pipeline into Round Valley proper, and turn right onto a doubletrack in the valley (**m7.8**). Fork left immediately onto singletrack to start the second climb, which also has plenty of switchbacks. Top out, swerve downhill through looping turns, and fork right on either

High Trail (first junction) or Kari's Trail (second junction). Neither trail is harder than the other, and both combine switchbacks and high-speed straightaways across the oak brush hills. After the trails merge, cruise past the junction with Rambler Trail, which forks left, and cross a doubletrack. More twisting trail takes you to the paved access road to the National Ability Center. Cross the road and whip through the sage to Round Valley's west trailhead (**m11.4**). (This section of trail may be rerouted.)

Take the frontage road right and hop onto the paved trail, which passes under UT 248. Connect with the dirt Richardson Flat road, and turn right on the paved Union Pacific Rail Trail. Spin for an easy 2 miles alongside Silver Creek back to the trailhead, noting the peculiar trailside artwork made of welded scrap metal.

**Option:** Round Valley out-and-back
This is a no-brainer. Forego the loop described above and simply ride from one trailhead to the other and back for 11.2 miles, round trip. While you're at it, explore peripheral trails like Rambler Trail on the east side; Matt's Flat, Cammy's, Backslide, and Nowhere Elks Trails on the south end; or Rademan Ridge and La Dea Duh Trails atop the climb from the western trailhead. (See *Park City Trail Map*, by Mountain Trails Foundation.) You can ride around for days and not duplicate your route. More trails are planned for Round Valley, so keep your eyes open and your ears tuned to local happenings.

**Option:** Round Valley-Lost Prospector Loop
If you feel like you just warmed up when it's time to cool down on the Rail Trail, then add on the nearby Lost Prospector Trail. You'll tack on 3 miles of excellent singletrack and 1.5 miles of paved bike trails and roads for a moderately strenuous, 18.6-mile loop.

One-half mile into the Rail Trail, fork left on Skid Row Trail, and gear down for a 0.8-mile climb up 13 switchbacks, gaining about 300 feet. Turn right on Lost Prospector Trail, and cruise westward with the Wasatch Crest in the distance and Prospector/Park Meadows below. Curve around a narrow hollow where S.O.S. Trail forks right and descends, and then gradually climb into a broader hollow, riding straight through the intersection with Gamble Oak Trail. Lost Prospector undulates across the hillside, passing into pretty aspen-clad hollows and swinging out across scenic oak brush slopes. After crossing Masonic Trail, Lost Prospector swings left/south and offers a fine view of Old Town Park City. Stay left on the higher lane where the trail splits, and roll to its end on paved Aerie Drive. Descend to Deer Valley Drive, go left (cross the road cautiously), and then turn right immediately onto lower Main Street to catch the paved Poison Creek Trail. Pass City Park, duck under Deer Valley Drive, and cross Bonanza Drive to return to the Rail Trail trailhead.

# Round Valley-Rail Trail

Left: Steve and Joe head up Round Valley Trail. Wasatch Crest in the background. Right: Jared gets his kicks on "Rambler Trail."

### ! Know Before You Go

- The trails in Round Valley typically melt out by mid- to late-April, depending on seasonal weather. Please allow the trails to dry completely before riding. By midsummer, Round Valley is too hot to ride during midday.
- The loop is marked throughout with sign posts.
- Round Valley is popular with hikers, runners, and equestrians, so ride cautiously and courteously, especially around blind corners.

### ? Maps & More Information

- USGS 1:24,000: Park City East and Park City West, Utah.
- *Park City Trail Map,* by Mountain Trails Foundation.

### Trailhead Access

*Union Pacific Rail Trail trailhead:* From Park Avenue (UT 224), take either Deer Valley Drive or Kearns Boulevard (UT 248) to Bonanza Drive. Turn onto Prospector Avenue, and you'll find the Rail Trail trailhead behind the Sun Crest Condominiums.

*Round Valley west trailhead:* From Park City, drive north on UT 224, and turn right onto Old Ranch Road, which is 0.4 mile north of Canyons Resort Drive and 2.4 miles south of I-80. Take Old Ranch Road 2.4 miles to the trailhead.

*Round Valley east trailhead:* From UT 224, take Kearns Boulevard (UT 248) 3 miles to the junction with US 40. (Kearns Boulevard is 1.2 miles north of Old Town Park City and 5.5 miles south of I-80.) Turn left onto the frontage road for the National Ability Center, just west of the interchange, to reach the trailhead. Alternatively, from I-80 take Exit 148 for US 40/Heber; then take Exit 4 for Park City/UT 248. Turn right immediately onto the frontage road for the National Ability Center to reach the trailhead.

# 6
# Union Pacific Rail Trail

**PARK CITY RIDES — JUST THE FACTS**

| | |
|---|---|
| **Location:** | Park City to Echo Reservoir or vice versa |
| **Length:** | 26.6 miles, one-way |
| **Tread:** | 2 miles paved trail, 24.6 miles dirt and gravel trail |
| **Physically:** | Moderate (Park City to Echo); moderately strenuous (Echo to Park City) |
| **Technically:** | 1-2 (smooth sailing the whole way, but gravel can get thick occasionally) |
| **Gain:** | 1,300 feet (Echo to Park City); loss: 1,300 feet (Park City to Echo) |
| **In a nutshell:** | Old railroad grade the whole way |

**Why Should U Ride This Trail?**

At nearly 30 miles long but a mere 100 feet wide, the Historic Union Pacific Rail Trail is one of Utah's most unique state parks. The park is centered on the abandoned Echo & Park City Railway, which served Coalville and Park City for nearly 100 years. This is Utah's first rail trail, and it sets the standard for future conversions. The route caters to all forms of non-motorized recreation, including bicycling, hiking and running, horseback riding, and cross-country skiing. You'll travel from the historic mining center of Park City through the rural communities of Wanship and Coalville and then along the Weber River to Echo Reservoir. With numerous trailheads along the way, you can choose to pedal all or part of it.

## Details

From the Park City trailhead behind Sun Creek Condominiums, pedal east along Silver Creek and behind homes and businesses. During Park City's heyday, the brook was dubbed "Poison Creek" because of its high concentration of heavy metals and other mine wastes. The eight-foot-wide trail is paved for about 2 miles to the crossing of the Richardson Flats road; thereafter, the old rail grade is packed dirt and gravel. Pass under US 40, and then use caution crossing UT 248. With Park City receding from sight, the trail crosses open spaces and comes to the Starr Pointe Trailhead, which was once the 500-person townsite of Atkinson (**m5.7**). This is a good place to turn around if you want to sample only a part of the trail.

Continuing on, the Rail Trail passes under the eastbound lane of I-80, curves into Silver Creek Canyon, and says goodbye to the distant Wasatch Range. The grade gets twice as steep, which isn't saying much considering that it was previously a meager one percent. Still, the canyon's two-percent grade allows you to alternate between pedaling and coasting and you'll click away the miles with ease. Although the route is wedged between the highway's separated lanes, many sections are buffered from the whir of traffic by thickets of willow, dogwood, wild rose, and even edible berries. Those interested in geology will notice the light purple, gray, and pale green outcroppings of volcanic rocks, which indicate that magma was once thrust into the surrounding bedrock. Nearly 4 miles down the canyon, the trail crosses under I-80's westbound lane and passes a quizzical sign warning of "rock chuck crossing." Should you watch out for roly-poly vermin or for rocks being chucked from the highway overhead? Roll into Wanship (**m14.2**) and briefly follow Wanship Road; then pick up the Rail Trail behind Spring Chicken Inn, which is renowned for its fried chicken. Lunch anyone?

The Rail Trail follows the fertile Weber River valley near Hoytsville.

From Wanship to Coalville, the Rail Trail wanders down the fertile Weber River valley at a nearly imperceptible grade. Today, livestock find good grazing in these ranch lands, but long before immigrants settled the land, mountainmen found the valley populated by Native Americans in teepee villages. Coalville (**m22.0**), like Park City, has a mining heritage, but the town's name reflects the fact that veins of black carbon were the sought-after commodity rather than semiprecious metals.

The last stretch crosses the inlet marshes of Echo Reservoir then follows the length of the reservoir alongside US 189, which gives you the option of pedaling on smooth pavement for the last couple of miles. The Rail Trail informally terminates near the reservoir's dam. Just around the corner, Echo Canyon was an immigration thoroughfare in the mid- to late-1800s that contained the Mormon Trail, the Pony Express, and the Transcontinental Railroad.

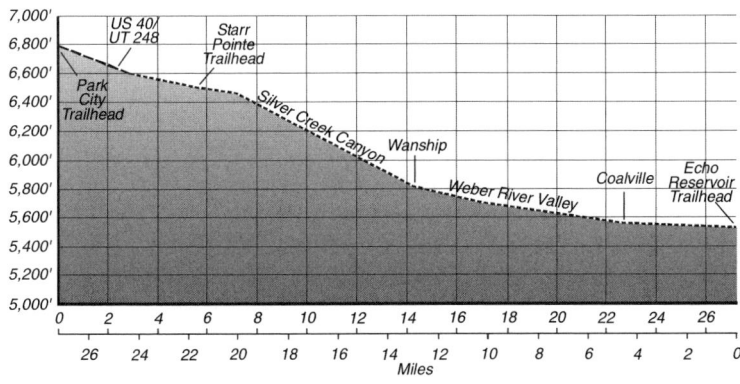

**48**  Mountain Biking Park City & Beyond

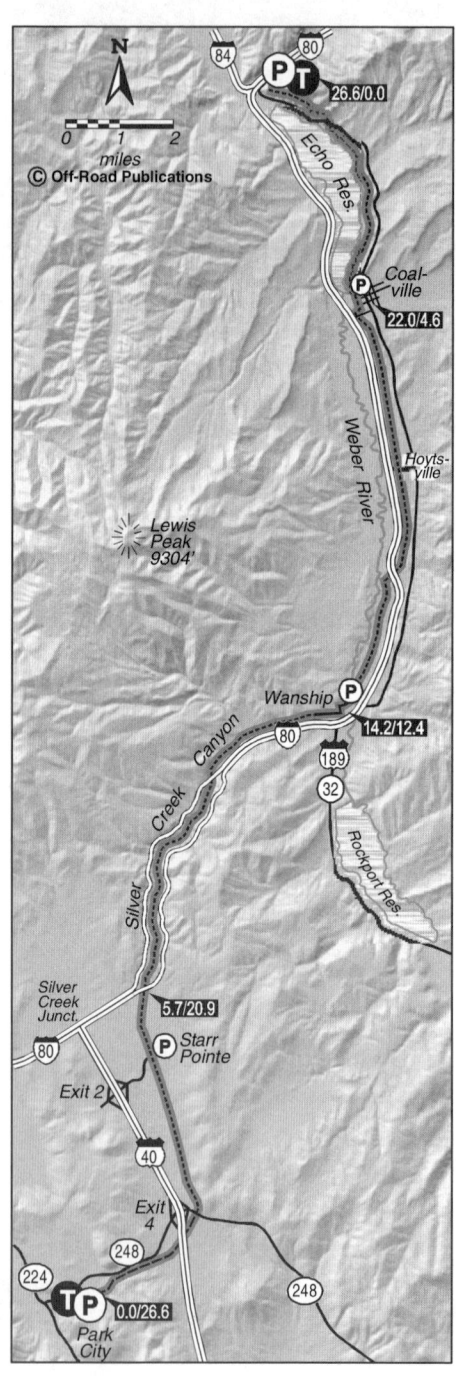

## Union Pacific Rail Trail

### ! Know Before You Go

- Trailheads have outhouses but no water taps. Park City, Wanship, and Coalville have visitor services.
- If you forego the shuttle between endpoints, then riding round trip is strenuous.

### ? Maps & More Information

- USGS 1:100,000: Salt Lake City, Utah.
- *Park City Trail Map,* by Mountain Trails Foundation.
- Historic Union Pacific Rail Trail State Park (brochure), c/o Mountain Trails Foundation

### Trailhead Access

*Park City trailhead:* From Park Avenue (UT 224), take Kearns Boulevard (UT 248) or Deer Valley Drive to Bonanza Drive. Turn off onto Prospector Avenue and find the trailhead parking area behind Sun Crest Condominiums. Observe parking restrictions and maximum parking times.

*Starr Pointe trailhead:* From Park City, take Kearns Boulevard (UT 248) to US 40 and go left/north; then take Exit 2 for Silver Summit. (From I-80, take Exit 148 for US 40 and drive south to Exit 2 for Silver Summit.) Take Silver Creek Drive and then Starr Pointe Road 1.1 miles to the trailhead.

*Wanship trailhead:* From I-80, take Exit 156 for Wanship and travel north through town on US 189. The trailhead is behind Spring Chicken Inn and Café.

*Coalville trailhead:* From I-80, take Exit 164 for Coalville. Upon exiting the highway, turn right onto 100 South then left onto Main. Turn left onto 200 North and find the trailhead one block down.

*Echo Reservoir trailhead:* From I-80, take Exit 169 for Echo and turn right. The trailhead is near the reservoir's dam just after passing under the railroad bridge.

# Lost Prospector-Rail Trail

## Just the Facts

| | |
|---|---|
| **Location:** | City Park to Prospector Park and back |
| **Length:** | 6.9 miles, loop |
| **Tread:** | 0.2 mile roads, 2.6 miles paved paths, 4.1 miles singletrack |
| **Physically:** | Moderate (short, steep climb on paved road then incremental climbs on rolling trail) |
| **Technically:** | 1-3+ (Lost Prospector is both smooth and choppy, ending in a steep descent with tight switchbacks, Rail Trail and Poison Creek Trail are paved) |
| **Gain:** | 600 feet |
| **In a nutshell:** | City Park-Poison Creek Trail-Aerie Drive-Lost Prospector Trail-Skid Row Trail-Rail Trail-Poison Creek Trail-City Park |

## Why Should U Ride This Trail?

*Ready to experience the joy of singletrack but don't want to climb an entire mountain in the process? Lost Prospector Trail serves up just the right amount of genuine singletrack to test your skills and endurance, but it's free from the anxieties that may come with venturing far into the backcountry. If you can endure the short, stiff climb up Aerie Drive– we're only talking about a couple hundred yards–then the rest is gravy. Lost Prospector Trail winds around the shady side of Masonic Hill on a rolling contour, weaving into lush hollows and out across open sunny slopes, where you'll enjoy views of Park City, its neighborhoods, and the Wasatch Crest. The climbs are moderate, short-lived, and always followed by spirited freewheeling. A short, twisting descent on Skid Row Trail takes you to the Rail Trail, where you then click away the remaining miles with ease. Of course, serious riders can use Lost Prospector as a stepping stone to a full day's ride of near epic proportions on trails through Solamere, Deer Crest, and lower Deer Valley Resort.*

## Details

Hop on the paved Poison Creek Trail behind Park City City Park (gotta love that name, huh?), and ride one-half mile up along the trickling creek. Pass under one vehicle bridge, but turn right before the second bridge and pop up onto lower Main Street. Go left onto Main and then left again onto Deer Valley Drive. (Use caution crossing the four lanes of traffic.) Turn right in a few hundred yards onto Aerie Drive, and crawl up the short but steep grade in your easiest gears. Just when you start to agonize, and near the first house, fork left on Lost Prospector Trail. Phew! What a way to start a ride.

Lost Prospector rises up a short, rocky ramp then goes straight through an X-junction on a gradually ascending traverse (tech 2-3). The left fork, which runs parallel to and below the main trail, is more technical (tech 3-4). It rejoins the main trail where Lost Prospector swings to the east and overlooks Prospector Square. Also at this point, Masonic Trail forks right and uphill (see "Option"). So, ignore the left fork, and stay eastbound on

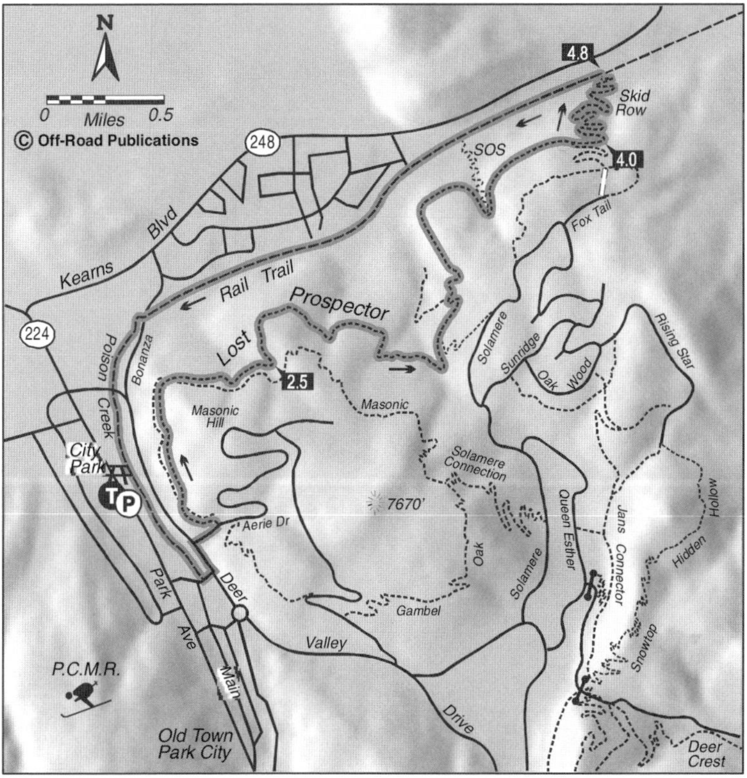

# Lost Prospector-Rail Trail 51

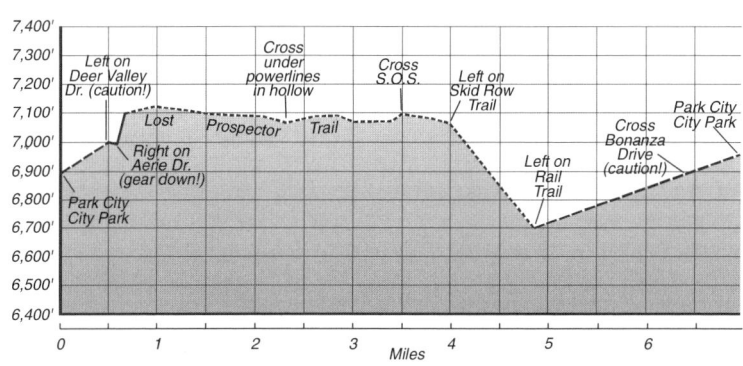

a rolling contour through the oak, maple, and aspen. Wind through the timbered hollows and swing out across the open hillsides. Climbs may require you to gear down, but they are rarely a burden.

Cross a doubletrack in a prominent hollow with a powerline overhead (**m2.5**); then go straight through the junction with Gamble Oak Trail. Watch out for a pair of tight curves on the fast, choppy descent (tech 3⁺) that might take you by surprise. Thereafter, the path overlooks Prospector Park before rising steeply into a tight hollow, where S.O.S. Trail forks left.

Want great singletrack without the anguish? Hit Lost Prospector Trail.

(S.O.S. descends to the Rail Trail via steep, wickedly tight, high-banked turns rated tech 4⁺-5.) Another nice contouring section takes you to a junction, where Skid Row Trail forks left and Fox Tail Trail goes straight/right (**m4.0**). (See "Option.")

Go left on Skid Row Trail and slither off the hillside around 13 switchbacks, some spaced more tightly than others (tech 3-4). It's good fun, and you'll quickly learn which way you turn with the most confidence. Cross a doubletrack at the bottom, and go left on the paved Rail Trail (**m4.8**). The Rail Trail makes a beeline up Silver Creek along the edge of homes and passes an array of peculiar sculptures made of welded scrap metal. Pass the Rail Trail trailhead after 1.5 miles, and cross Bonanza Drive to connect with the paved Poison Creek Trail. The path dips under Deer Valley Drive and returns to City Park to complete the loop.

**Option:** Solamere-Masonic Hill Add-on
Do you prefer going clockwise on a loop, or are you looking for more singletrack? If so, then this 12-mile option, which links together five trails in the Solamere area, is for you. None of these trails is worthy of its own chapter, but together they make a logical, continuous route. Directions tend to be exasperating, especially when winding through the streets of

Awesome singletrack is always just a stone's throw away in Park City.

Solamere, so previous knowledge of this area is a benefit. If you navigate this route successfully, then you'll climb a few extra hundred feet, cross over the top of Masonic Hill, and then descend on a tight, technical trail back to Lost Prospector. Newbies and even those with budding skills should stick to the main Lost Prospector loop.

At the end of Lost Prospector Trail, where you would normally fork left down Skid Row Trail, stay straight/right and climb moderately for one-half mile up Fox Tail Trail. Go straight across a doubletrack, and exit onto a paved residential road also called Fox Tail Trail. (Access to the road may change due to future residential development.) To get back on dirt trails, you must first zigzag on paved roads: Go right on Fox Tail Trail (paved road), left on Solamere Drive, left again on Solamere at the corner of Hidden Oaks Cove, right on Sunridge Drive, left on Oak Wood Drive, and right on Oak Wood Drive at the intersection with Rising Star Lane. Just past 3610 Oak Wood Drive, pick up the Wood Chip Trail forking left (might not be signed). Are you with me?

The soft, crunchy, dirt-and-bark-chip trail contours high above Solamere and Deer Valley Meadows with inspiring views of lower Deer Valley Resort. Stay straight through two junctions, descend slightly around the knoll, and exit onto paved Rising Star Lane, where you can view the Uinta Mountains and Jordanelle Reservoir to the east. Coast down to the road's end, and fork right onto a trail that rises uphill under a rope tow. A fast straightaway descent through the brush dumps you out at the lower Deer Crest entrance gate. Go right on Queen Ester Drive, left on Telemark Drive, and left on Solamere Drive. Pick up Solamere Connection Trail on the right, across from the club house. (See chapter "Solamere.")

Moderate grades and 13 sharp, mostly ridable switchbacks take you 350 vertical feet to the top of the knoll and to a four-way junction with Gambel Oak Trail. Turn right, cross a doubletrack, and drop quickly down six tight turns through the oak brush (tech 4). Contour a bit, and then drop like a pinball down more angular, eroded turns as roots nip at your tires. Additional technical turns drop you onto Lost Prospector Trail. Go left and retrace your incoming tracks to Aerie Drive and City Park.

**Option:** Deer Crest Add-on

But wait, there's more! Before climbing Solamere Connection Trail up Masonic Hill, add 8 miles of sweet singletrack through Deer Crest. (Consult the "Deer Crest" chapter and begin this side trip by riding backwards from **m7.2**.)

In a nutshell, go southeast on Hidden Hollow Trail from the end of Rising Star Lane, climb over Snow Top knoll, and descend to the upper Deer Crest gate at McKinley Gap. Charge over Heinous Hill to Roosevelt Gap, climb Outlook Trail, and descend Spin Cycle. Upon climbing Village Trail back to the upper Deer Crest gate at McKinley Gap, go around the *west* side of Snow Top knoll on Jans Connector Trail, and descend to the lower Deer Crest gate at Queen Esther Drive. Now climb Solamere Connector Trail and descend Masonic Trail to Lost Prospector. Retrace your tracks to Aerie Drive and City Park. Whoa! That's 20-plus miles and a couple grand of elevation gain.

### ! Know Before You Go

- Lost Prospector Trail is popular with hikers, so ride cautiously and courteously, especially around blind corners.

### ? Maps & More Information

- USGS 1:24,000: Park City East and Park City West, Utah.
- *Park City Trail Map,* by Mountain Trails Foundation.

### Trailhead Access

Begin at Park City City Park, which is located on Park Avenue between 13th and 14th Streets.

# 8
# Solamere

**JUST THE FACTS**

| Location: | Deer Valley Resort-Solamere |
|---|---|
| Length: | 7.5 miles, loop |
| Tread: | 1.5 miles pavement, 6 miles singletrack |
| Physically: | Moderately strenuous (four moderate climbs, four switchbacking descents) |
| Technically: | $2^+$-$4^+$ (good trails throughout; tight switchbacks; descent off Heinous Hill is short but wicked) |
| Gain: | 830 feet |
| In a nutshell: | Snow Park Lodge-Gambel Oak-Solamere Connection-Jan's Connector-Hidden Hollow-Snow Top-Gap Trail-Snow Park Lodge |

This loop takes you around Solamere on trails that demonstrate how the concerted efforts of individuals, planners, and developers have made recreational paths an integral part and valuable amenity to this mountain community. Granted, you won't experience the solitude of true backcountry trails on this route because condominiums, custom homes, and paved roads are almost always in sight. Although contrived, these singletracks are excellent, and you'll quickly appreciate the locals' commitment to improving their quality of life through recreation. Four climbs hallmark the loop, none of which is overly taxing. Each is offset with an exciting descent, blending full-throttle straightaways and tricky switchbacks. Typical of Park City, you can tack on peripheral trails to the Solamere loop and ride to your heart's and legs' content.

## Details

Start out from Deer Valley Resort's Snow Park Lodge with an easy 0.6-mile glide down Deer Valley Drive South, and then fork right onto Meadow Mountain Road (just past the junction with Deer Valley Drive North). The sharp grade will start your heart pumping. Go right onto Gambel Oak Trail, just past the junction with Sunnyside Drive. The dirt-and-pebble trail rises moderately around three pairs of switchbacks and through the trail's namesake foliage (tech 3). (You may encounter trail detours due to residential developments.) One rocky stretch near the top will test your muscle and balance (tech 4). Top out at a four-way junction in a small clearing on the east side of Masonic Hill (**m1.7**), and go right onto Solamere Connection Trail to undue the previous climb. Hastily descend 13 tight switchbacks (plus a few squiggles at the bottom) on smooth and choppy tread (tech 3-4) to Solamere Drive opposite the tennis courts. Take Solamere Drive left, turn right onto Telemark Drive and then onto Queen Ester Drive. Take the bypass trail around the Deer Crest entrance gate (**m3.4**), go up the road a couple hundred feet, and turn sharply left to resume on singletrack.

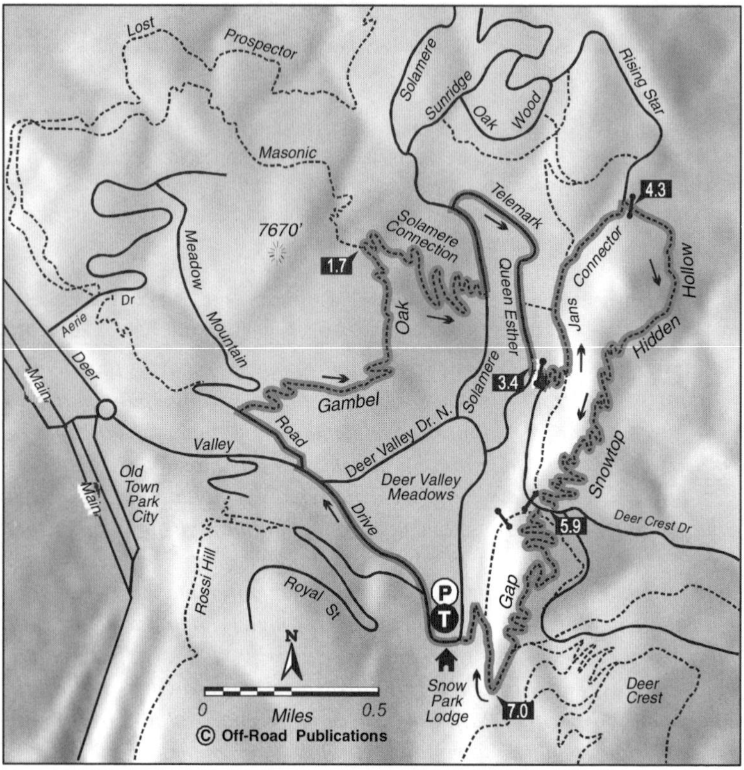

**56** Mountain Biking Park City & Beyond

Climb six switchbacks; then fork left from the seventh turn (a right-hander) onto Jan's Connector Trail. Continue climbing moderately, staying right at all junctions, and exit to the cul de sac on Rising Star Lane (**m4.3**). Stay to the right of the gate, and hop onto Hidden Hollow Trail for an effortless glide on buffed trail through towering aspens. You'll catch a quick glimpse of Jordanelle Reservoir and the eastern Uinta Mountains as you round the knoll. Ready for climb number three? More than one

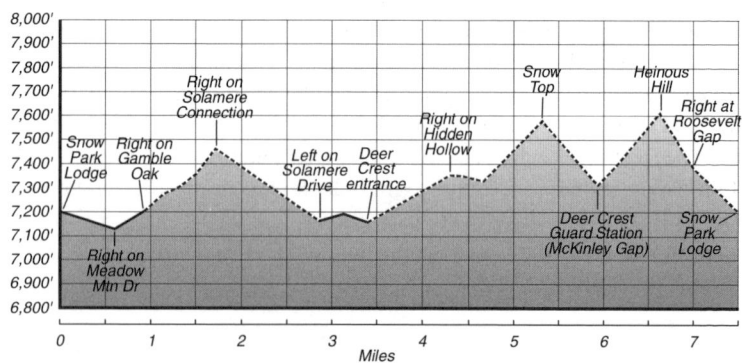

James charges up Snowtop Trail; Deer Valley Meadows below.

dozen switchbacks effectively ease the grade, but you'll need good balance and strong legs to clean the sharp turns. In between, the trail is smooth and gently pitched. Stop at the top to enjoy the panoramic view of this mountain community because once you begin descending you'll need to turn your attention to the trail beneath your wheels. Eight tight turns (tech 4) take you off the knoll to another gated station for Deer Crest at McKinley Gap (**m5.9**).

Cross the paved road, hop up the embankment, and begin the loop's fourth and final climb up Heinous Hill on Gap Trail. (You can bypass this last climb by taking the trail to the right around the knoll.) Moderate grades and biker friendly turns might have you wondering, "what's so heinous about this hill?" Your question will be answered when you roll off the top and drop through tight, steep, rough switchbacks (tech 4[+]) that have forced elite racers to dab a foot or dismount. Whoa! Lastly, go right at Roosevelt Gap (**m7.0**) and descend to Snow Park Lodge. (Roosevelt Gap Trail is notorious for being rerouted because of ongoing construction at Deer Valley Resort, so watch for trail markers and obey travel restrictions.)

**Option:** Deer Crest Add-on

Keep going, and take in some riotous singletracks along the way. You'll add about 5 miles and climb another 800 feet. When you reach Roosevelt Gap, climb Outlook Trail to the left, and make your way over to the famed Spin Cycle Trail (see the chapter "Deer Crest"). True to its name, the luge-style trail is wound tighter than a corkscrew, but you must pay dues for the roller coaster ride by climbing the long-winded Village Trail back to McKinley Gap. Finish off the ride by either going over or around Heinous Hill.

### Know Before You Go

- Stay on designated trails and be mindful of private property. Watch for detours around construction areas. This loop is signed with trail markers that correspond to *Park City Trail Map*.

### Maps & More Information

- USGS 1:24,000: Park City East, Utah.
- *Park City Trail Map,* by Mountain Trails Foundation.

### Trailhead Access

From Park Avenue (at Jans and Cole Sport), take Deer Valley Drive to Deer Valley Resort's Snow Park Lodge (resort base). From Old Town Park City (Main Street), take Heber Avenue to the roundabout, and then take Deer Valley Drive to Snow Park Lodge.

## 9
## Deer Crest (Spin Cycle & more)

**JUST THE FACTS**

| | |
|---|---|
| Location: | Lower Deer Valley Resort |
| Length: | 9.7 miles, loop |
| Tread: | 0.6 mile paved roads, 0.5 mile doubletrack, 8.6 miles singletrack |
| Physically: | Moderately strenuous (steady climbs on good trails) |
| Technically: | $2^+$-$4^+$ (good trails throughout; tight switchbacking descents on Spin Cycle, Snowtop, and Gap Trails) |
| Gain: | 1,800 feet |
| In a nutshell: | Snow Park Lodge-Roosevelt Gap-Outlook-Spin Cycle-Village Trail-Snowtop-Hidden Hollow-Jans Connector-Heinous Hill-Roosevelt Gap-Snow Park Lodge |

**WHY SHOULD U RIDE THIS TRAIL?**

The legendary Spin Cycle Trail lives on, but in a new location in the exclusive Deer Crest subdivision—formerly Telemark Park. This luge-style trail, with its dozens of dizzying, high-banked turns, is better than ever. The difference is that the "new and improved" Spin Cycle takes more effort to get to and from. It's all good because in the real world of mountain biking, downhills are meant to be earned. Don't freak out; we're not talking about lung-searing, leg-cramping grinds of interminable length but of "comfortably strenuous" climbs on wooded singletracks. The entire loop, with its blend of steady climbs and switchbacking descents has race course written all over it. In fact, these trails have been integral parts of mountain bike races, including the annual Park City Pedalfest and past NORBA National Championship Series. If you're riding with others, it's almost inevitable that the pace will gradually quicken until you are all going full-throttle in an undeclared race.

### Details

Start out by making the half-mile-long, switchbacking climb on Roosevelt Gap Trail (tech $2^+$). It begins on the Black Diamond entry road between Powder Run Condominiums and Snow Park Lodge. Construction in this area may close the trail temporarily. If so, then you'll have to access the Deer Crest trails via Little Stick (the steep dirt service road/ski run behind the lodge) or via Queen Esther Drive at the lower Deer Crest entrance gate (0.5 mile north of the lodge).

From Roosevelt Gap, descend toward the vehicle bridge but don't go under it; fork right and climb Outlook Trail. (Pipeline Trail, which passes under the bridge, is an optional return route when climbing Village Trail.) The trail rises moderately, but you'll have to muscle your way around the switchbacks (tech 3-4). Ignore Deer Crest Trail, which forks right at the second turn, and keep climbing Outlook. At the seventh turn, fork left to stay on Outlook (**m1.3**), which contours the hillside and affords a gaping view of Jordanelle Reservoir. Power up a short hill, and top out on an emergency access road. Go left and descend the road under a bridge to an intersection marked with a stop sign. (Watch for trail markers directing

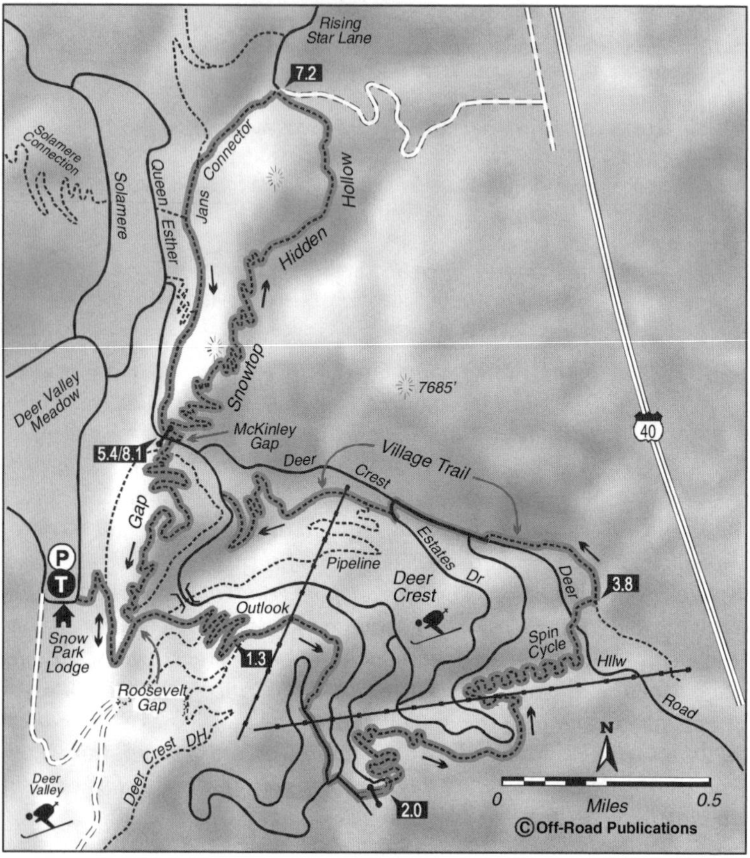

**60** Mountain Biking Park City & Beyond

you through the streets.) Turn left; then turn right immediately on Home Run Court. After the first house, turn left onto a service road and go around a gate. You'll find an antique washing machine on the right marking its namesake trail (**m2.0**).

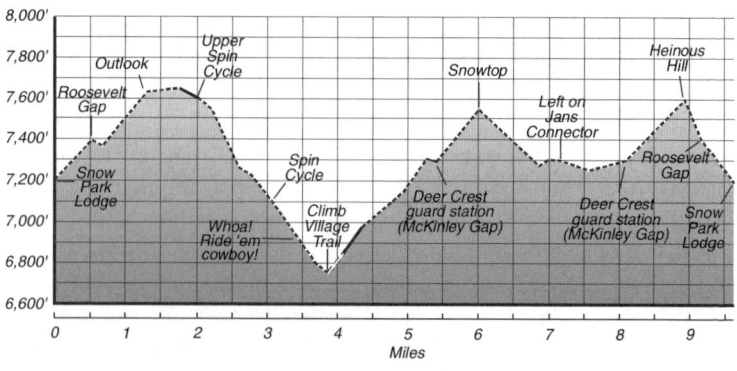

Whoa, cowboy, you're not there yet. First, find your groove by curving down the lush hollow, which is striped with tall, pretty, bleach-white aspens. This is just a teaser of things to come. Join with a doubletrack/ski run, and go under a bridge with the distant Jordanelle Reservoir in your sights. After the

Chris heads down Spin Cycle—in haste.

road/ski run bends right, watch for a singletrack forking left under a ski lift. Dive into the hollow again, and hold on tight. It's Friday night on the PBR circuit (that's Pro Bull Riding), and Spin Cycle's twisting trail will try to buck you from your saddle (tech 4). Yee-ha! As you bank back and forth down the gully, you'll get the feel for feathering your brakes as gravity pulls you around each turn. There's no need to skid! Just when you've tamed the beast, the rodeo ride ends. Go left around the maintenance building, cross paved Deer Hollow Road, descend a bit more on dirt to a wide doubletrack/ski run, and start your climb up Village Trail (**m3.8**). Village intersects paved Deer Hollow Road in a few hundred yards, and you'll ride briefly on pavement.

Spin up the road, go under a bridge, turn left on Deer Crest Estates Drive, and find the continued Village Trail immediately on the right. Climb steadily through the mixed woods (tech 3) and stay right at the junction with Pipeline Trail, unless you want to shortcut the loop to Roosevelt Gap. Cross under Deer Crest Lift, duck back into the woods, and keep chipping away at the climb. Just think, elite racers charge up this trail in middle chainring. Ouch! Pop out to a paved road, and go right to Deer Crest's gated guard station at McKinley Gap (**m5.4**).

Pick up Snowtop Trail to the right of the gate, and climb in earnest around tight turns (tech 3-4). (You'll return on the left fork, Jan's Connector.) A fast, mile-long switch-

The NORBA circuit comes to Deer Crest.

Brad drops into Spin Cycle.

backing descent on Hidden Hollow Trail (tech 3-4) takes you off the knoll's east side; then it levels for a sweet ramble through towering aspens. Exit to the paved cul de sac on Rising Star Lane (**m7.2**), and then take the trail to the left and under the rope tow lift. Jan's Connector Trail traverses around the knoll's west side and high above the Solamere community. Stay left at all junctions and return to the Deer Crest gate at McKinley Gap (**m8.1**).

Cross the road at the gate and head up Heinous Hill on Gap Trail, following signs for Solamere Loop. (Trails to the right and left contour around the knoll.) Moderate grades and smooth turns hardly make the climb "shockingly brutal or cruel" as the hill's name suggests, but the rugged descent to Roosevelt Gap is another story. The trail's rough, angular switchbacks require exact wheel placement and dialed-in balance (tech 4⁺). Even top racers are known to dab once or twice. Retrace your tracks from Roosevelt Gap to Snow Park Lodge to finish the loop.

## Know Before You Go

- Be alert to vehicle traffic on paved roads and to construction throughout Deer Crest.
- Deer Crest is a private community that has graciously provided for public recreation. Stay on designated trails, and respect private lands.
- A helmet is required when biking at Deer Crest.

## Maps & More Information

- USGS 1:24,000: Park City East, Utah.
- *Park City Trail Map,* by Mountain Trails Foundation.
- Deer Crest: (435) 655-8215.

## Trailhead Access

From Park Avenue (at Jans and Cole Sport), take Deer Valley Drive to Deer Valley's Snow Park Lodge (resort base). From Old Town Park City (Main Street), take Heber Avenue to the roundabout, and then take Deer Valley Drive to Snow Park Lodge.

## 10 Deer Valley Resort

**JUST THE FACTS**

| | |
|---|---|
| Location: | Silver Lake Express Lift at Snow Park Lodge (base) and Sterling Lift at Silver Lake Village (mid-mountain) |
| Length: | Up to 50 miles |
| Tread: | Singletracks with a bit of doubletracks |
| Physically: | Moderately easy to strenuous (resort trails are between 7,200 feet and 9,400 feet in elevation) |
| Technically: | 3-5 (maintained singletracks to extreme downhill routes) |
| Loss: | 1,300 feet (Sterling Lift); 1,200 feet (Silver Lake Express Lift) |
| In a nutshell: | See below |

**WHY SHOULD U RIDE THIS TRAIL**

Renown as one of the nation's most sophisticated ski resorts, Deer Valley Resort (DVR) has also emerged as one of the nation's premier mountain biking venues. With its summer trails program now more than a decade old, DVR boasts of over 50 miles of designated bike trails that are accessed from two lifts running tandem up two mountains: Silver Lake Express from the resort base at Snow Park Lodge and Sterling Lift from mid-mountain at Silver Lake Village.

Lift-served access means downhill cruising is the name of the game, and DVR offers a variety of trails that require nary a pedal stroke, ranging from meandering singletracks geared for first-time bikers to world-class descents reserved for expert downhill racers. You'll even find a small "terrain park" on the upper mountain, including ramps, teeters, skinnys, and other pre-fabbed stunts. Although DVR caters to the freeride crowd, the resort has remained dedicated to keeping the "biking" in mountain biking and offers miles of excellent cross-country-style trails, many of which have played roles in local and national mountain bike race courses.

### Details

**Lower DVR Trails** (Silver Lake Express Lift at Snow Park Lodge):
**(1) Lakeside Trails** (1 mile, easy, tech 1): These paved trails circle the lakes of Deer Valley Meadows north of the parking lots. They are perfect for families with children, and the lakes provide picturesque picnic spots.

**(2) Tour de Homes** (2.5 miles, moderate, tech 2-3⁺): TdH is a blend of dirt service roads and singletracks linking Snow Park Lodge and Sterling Drive at Silver Lake Village. Over the years, it's been the out-of-the-starting-gate climb for the annual Park City PedalFest mountain bike race. As the trail's name implies, you'll ride past custom homes that line the resort's ski runs.

To climb from Snow Park Lodge, head up the service road under Silver Lake Express Lift and veer right to climb steeply on a gravel road. You'll fork right from the road into some tall pines and pedal up smooth singletrack. Watch for trail signs directing you over and under skier bridges and to Sterling Drive at Silver Lake Village. Gain is about 800 feet.

**(3) Four Point** (1 mile, moderate, tech 3-4): This singletrack connects Silver Lake Village with the Deer Crest trail system. To make a cross-country loop around the lower resort, first climb Tour de Homes and then link to Four Point, which takes off from the dirt service road running under Silver Lake Express Lift from Silver Lake Village. The trail combines smooth and rocky tread with tight switchbacks, and it takes you across ski runs and through patches of dense timber to the Little Stick and Deer Crest Downhill trails, passing Devo and NCS Trails along the way.

**(4) Deer Crest Downhill** (2.5 miles, moderate, tech 3): This wide singletrack, accessed from Four Point, connects Bald Eagle Mountain and Snow Park Lodge with the Deer Crest trail system. You'll find scenic views of Jordanelle Reservoir to the east, the Wasatch Crest to the west, and lower DVR and Solamere to the north. As you head down Deer Crest, fork left at the junction with Outlook Trail to reach Snow Park Lodge, or fork right on Outlook to head over to the famed Spin Cycle Trail. (See chapter "Deer Crest.")

**(5) Little Stick** (0.75 mile, moderate, tech 3): If you like speed, then point your wheels down Little Stick. This dirt and gravel service road takes off from near the junction of Four Point and Deer Crest Downhill Trails and takes a "direct" line to the base at Snow Park Lodge. A high speed straightaway precedes a hairpin turn left, so ride attentively; then a steeper descent crossed by speed bumps takes you to the base.

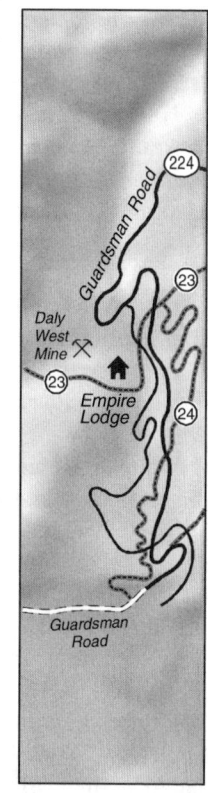

**(6) Bone** (0.5 mile, moderate, tech 4-5): This singletrack is a steep, twisting, technical connector trail between Four Point and Little Stick. A short uphill section requires you to put power to the pedals while tight turns and rough tread demand deft handling.

**(7) Devo** (2 miles, moderate, tech 3⁺-4⁺): Dropping 1,200 feet from Bald Eagle Mountain to the base at Snow Park Lodge, Devo is an extreme-level "cross-country downhill," or in today's terminology, a "freeride" trail. It's steep, rough, and requires expert skills. Parts of the trail have been used in local and national races.

Devo takes off from near the top of Homestake Lift on Bald Eagle Mountain and forks left where NCS forks right. You'll cross Four Point, dive into the thick timber, and switchback down under Silver Lake Express Lift.

Deer Valley Resort **65**

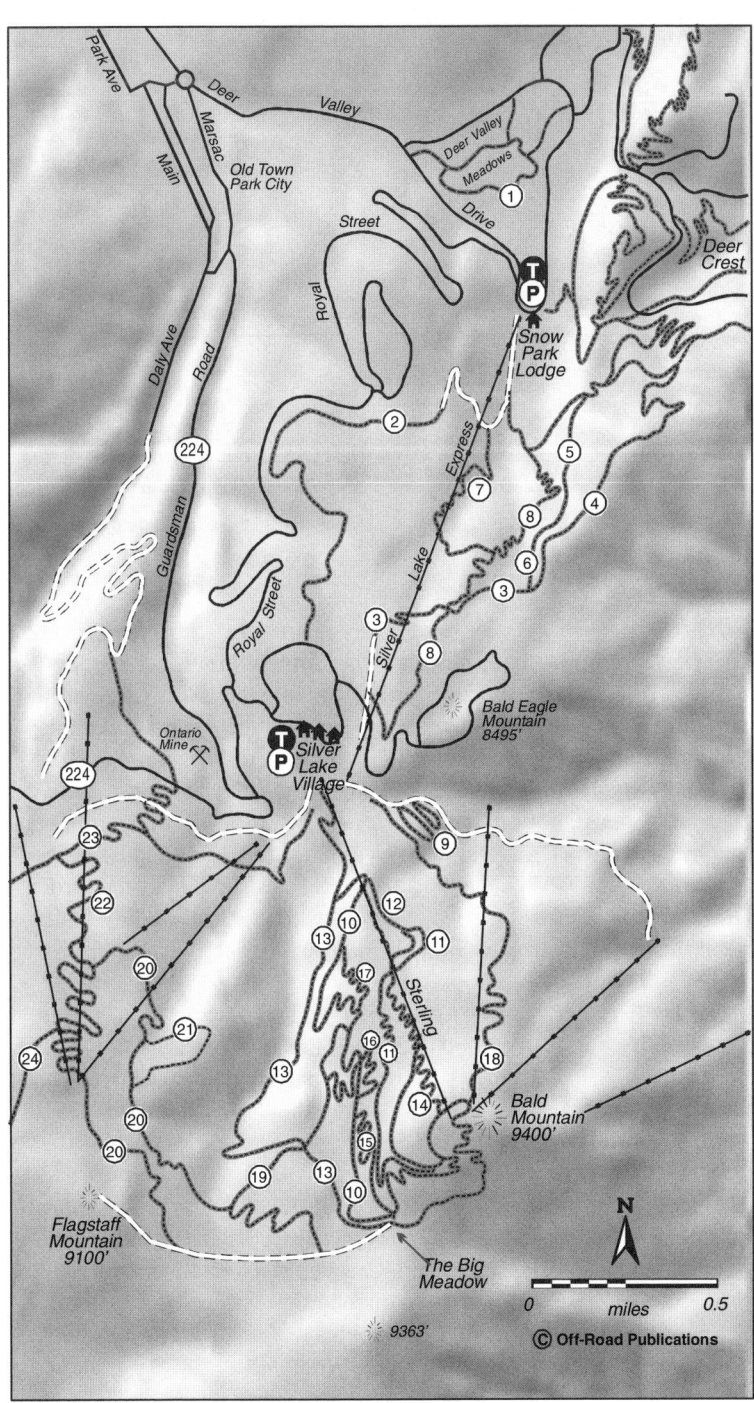

The gang takes a lap around Flagstaff Loop.

Steve makes the big root drop on Freestyle look easy.

**(8) NCS (National Championship Series Downhill)** (1.5 miles, strenuous, tech 5+): Built for the 2001 NORBA Nationals, NCS is one of the most difficult downhill race courses in the country. It's steep and extremely technical, so it's recommended only for the expert rider or pro downhill racer. A downhill-specific bike and protective gear are recommended.

Out of the starting gate, you'll catch air off a big rock jump then plummet down a rock waterfall (sans water). A section in the middle, dubbed "Barney Rubble," is a boulder field that would make Fred Flintstone proud. The bottom is marked by steep, tight switchbacks followed by a high-speed run out to the base. Scout this route before you ride it.

**Upper DVR Trails** (Sterling Lift at Silver Lake Village)
**(9) McHenry's Practice Loop** (1.5 miles, moderately easy, tech 2): This quick loop is the perfect trail for beginners to practice their skills and check out their bikes. Access it by taking the dirt road located east of Sterling and Homestake Lifts and at the top of McHenry's ski run.

**(10) Naildriver** (2.1 miles, moderate, tech 3): Naildriver is the main downhill route from the top of Sterling Lift. The wide path winds through groves of aspens and affords views of Park City below. Control your speed and be watchful of loose gravel, sharp turns, and slower riders. Access the trail by following Sunset ski run off Bald Mountain and by heading towards the multiple junction in the big meadow.

Deer Camp Trail is even better in color.     Miners were here first.

**(11) Sunset** (2.5 miles, moderate, tech 3): Like Naildriver, Sunset is one of the least difficult downhill routes. Still, the switchbacks near the top can be tricky and the lower sections can have choppy rocks and gravel. Overall, the trail is biker friendly and passes through glorious aspen groves and across scenic ski runs. If you find upper Sunset to be a piece of cake, then veer onto Freestyle for a more exciting finish.

**(12) Freestyle** (1.5 miles, moderate, tech 4-5): Freestyle is designed for riders who like steep, twisting singletrack through tight trees, with an exciting (and surprise) drop near the end. Access it from Sunset or Aspen Slalom where the trails converge under Sterling Lift.

**(13) Homeward Bound** (3 miles, moderate, tech 3-4): This is the longest downhill route from the top of Sterling Lift, so you get maximum bang for your buck. Tight switchbacks up top give way to curvy turns in the middle and speedy straightaways near the bottom. You can test your skills in the small terrain park near the bottom, which has ramps, teeters, skinnys, and other freeride features. The terrain park is a work in progress and may expand in the future. Access the trail from the top of Sterling Lift by heading to the reflector shields and then riding through the big meadow.

**(14) Aspen Slalom** (2 miles, moderate, tech $3^+$-$4^+$): This tight singletrack features slalom-like turns through dense aspens. Since it follows under

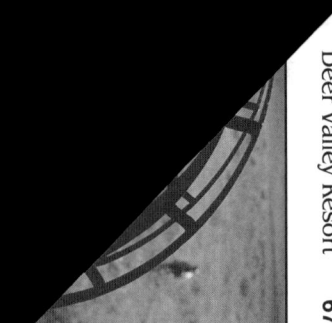

& Beyond

to those on the lift above. Finish off on

...derate, tech 3-4): This singletrack fea-
...ens and is accessed from Naildriver by
...ink to G.S. Trees, lower Naildriver, and
...gletrack descent.

...ate, tech 3-4): If you like the thrill of
...ur sights on G.S. Trees. Turns are plen-
tiful and playful on this tight singletrack, which runs through dense aspens. Get to G.S. Trees from Super G Trees or by veering from Naildriver after crossing Sunset West ski run.

**(17) Twist and Shout** (0.5 mile, moderate, tech 4-5): Once the acid test of skill and courage, Twist and Shout has been overshadowed by other downhill-specific trails, like Fire Swamp and Thieves Forest. Still, Twist and Shout is a daring drop through radical turns and side-swiping trees. Twist down this singletrack without "dabbing" a foot (or bailing out altogether) and you'll have something to shout about! The trail forks right from Naildriver about halfway down; otherwise, you can get primed for action by first descending Super G Trees and G.S. Trees to the trail junction on Naildriver.

**(18) Thieves Forest and Fire Swamp** (1.5 miles each, strenuous, tech 5): Although two separate trails, Thieves Forest and Fire Swamp share a common thread: both are expert-level descents geared for fearless riders on downhill-specific bikes. Protective gear is recommended. Expect to find radical drops over rocks and logs, eroded tread, and hang-your-butt-off-the-back stunts. Needless to say, these trails rate high on the "pucker scale." If you dare lift your eyes from the trail, however, you'll find scenic views of the Jordanelle Reservoir valley below.

**(19) Deer Camp** (3.5 miles, moderately strenuous, tech 3⁺): Deer Camp loops through a dense grove of aspens and is a "must ride" during autumn when aspen leaves sprinkle the trail like gold doubloons. With a blend of tight and open turns, dips, and doodles, you'll flow around this singletrack like a surfer catching a wave. Link together Deer Camp and upper Homeward Bound for a small loop near the big meadow, tap into G.S. Trees for a downhill run, or head over to Flagstaff Loop for a longer cross-country tour. Watch for two-way traffic.

**(20) Flagstaff Loop** (4 miles, moderately strenuous, tech 3-4): If you like to "ride" your mountain bike, instead of being a mere victim of gravity, then you'll find excellent cross-country-style pedaling on Flagstaff Loop.

Big air!

A DHer finds his "groove."

You'll stay high on the mountain and make a big loop to the top of Red Cloud Lift and back. Portions have been used in race courses, so you can expect a blend of full-throttle straights, twisting turns, and technical stunts all on rolling singletrack. Flagstaff takes off a short ways down Deer Camp. Watch for two-way traffic. (Portions of this trail will be rerouted due to construction of the Red Cloud subdivision. Therefore, portions of the trail may be temporarily closed.)

**(21) Ontario Loop** (0.5 mile, strenuous, tech 4) This side loop to Flagstaff traverses around Ontario Bowl on singletrack with quick climbs and choppy tread. It affords good views of Silver Lake Village along the way.

**(22) TBB (Team Big Bear)** (2.2 miles, moderate, tech 3+): TBB is a cross-country-style downhill that combines fast straightaways and sharp turns. You'll venture to the outer limits of the mountain bike park and meander through pristine woods and across sunny ski runs.

Access TBB from the west side of Flagstaff Loop by taking the Tour des Suds/Team Big Bear Connector. After you wrap around the knoll where several lifts converge, your brakes will become your greatest allies as gravity takes over. Go right on Mid Mountain Trail to return to the base of Sterling Lift. (All or part of TBB will be rerouted due to construction of the Red Cloud subdivision. Therefore, portions of the trail may be temporarily closed.)

Chillin' on the lift at Deer Valley.

**(23) Mid Mountain Trail** (4 miles or more, moderate, tech 3): Mid Mountain Trail (MMT) takes you away from the mountain bike park on a cross-country tour to Empire Lodge and back. From the lodge, you can continue on MMT to Park City Mountain Resort (or all the way to The Canyons Resort) or link to a variety of trails around Daly (Empire) Canyon. To get to MMT, descend west on the dirt service road from the base of Sterling Lift, and fork left onto the trail under the skiers' bridge. No chairlift access. (See chapter "Mid Mountain Trail-South.")

**(24) Tour des Suds** (5.5 miles, moderate, tech 3+): Tour des Suds takes you away from the mountain bike park on a roundabout tour of Deer Valley's upper mountain and to the base of Sterling Lift. (Portions of this trail will be rerouted due to construction of the Red Cloud subdivision. Therefore, expect closures.)

Access upper Tour des Suds ("new Suds") from Flagstaff Loop and upper Team Big Bear (TTB). Take TTB around the combined summits of Quincy, Silver Strike, Northside, and Ruby Lifts, fork left on Upper Suds/ TBB Connector Trail and descend gradually to Guardsman Road. Cross the road and dive down the upper stretch of TDS. Cross back over Guardsman Road, and angle down the mountain around a half dozen switchbacks on "new Suds" to MMT. Fork right on MMT and roll back to the base of Sterling Lift. Better yet, save a few bucks, snub the lift altogether, and *climb* Tour des Suds. Take a lap around Flagstaff Loop, connect with Deer Camp, and descend G.S. Trees and Twist and Shout for a superb cross-country ride.

**The BIG Loop** (11 miles, strenuous, tech 3+): Got legs? Test your mettle and might against this ultimate cross-country loop from Snow Park Lodge to the top of Bald Mountain and back. You'll gain almost 2,500 feet in the process and take in some of the finest trails at DVR.

Start at Snow Park Lodge by climbing Tour des Homes to Silver Lake Village. Hop on MMT, climb Tour des Suds, and take a lap around Flagstaff Loop on the upper mountain. Now that you've built up all that potential energy, let kinetics take over by descending Deer Camp to G.S. Trees to Twist and Shout to Naildriver to Silver Lake Village. One short climb up the service road under Silver Express Lift takes you to Four Point, where you continue the cross-country descent. Link to Deer Crest Downhill and cruise back to Snow Park Lodge. That's what mountain biking is all about.

Want more? Instead of returning to Snow Park Lodge on lower Deer Crest Downhill, fork right on Outlook and then slip down Spin Cycle's singletrack luge run. Keep in mind that if you do, you'll have to climb about 600 vertical feet up Village Trail to return to Snow Park Lodge.

### ❗ Know Before You Go

- Sterling and Silver Lake Express Lifts operate 10 a.m. to 5 p.m. daily from mid-June to Labor Day, and then Saturday and Sunday only through late September, weather permitting.
- Chairlift rates are $20 for an all-day bike pass, $12 for a single-ride pass, and $250 for a Summer Season Pass.
- Helmets are required for all bikers.
- Trails may be temporarily closed without notice. Stay on designated bike trails and obey all trail signs.
- Always yield to vehicles, horses, hikers, and riders pedaling uphill.
- Don't stop where you might obstruct a trail or are not visible to others.
- Trails are not regularly patrolled.
- Notify the lift operator for first-aid assistance, or call (435) 645-6733.
- Smoking is not permitted on the mountain.
- Mountain bike rentals, accessories, and protective clothing are available at Deer Valley's Bike Rental Shop at Silver Lake Lodge. For more information, call (435) 645-6648.
- Deer Valley Mountain Bike School offers group and individual tours and skills clinics. For more information, call (435) 645-6648.
- For lodging, dining, and vacation packages: (800) 558-DEER (3337).

### ❓ Maps & More Information

- USGS 1:24,000: Brighton, Heber City, and Park City East, Utah.
- *Park City Trail Map,* by Mountain Trails Foundation.
- *Deer Valley Resort Summer Trail Map,* by Deer Valley Resort: (800) 424-DEER (3337) or (435) 649-1000, www.deervalley.com.

### Trailhead Access

*Snow Park Lodge (Silver Lake Express Lift):* From Main Street in Park City, take Heber Avenue to the roundabout, and then take Deer Valley Drive to Snow Park Lodge. *Silver Lake Village (Sterling Lift):* From the roundabout on Deer Valley Drive, take Marsac Avenue to Guardsman Road (UT 224), and drive up Ontario Canyon. Just past the historic Ontario Mine, turn left onto Guardsman Pass Connection then right at the junction with Royal Street West to reach Silver Lake Village. Alternatively, from Snow Park Lodge, drive up Royal Street and Royal Street West.

# 11
# Tour des Suds

**JUST THE FACTS**

| | |
|---|---|
| **Location:** | Daly (Empire) Canyon |
| **Length:** | 6.4 miles (approximate), one-way |
| **Tread:** | 0.7 mile paved bike path, 1 mile paved road, 1.7 miles doubletrack, 3 miles singletrack |
| **Physically:** | Strenuous (one long, steady climb; sharp switchbacks) |
| **Technically:** | 1-3+ (smooth and rough singletracks; tight switchbacks) |
| **Gain:** | 2,050 feet |
| **In a nutshell:** | Poison Creek Trail-Main Street-Daly Canyon-TDS-Ontario Bypass-MMT-TDS |

**WHY SHOULD U RIDE THIS TRAIL?**

Tour des Suds (TDS) is a long-standing Park City tradition dating back to 1983. It began as an impromptu event held by a handful of local road racers, who hopped on their "clunkers" for a day of spirited off-road racing through Park City's mountains. Today, the fall classic attracts hundreds. Although many participants are devoted racers, most are admitted non-competitive types who simply enjoy the camaraderie of fellow bikers. Some go full tilt and ride in the wackiest of costumes—just for grins. The Tour has maintained its light-hearted, tongue-in-cheek appeal, for it is every bit as much a social event as it is a timed race. And it's still highlighted by a post-race picnic with plenty of "suds."

Tour des Suds is a great ride other than on race day, too, if you like hill climbs. You'll warm up on paved roads, and then climb steadily on doubletracks and singletracks. You'll enjoy copious freewheeling on the return, whether you retrace your tracks or follow nearby trails.

### Details

Tour des Suds can be a navigational nightmare because some sections, especially at Deer Valley Resort (DVR), get booted around faster than a soccer ball at the mercy of Mia Hamm. But DVR is committed to upholding the legacy of TDS and to providing a through route. The directions that follow are exasperating, so be patient.

Although the official TDS race goes up Park Avenue from City Park, take the paved Poison Creek Trail from the park instead and climb gently along the willow-lined hollow and behind condominiums. When you reach Heber Avenue (near the roundabout), turn right then left, and sprint up historic Main Street, as racers do during the timed event. (Alternatively, go up Swede Alley.) Stay straight at the top of Main and continue on Daly Avenue, passing renovated miners' homes that are designated as national historic landmarks.

Go around the United Park City Mines gate, shortly after the pavement turns to dirt (**m2.0**), and pump hard up the steep, gravel road (tech 2+). (United Park City Mines has graciously welcomed public recreation on its land, so they deserve our sincere thanks.) Bend left around the big

Left: TG 1 Trail slips through crook-neck aspens. Right: crossing Daly Bowl on TG 1.

beige water tank, and continue straight at the intersection where "Town Trail" forks right and leads to the Judge Mine. Climb the dirt road to the top of the hill and under the power lines; then hop onto the Prospect Ridge singletrack and climb steeply on rough tread (tech 3⁺). (Contruction might alter this section.) Pop out to a doubletrack, and either take it left high above Ontario Canyon (easier) or continue climbing the Prospect Ridge trail (harder). If you chose the former, then follow the road around a right bend after it passes under the power lines and intersect the Prospect Ridge trail. If you chose the latter, chug up the steeply pitched trail and cross over the doubletrack. Regardless, both routes now follow the Ontario Bypass Trail (tech 3). (If you reach a washout in the doubletrack that overlooks the big beige water tank in Daly Canyon, then you missed the Ontario Bypass Trail by a couple hundred feet.) The singletrack rises through the aspens, exits to a doubletrack next to two old wooden water tanks, and intersects paved Guardsman Road. Phew! Are you with me?

Climb Guardsman Road about 50 feet; then fork left onto the singletrack (tech 3⁺). Exit to a dirt road, go right and climb about 150 feet, and then fork left onto the continued trail. Climb several switchbacks to the intersection with Mid Mountain Trail (MMT, **m4.2**) and go right. Climb

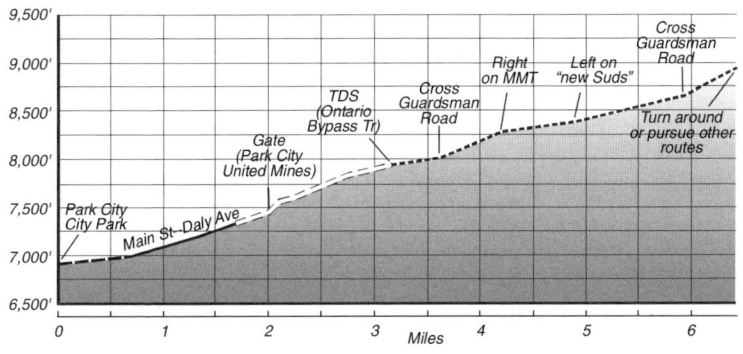

**74** Mountain Biking Park City & Beyond

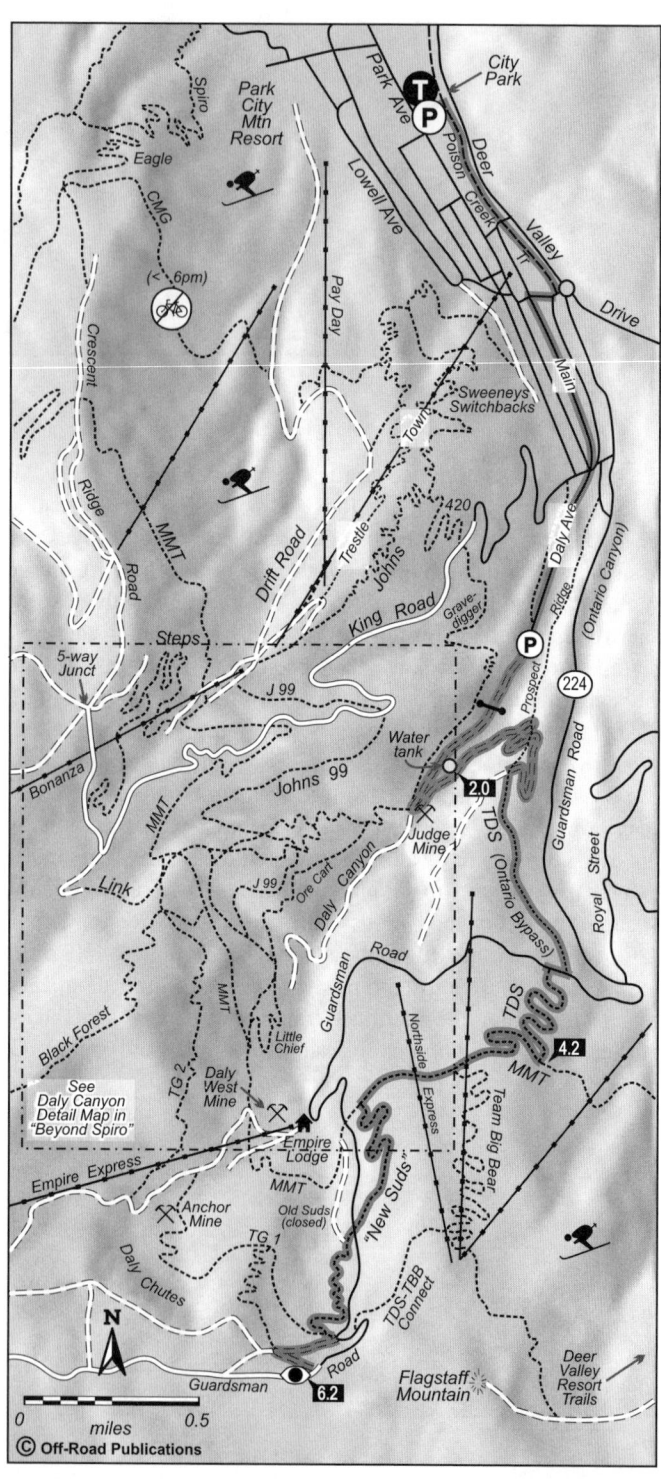

gradually across ski runs and through islands of timber, and fork left on the new-and-improved "new Suds," just before MMT crosses Guardsman Road. Are you still with me? (The old route goes left on the other side of Guardsman Road. Watch for trail markers.)

The rest of TDS is a guessing game because "new Suds," is a work in progress. At the time of publication, "new Suds" was planned to stay on the *east* side of Guardsman Road for another 0.9 mile (to about 8,680 feet) and then cross to the west side of Guardsman Road to tie into the top of the old trail. Much of the old TDS above Empire Lodge will be abandoned due to new road construction. You should cross another paved road before you come to the junction with TG Trail. Go straight and pump uphill to Guardsman Road where the road bends left. Clear as mud, right?

Although you might have had enough of these navigational shenanigans, TDS is not officially over. Fork right onto a doubletrack, and climb a few hundred yards to the top of the ridge (**m6.2**). There, you can breathe a victorious sigh of relief, while overlooking Daly Bowl to the north, the backside of Brighton Resort to the west, and the fertile meadows and glorious aspens of Bonanza Flats to the south. It's all downhill back to town. Retrace your tracks, provided you memorized the way, or follow one of the options below.

**Option:** Deer Valley Resort
Return to the left bend on Guardsman Road. Cross the road and link to the new "Upper Tour des Suds/Team Big Bear Connector Trail," which ties into Deer Valley Resort's Team Big Bear Trail and Flagstaff Loop. All of these trails are "new-and-improved" due to development of the Red Cloud Subdivision on Deer Valley Resort. Your choices for descending through Deer Valley Resort are endless (see chapter "Deer Valley Resort").

**Option:** TG 1-MMT
These trails take you across the top of Daly Canyon and return you to the junction of MMT and the "new Suds."

From the ridge at the top of TDS, take TG 1 Trail (singletrack) on a contour across the canyon's uppermost slopes (tech 3⁺), and bank down tight, rocky switchbacks (tech 4) to a T-junction with TG Trail. (If you go right, then you'll return to TDS.) Go left, slip through a stand of crookneck aspens, and exit the timber beneath the cliffs of Daly Bowl—a skier's haute route. Watch for moose, which are known to inhabit these moist meadows. The trail passes beneath the huge tailings of the old Anchor Mine (talk about a perfectly pitched powder run) and intersects the upper Daly Canyon dirt road. Descend like wind-fanned wildfire toward Empire Lodge, but not all the way. Watch carefully for Little Chief/MMT crossing the dirt road. Take the combined trails to the right, circle around Empire Lodge, and cross Guardsman Road. Finish off the descent on lower TDS.

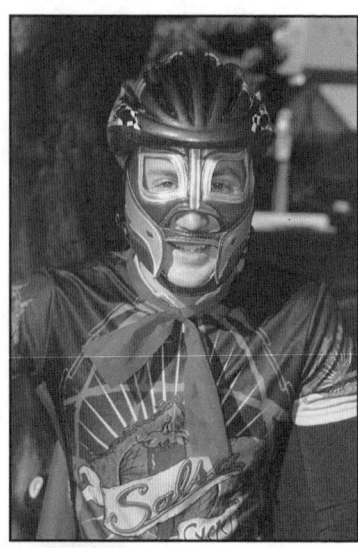

It's a race, it's a party, it's a freak show. No, it's the Tour des Suds.

Alternatively, if you go left on Little Chief/MMT, you can descend to town through lower Daly Canyon via Ore Cart, Shovel, or Speed Bag Trails. All are steep, tight technical trails that rate tech 4⁺. (Beware of closures in Daly Canyon.) You'll pop out of Daly Canyon at the Judge Mine near the familiar beige water tank. If you stay on Little Chief/MMT, you'll eventually reach Park City Mountain Resort, where you'll have the option of taking John's Trail, Trestle Trail, and Sweeney's Switchbacks back to town (all rate tech 4). (See Daly Canyon Detail Map in the chapter "Beyond Spiro.")

**Option:** TG 2-Black Forest

Venture still farther into Park City's backcountry on seldom-traveled trails by descending TG 2 and Black Forest Trails. Take TG 1 Trail across Daly Bowl as described above to where it intersects the Daly Canyon dirt road. Don't descend; rather, climb the road, and fork right from the first left bend, following a resort sign for "Supreme." There, TG 2 Trail darts into the woods and becomes tight and exacting (tech 3-4); then it joins with Black Forest Trail amidst a picturesque grove of aspens. Drop down a steep shot to the intersection with MMT and Link Trail. Below Link, Black Forest winds playfully through the aspens then out across a sloping meadow to the intersection with John's '99 Trail. Below John's '99, Black Forest drops radically into Daly Canyon (tech 4-5). Whoa! Some sections are precipitous, so look before you leap. Go to the familiar beige water tank and coast down Daly Canyon back to town. Or link to Town Loop near the beige water tank and pursue still more singletrack.

### ❗ Know Before You Go

- Construction in Daly Canyon and at Deer Valley Resort may cause TDS to be rerouted or temporarily closed. Consult *Park City Trail Map* for trail updates. Watch for detours, and obey travel restrictions.
- Use caution crossing Guardsman Road.
- Upper TDS is planned to be rerouted as "new Suds." Watch for trail signs.

### ❓ Maps & More Information

- USGS 1:24,000: Brighton, Heber City, Park City East, and Park City West, Utah.
- *Park City Trail Map,* by Mountain Trails Foundation.

### Trailhead Access

Tour des Suds (race course) begins at City Park on Park Avenue. To skip the initial paved-road section, and thus one-third of the climb, drive up Main Street and then up Daly Avenue, and park where the pavement turns to dirt. Pick up the description above at **m2.0** at the gate.

## Town Loop

**JUST THE FACTS**

**Location:** Daly (Empire) Canyon
**Length:** 6.8 miles, loop
**Tread:** 1.7 miles paved road, 0.7 mile paved bike path, 0.8 mile dirt road, 3.6 miles singletrack
**Physically:** Moderately strenuous (steady climbs on paved and dirt roads then incremental climbs on singletracks)
**Technically:** 1-4+ (rugged, twisting singletracks; gravel dirt road)
**Gain:** 1,000 feet
**In a nutshell:** City Park-Poison Creek-Main Street-Daly Avenue-Gravedigger-4:20-John's-Sweeney's Switchbacks-Empire Avenue-City Park

### Why Should U Ride This Trail?

*Short on time? Looking for a quick, solid workout? Want to perfect your technical riding skills? If so, then Town Loop is your ride. This loop stays close to town, thus its name, and links together four different singletracks between Daly Canyon and Old Town. First, you'll jump start your heart, lungs, and legs by chugging up Main Street and Daly Canyon; then you'll hop onto the dicey Gravedigger and 4:20 singletracks and traverse the hillsides right above town. John's Trail and Sweeney's Switchbacks are twisting technical downhills that will return you to town. If you're fortunate enough to be on an extended lunch break, then you can add more miles to your heart's and legs' content.*

### Details

For the sake of simplicity, this loop begins at City Park, and you start out on the paved Poison Creek Trail behind the old Miner's Hospital. (You can start from anywhere in town, though.) The path rises gently along a willow-lined hollow and behind condominiums. When you reach Heber Avenue (near the roundabout), turn right then left, and head up historic Main Street. (Alternatively, you can pedal up Swede Alley.) Stay straight at the top of Main, and continue up Daly Avenue past some renovated miner's homes, which are designated national historic landmarks. After pavement turns to dirt, go through the gate for United Park City Mines, and pump hard up the steep, gravelly hill (tech 3). Bend left around the big beige water tank; then fork right on a dirt road signed for Town Loop, which takes you past the historic Judge Mine (**m2.4**).

Cross Daly Canyon and pick up Gravedigger Trail on the right side of the fenced-in power substation. The singletrack is easy at first, as it crosses the tops of mine tailings; then the trail angles up two short, remarkably steep hills (tech 4+). Tight rocky turns and chunky trail, thereafter, require that you be on top of your game, or you might "dig" your own "grave" (tech 4). Descend a gravelly doubletrack in Woodside Gulch (tech 3+) for 100 yards, fork left on a singletrack rising into the aspens, and exit to the dirt King Road (**m3.5**).

N
0 miles 0.25
© Off-Road Publications
Park Ave
Poison
City Park
Park City Mountain Resort
Lowell
Empire
Creek
Trail
Deer
Valley
Drive
Pay Day
Drift Road
CMG
(< 6 pm)
Flat Cable
Sweeneys Swbks.
Swede Alley
Main
5.0
Town
Johns
420
3.5
Trestle
Johns
Drift Road
Old angle station
MMT
Woodside
Gul
Daly Ave
Daly Bypass
(Ontario Canyon)
King Road
Johns '99
Silver King
Gravedigger
Water tank
Guardsman Road
Johns '99
Sub-station
Walker - Webster Gul
2.4
Judge Mine
Daly Cyn
MMT
TDS

8,400'
8,200'
8,000'
7,800'
7,600'
7,400'
7,200'
7,000'
6,800'
6,600'
Park City City Park
Gate (United Park City Mines)
Right on Gravedigger at Substation
Cross King Road on 4:20 Trail
Right on Johns Trail
Left on Sweeneys Switchbacks
Exit to Lowell-Empire Aves
Park City City Park
0
1
2
3
4
5
6
Miles

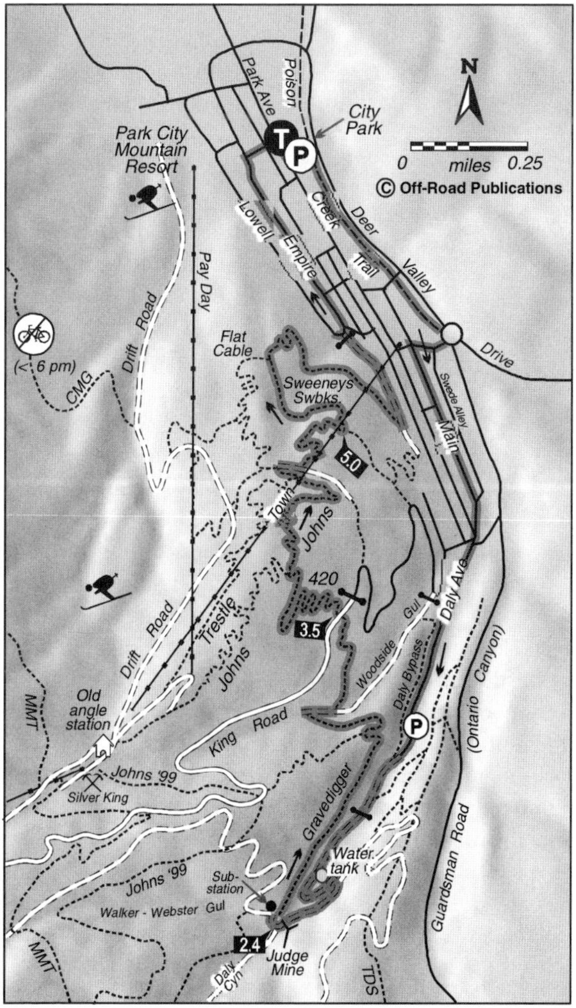

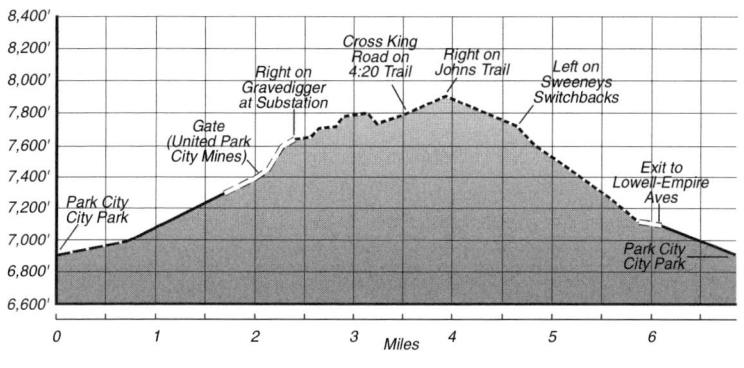

Thus it's called "town" loop.

If you've met your match, then you can bail out by descending King Road to upper Main Street in town. If you're jonesing for still more challenging singletrack, then cross King Road and hit 4:20 Trail. The steep entry ramp with a huge rock in the middle of it is almost impossible to ride (tech 5), so save your energy and dismount; 4:20 then curves playfully up through the oaks, maples, and aspens (tech 3+) to the intersection with John's Trail.

The climbing is done, unless you pursue upper John's Trail (see "Option" below). Go right and descend John's through tightly packed aspens (tech 3) to the lower junction with Trestle Trail. Now, go down to the doubletrack right below you and look for Sweeney's Switchbacks forking left, next to the old tramway trestle and under the newer Town Lift. Bank down through the timber on smooth and choppy tread (tech 3-4+), and stay left at the junction with South Sweeney's next to the "lone pine" (**m5.0,** see "Option"). More rock-hopping and switchback-dancing take you across Creole ski run and into a dark, dense stand of oaks and maples. Fork right, turning back under the lift and across lower Creole. Exit Sweeney's to a dirt road, and take it left to a cable gate on the horseshoe bend where Empire Avenue meets Lowell Avenue. Go right and coast down Empire, turn right on 14th Street, and turn right again on Park Avenue to return to City Park.

**Option:** John's-Trestle Add-on
If switchbacks are your game and you made easy work of Gravedigger and 4:20 Trails, then you'll love upper John's Trail because it's a veritable slalom course through the aspens. But you won't riding fast like a speeding skier; rather, the innumerable turns and multitude of roots demand a slow, calculated approach (tech 3-4+).

From the junction with 4:20, upper John's rises 1.4 miles to a knoll overlooking Town Lift. Fork sharply right, bend left past the top of Payday Lift, and fork right on Trestle Trail just down the dirt road. Aptly named, the trail follows the old support towers of the tramway that once hauled ore from the Silver King Mine down to town. The tread is choppy and the switchbacks are wickedly sharp (tech 3-4+). Pass directly under the supports of an old mine hoist and intersect the bottom of John's Trail. Take Sweeney's down to town as described above.

How wide are *your* handlebars?

**Option:** Return to Daly Canyon

If you park on Daly Avenue, where pavement turns to dirt, you can skip the climb up Poison Creek Trail and Main Street and still make this ride a loop. Ride as described above all the way over to the junction with South Sweeney's at the "lone pine." Take South Sweeney's to King Road. Descend King Road past Sampson Avenue and to the junction with Ridge Avenue. Go right on a dirt road up Woodside Gulch and climb past a gate. In a couple hundred yards, fork left on Daly Bypass Trail (might be unsigned), and cross a dry creek, which is streaked with rusty pigments. You'll wrap around the hillside high above Daly Canyon, traverse past old mines, and exit to the Daly Canyon dirt road close to where you parked.

### Know Before You Go

- Be alert to construction and trail closures in Daly Canyon.
- Be cautious of vehicle traffic on Main Street.
- Never enter mine structures, as they can be hazardous.

### Maps & More Information

- USGS 1:24,000: Park City East and Park City West, Utah.
- *Park City Trail Map,* by Mountain Trails Foundation.

### Trailhead Access

Begin at Park City City Park, which is located on Park Avenue between 13th and 14th Streets. Alternatively, you can park on Daly Avenue where pavement turns to dirt to eliminate the paved road sections. (See "Option: Return to Daly Canyon" above.)

## 13
# Sweeney's Switchbacks

| | |
|---|---|
| **Location:** | Park City Mountain Resort |
| **Length:** | 5.9 miles, loop |
| **Tread:** | 0.1 mile doubletrack, 5.8 miles singletrack |
| **Physically:** | Strenuous (moderately steep, switchbacking climb with smooth and rough tread) |
| **Technically:** | 2-4+ (innumerable turns on rough and rooted trails) |
| **Gain:** | 1,100 feet |
| **In a nutshell:** | Sweeney's-John's-Trestle-Flat Cable-Sweeney's |

Sweeney's Switchbacks is one of Park City's legendary trails. The trail rises quickly right from Old Town's back door and, as the name suggests, takes a less-than-direct line up the hillside. The tight turns and overall rocky tread require finesse and power.

John's Trail takes Sweeney's switchbacking theme and "kicks it up a notch," as chef Emeril Lagasse would say, taking 2.2 miles to cover 0.6 mile as the crow flies. There is nary a straightaway, to say the least. Roots from trail-side aspens swarm the tread, so you must also be well versed at popping wheelies.

There is never a dull moment on the loop's second leg, a descent on Trestle and Flat Cable Trails. Trestle starts with a fast straightaway, but then it dives down sharp, rough turns. Flat Cable is more forgiving, with gooseneck turns on softer tread.

Not only is this short loop packed with action, it also offers a lesson in local history. The route curves under the path of the modern-day Town Lift, which follows the same line as the century-old mine tram. Although the tramway is defunct, its trestles still stand as a legacy to Park City's mining heritage. Not far from the trail, skiers took to the air by jumping from the old Creole Mine dump, heralding a new era for Park City.

### Details

For the sake of simplicity, this route starts at the horseshoe bend where Lowell Avenue and Empire Avenue join (about 0.5 mile from Park City Mountain Resort's base facilities). Go around the steel cable gate and climb the dirt road. Shortly after crossing under Town Lift, fork sharply right onto Sweeney's Switchbacks.

The steep, rocky ramp at the entrance temporarily gives way to smoother, gentler trail (tech 3). Climb around three turns, and fork left at a junction in a grove of scrub oaks and maples. Remember this junction because it's crucial on the return. Pass Flat Cable Trail on the right (your return route), cross Creole ski run, and enter the conifers. (An interpretive plaque on the edge of Creole explains how the nearby Creole Mine was converted to a ski jump after it closed and how Utah's legendary Alf Engen

## Sweeney's Switchbacks

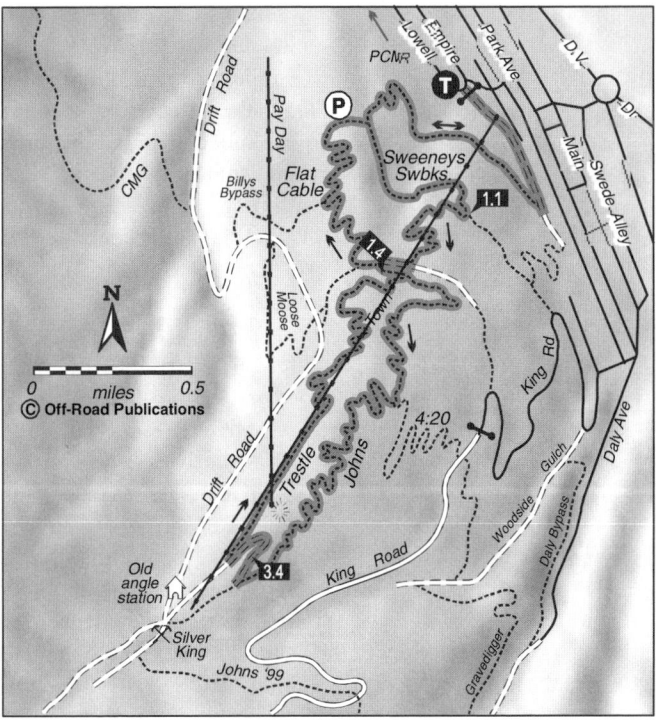

organized competitions here in the 1920s.) Battle a section of choppy bedrock (tech 4+), fork sharply right at the junction with South Sweeney's (**m1.1**), and keep chugging up the choppy trail and around more switchbacks.

Sweeney's intersects a doubletrack/cat track next to an old tram tower and where trails go every which way. Take the doubletrack to the right for about 200 feet; then fork left on a trail that leads to the multiple junction with John's Trail and Trestle Trail (**m1.4**). (Ignore Flat Cable Trail for now, which forks to the right from the doubletrack.) Go left and climb John's; you'll return on Trestle.

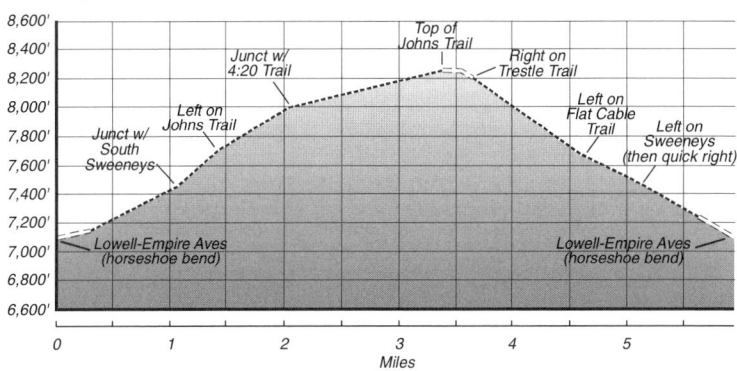

The old tramway trestles stand as a tribute to P.C.'s mining days.

John's Trail (tech 3⁺) rises moderately up multiple switchbacks for 0.4 mile to the junction with 4:20 Trail; thereafter, John's continues rising moderately but the turns become innumerable, the trail is laced with roots, and the aspens become claustrophobically confining (tech 3-4⁺). During autumn, the aspen canopy transforms to a golden veil. Fork sharply right at the top of John's Trail (**m3.4**), take the dirt road past the top of PayDay Lift, and fork right on Trestle Trail.

Trestle makes a beeline through a swath in the aspens that delineates the old tramway, and then the trail dives down the hill through sharp, rough switchbacks (tech 4⁺). After crossing ski runs and reentering the trees, the trail goes directly under the support legs of an old mine tower and returns to the familiar junction with John's and Sweeney's (see **m1.4**). Go to the doubletrack/cat track and fork left on Flat Cable Trail. Less hectic than Sweeney's, Flat Cable Trail loops gracefully down across the ski runs for a mile before rejoining Sweeney's. Fork left on Sweeney's, enter the familiar grove of oaks and maples, and fork right immediately to descend lower Sweeney's to the bottom.

### ❗ Know Before You Go

- Sweeney's Switchbacks is very popular with hikers, so ride cautiously and courteously. Descending bikers should yield to ascending bikers.
- Portions of Sweeney's Switchbacks may be altered or closed near the junction with John's Trail due to resort construction.

### ❓ Maps & More Information

- USGS 1:24,000: Park City East and Park City West, Utah.
- *Park City Trail Map,* by Mountain Trails Foundation.

### 🏁 Trailhead Access

To ride to the trailhead from Old Town, take Crescent Tram/8th Street up to Empire Avenue. Go left on Empire to the horseshoe bend, and start at the cable gate. By vehicle, park at Park City Mountain Resort and pedal 0.5 mile up Lowell Avenue to the horseshoe bend where it becomes Empire Avenue.

# Park City Mountain Resort

**JUST THE FACTS**

| | |
|---|---|
| Location: | Park City Mountain Resort |
| Length: | Over 30 miles of designated trails |
| Tread: | Singletracks, doubletracks, and dirt roads |
| Physically: | Moderately easy (lift served) to strenuous (cross-country) |
| Technically: | 2-4+ (full gamut of trail conditions from buffed to rocky) |
| Gain: | As much or little as you want |
| In a nutshell: | See below |

**WHY SHOULD U RIDE THIS TRAIL?**

Park City Mountain Resort (PCMR) takes the one-stop-shopping, mega-superstore approach to summer fun. Town and PayDay Lifts provide mountain bikers with uphill access to the resort's 30 miles of designated trails, which range from smooth dirt service roads to technical downhills to rolling cross-country tours to heart-pounding alpine climbs. But wait, there's more to do at PCMR. Gravity seekers other than mountain bikers will find thrills on the alpine slide, Ziprider cable, and Diggler scooters. For families and those less daring, the base area offers a variety of activities, including miniature golf, human maze, climbing wall, legacy launcher trampoline, and little miner's amusement park. You can even take a guided horseback tour. And when it comes time to satisfy your hunger and quench your thirst, you'll find plenty of culinary choices.

PCMR offers so many mountain biking routes that describing them all would necessitate a small guidebook in itself. Here is the lowdown on the most popular trail combinations. One note: Town Lift, rather than PayDay, is recommended for bike-lift access to the resort's trails. So if your ride ends at the resort base, you'll have to pedal up Park Avenue back to Town Lift. You can take your bike up PayDay Lift, but it's slower.

## Details

**Billy's Bypass** (2.2 miles, easy, tech 2-3): Billy's Bypass-Drift Road is the easiest way down from the top of Town and PayDay Lifts. Although the technical difficulty is low, you can reach near highway speeds if you don't use your brakes, so be cautious. Watch for loose gravel and for erosion control ditches across the road.

If you are riding PayDay Lift, then go down Bonanza Access Road to the top of Town Lift. From there, turn right on Drift Road (tech 2+). Descend across PayDay ski run to the junction with Sweeney's Switchbacks, and fork left on Billy's Bypass Trail. Dart into the trees, exit to the bottom of the winter terrain park, and reenter the trees. Connect with Blanche Road (tech 3), which takes you quickly to the base.

Left: CMG is the way. Right: dudes on Digglers.

**Sweeney's Switchbacks** (2.1 miles, tech 3-4⁺): Switchbacks are the name of the game on this twisting descent, which combines smooth dirt and rough, rocky tread.

If you are riding PayDay Lift, then go down Bonanza Access Road to the top of Town Lift. From there, turn right on Drift Road (tech 2⁺) and cross PayDay ski run. Where the road bends and descends sharply, look for Sweeney's forking right and entering the timber. Pass the junction with John's Trail, take the doubletrack/cat track for a couple hundred feet, and look for the singletrack forking left next to the old tramway towers. Go left at the junction with South Sweeney's, and after crossing Creole ski run, turn right at a junction in the midst of a dense grove of oak and maples. (It's just past Flat Cable Trail, which forks left.) You should now be heading back underneath Town Lift. Exit to a dirt road and go left to a cable gate where Lowell Avenue (left) joins Empire Avenue (right) on a horseshoe bend. Coast down Lowell to the resort base and to PayDay Lift, or go right on Empire and then right on Crescent Tram/8th Street to return to Town Lift.

**John's Trail-Sweeney's Switchbacks** (3.1 miles, moderate, tech 4): John's snakes through a grove of tightly spaced aspens, taking 2.2 miles to cover about 0.6 mile as the crow flies. Turns are plentiful, needless to say, and you'll need deft handling skills to manage the rooted trail (tech 3-4⁺). The aspens are so thick that you'll feel like you're magically lost in a Bev Doolittle painting.

If you are riding PayDay Lift, exit to the left, go along the top of the knoll, and fork left on John's Trail. If you are riding Town Lift, then pedal up the steep gravel trail on the right/east side of the lift to the top of the knoll to catch John's. Stay left at the junction with 4:20 Trail, and continue down to the multiple junction at the bottom of Trestle Trail and the top of Sweeney's Switchbacks. Descend Sweeney's (look for the trail junc-

Eagle Trail.

tion next to the old tramway tower), and either go left on Lowell Avenue to return to the resort base and to PayDay Lift, or go right on Empire and right again on Crescent Tram/8th Street to return to Town Lift.

**Trestle Trail-Flat Cable Trail** (2.3 miles, moderate, tech 3-4): Trestle-Flat Cable offers an alternate to descending John's Trail-Sweeney's Switchbacks. Trestle Trail follows the path of the old tramway, which once carried ore from the mountain's mines to town. Many of the tram's towers still stand as a legacy to the area's mining heritage.

If you are riding PayDay Lift, then go right and down the Bonanza Access Road for 200 yards, and turn right on Trestle Trail. If you are riding Town Lift, then exit to the right, climb the Bonanza Access Road toward the top of PayDay Lift, and fork left on Trestle. Trestle Trail runs through a swath in the aspens cut for the old tramway. Parts of the trail are smooth while others are rough and choppy, especially at the tight switchbacks (tech 4-5). After passing an old mine structure, you'll come to the multiple junction at the bottom of John's Trail and the top of Sweeney's Switchbacks. Go left on Flat Cable Trail (don't descend Sweeney's), curve down the ski runs, and pass Billy's Bypass, which forks left. Descend more turns and fork left on Sweeney's near Creole ski run. Enter a thick grove of oaks and maples; then turn right immediately to continue on lower Sweeney's, which takes you to the horseshoe bend on Lowell and Empire Avenues.

Return to the base and PayDay Lift by going left on Lowell Avenue, or return to Town Lift by going right on Empire and Crescent Tram/8th Street.

**Steps Trail** (1 mile plus options, moderately strenuous, tech 3+): Steps Trail is a steep switchbacking climb that takes you from the old angle station to the top of Crescent Ridge. The climb will make you sweat, especially since most of the trail crosses sunny slopes of brushy oak.

Go to the multiple junction of dirt roads at the top of Town Lift, and climb the dirt road to the right of the old angle station. Pass Mid Mountain Trail (MMT) and fork right on Steps. Gear down and climb. At the top, take the doubletrack to the left to the Five-way Junction and the yurt on Crescent Ridge.

From there, your options are many: 1) Roll out the dirt Crescent Ridge road, and loop back to the angle station by forking right and descending MMT. Total distance is about 3 miles. 2) Do the same,

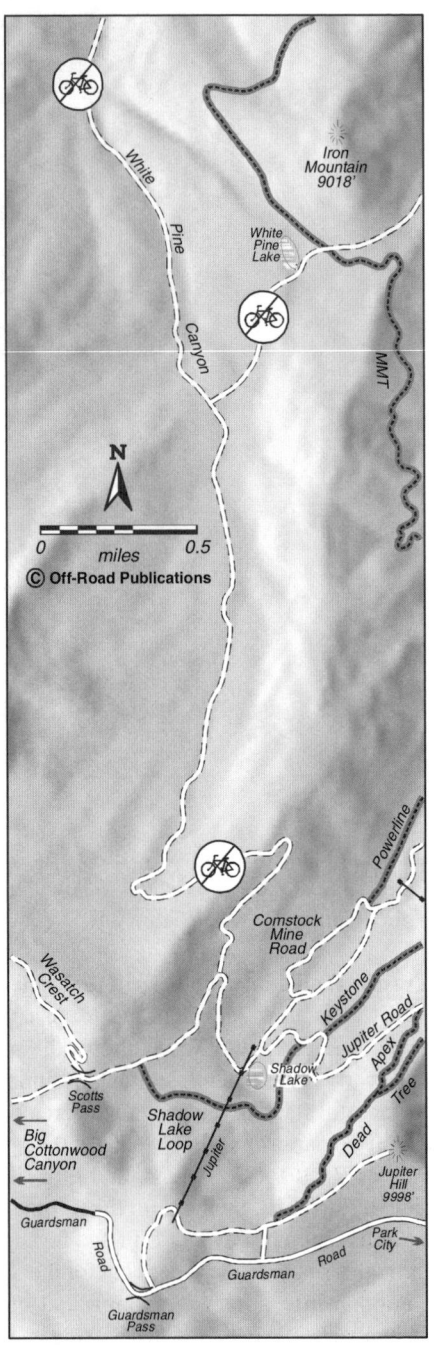

# Park City Mountain Resort 89

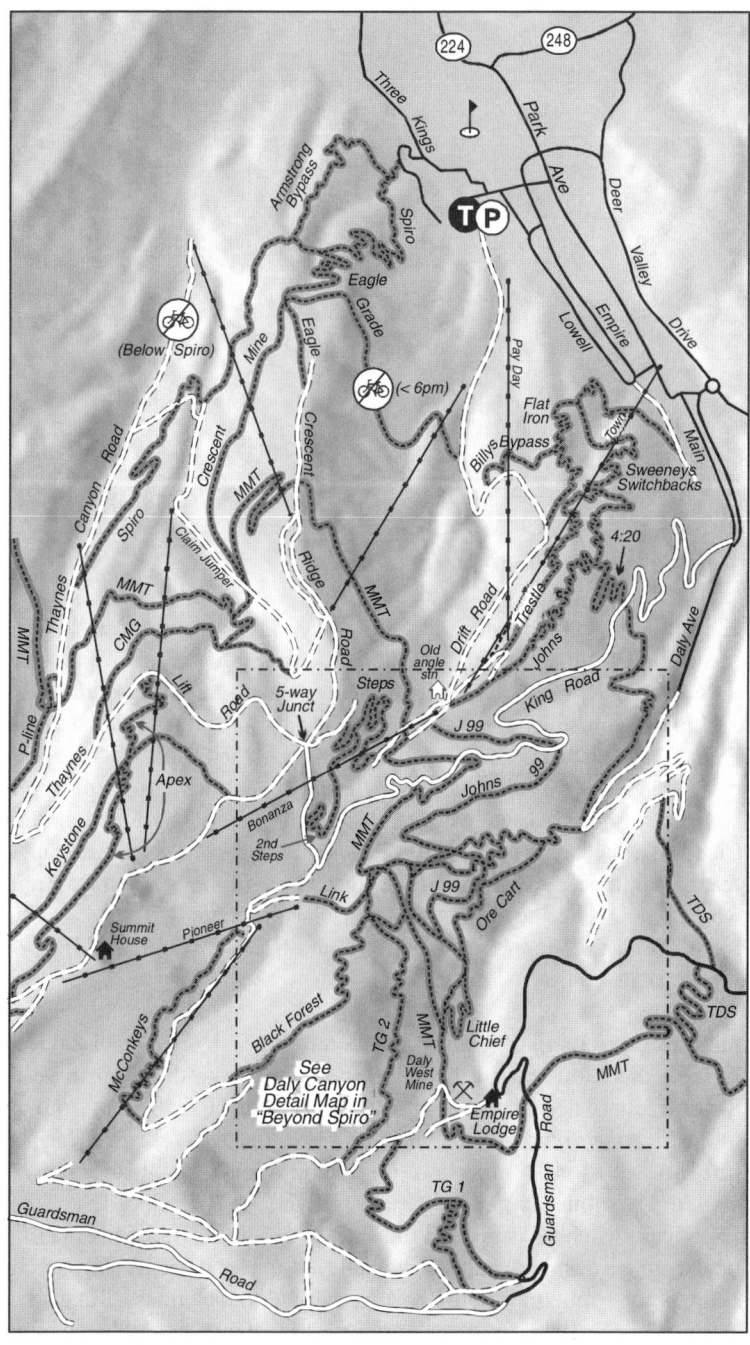

The all-important Five-way junction at PCMR.

but fork left and descend MMT all the way to the Thaynes Canyon jeep road. Go right, link to Spiro Trail, and descend Spiro to town. Upon exiting Spiro Trail, go left on Crescent Road, right on Three Kings Drive next to the golf course, and left on Silver King Road to return to the resort base. Total distance is about 7 miles. 3) Roll out the Crescent Ridge road past MMT, and fork left on Eagle Trail. Eagle is a steep, rough, downhill straightaway through the trees (tech 4+). Go right at the junction with Crescent Mine Grade (both trails merge as one) then fork left in about 50 feet to continue down Eagle. Five tight turns drop you to Spiro Trail, which you take to the bottom. Total distance is about 4.2 miles. 4) Use Steps Trail as a "stepping stone" to reach Shadow Lake, Dead Tree, or McConkey's Trails.

**Shadow Lake Loop** (8.8 miles, strenuous, tech 3): Use Town or PayDay Lifts to knock off half of the 2,400-foot climb from the resort base to Shadow Lake. (See chapter "Shadow Lake Loop.") Climb Steps Trail up to the Five-way Junction and yurt on Crescent Ridge. Take the Thaynes Lift road west for 0.5 mile, and fork left on Apex Trail, next to a resort sign for Dynamite ski run and just past Silverlode High-Speed Six-Pack Lift. Apex switchbacks up a ski run and enters some mixed timber before intersecting Keystone Trail. Go right on Keystone and pedal easily across ski runs for 1 mile to the Jupiter Access Road (doubletrack). Take a lap around Shadow Lake and retrace your tracks to the Five-way Junction on Crescent Ridge. Return to the base on Steps-Sweeney's, Eagle-Spiro, or MMT-Spiro.

**Mid Mountain Trail-Spiro Trail** (6.8 miles, moderate, tech 2-3): For mountain bikers, the completion of MMT across PCMR has provided the long-awaited missing link between Daly Canyon (Deer Valley Resort) and Thaynes Canyon (Park City Mountain Resort). Now, instead of roundabout trails up and down the hillsides, a straightforward, cross-country traverse exits. A ride up Town Lift plunks you right in the middle of MMT.

MMT-Spiro Trail takes you across the west half of PCMR, starting with a short ascending traverse and ending with a bomber downhill. From either PayDay or Town Lifts, go to the base of Bonanza Lift, and climb moderately up the doubletrack running along the right side of Bonanza for 0.1 mile. Fork right on MMT, and climb gradually on excellent singletrack (tech 2⁺). Intersect another doubletrack (coming up from the old angle station), go left then immediately right, and continue on MMT, which rises moderately through patches of aspens and affords spectacular views of Park City. Hop over a rock obstacle smack-dab in the middle of the tread (tech 4), and cross the Crescent Ridge road.

Switchback down across ski runs and cross the Claim Jumper jeep road. Climb two tight turns, and enjoy a gradual descent on a sweet trail across more ski runs. Go right on the Thaynes Canyon jeep road, and fork right on Spiro Trail after 0.3 mile. Coast for about a mile, climb a small hill, and freewheel down to town. Upon exiting Spiro Trail, go left on Crescent Road, right on Three Kings Drive next to the golf course, and left on Silver King Road to return to the resort base. Alternatively, make a sharp right onto Crescent Mine Grade upon intersecting the Claim Jumper jeep road. Tight singletrack descends gradually right back to the resort's base facilities. (Bikes allowed on lower CMG after 6 p.m. only.)

**Mid Mountain Trail-John's '99 Trail** (5.1 miles, moderate, tech 2-3⁺): If you feel that a mountain bike is meant to be "ridden" instead of being used as a simple commodity of gravity, then you'll love this cross-country loop, which has only moderately difficult climbs. It takes you across the east half of PCMR to Daly Canyon and back on superb singletrack and through lush forests. Be forewarned, this route can be confusing because of the many trails it crosses along the way.

From either Town or PayDay Lifts, go to the base of Bonanza Lift and pedal up the doubletrack on the right side of the lift. Fork left on MMT and duck into the woods; then cross both a jeep road and the dirt King Road. MMT switchbacks right, goes behind the resort's maintenance buildings, and winds its way up two steep turns amidst thick aspens. When it enters the conifers, MMT rises moderately to an overlook of Daly Canyon and Deer Valley Resort.

To return to PCMR, turn left on Little Chief Trail, and descend a handful of switchbacks. Cross Ore Cart Trail by dodging quickly right then left, and go straight on John's '99 Trail, where Link Trail forks left/uphill and Shovel Trail forks right/downhill. John's '99 catches a contour,

Left: Link Trail. Right: the author is happy to be alive on Dead Tree Trail.

narrows to a thin thread of dirt, and squeezes through tightly spaced aspens, where roots in the trail will be a nuisance for some riders and a hoot for other (tech 3+). Cross the dirt King Road and return to Bonanza Lift on one last stretch of sweet singletrack. The interpretive plaques at the old Silver King Mine near Bonanza Lift are a must-read.

**Dead Tree Trail** (14 miles, strenuous, tech 2-5): Dead Tree Trail, proper, is less than a mile long and gains just over 350 feet, so you might wonder, "what's so strenuous about it?" Dead Tree Trail is "relatively" easy, but like trying to explain the theory of "relativity" to fifth graders, *getting* to Dead Tree Trail is a monumental task geared only for gifted individuals. Like Wasatch Crest Trail, Dead Tree Trail takes you to Park City's highest elevations, reaching nearly 10,000 feet. That's 3,000 feet above town, and knocking off 1,200 feet on Town Lift does little to reduce the ride's overall difficulty. If you make the effort, however, you will be duly rewarded with colossal views of Park City's environs and of neighboring Big Cottonwood Canyon on the Salt Lake side of the Wasatch Range.

From Town Lift, climb the doubletrack on the right side of the old angle station, pass MMT, and fork right on Steps Trail. Gear down and climb. At the top, take the doubletrack left to the Five-Way Junction and the yurt on Crescent Ridge. Take the Thaynes Lift road west for 0.5 mile, and fork left on Apex Trail, next to a resort sign for Dynamite ski run and just past Silverlode High-Speed Six-Pack Lift. Apex switchbacks up the ski run and darts into the timber before intersecting Keystone Trail. Go right on Keystone for 50 feet; then fork left on middle Apex. Switchbacks take you up under Motherlode and Thaynes Lifts to Jupiter Access Road (doubletrack).

Go left and climb the rocky Jupiter road to Pioneer Ridge; then fork right on the Pioneer Ridge jeep road and climb past the avalanche control towers. (Alternatively, you can cross the Jupiter road and stay on Apex. It rises steeply and connects with the new "Perrier Pass Trail," which also takes you to the avalanche control towers on Pioneer Ridge.) Just before the ridge road becomes unbearably steep, you'll pass a dead tree on the left, so fork right, fittingly, on Dead Tree Trail.

Dead Tree Trail (tech 3+) makes an ascending traverse high on the slopes of Jupiter Bowl, passing upper Apex Trail along the way. Cross over the ridge, descend a doubletrack to Guardsman Road (all-weather dirt), and take Guardsman up to the pass. To get back to PCMR you must first descend Guardsman Road for 1.1 miles to the first left-hand switchback. (Cars are usually parked here.) Fork right onto a dirt road and descend to a red steel gate, which is locked so you must lift your bike over. Climb the doubletrack for 0.8 mile to Scotts Pass. (The old ridge trail between Jupiter Bowl and Scotts Pass is closed for revegetation.)

Go straight over Scotts Pass and descend the pebbly doubletrack for 0.3 mile, fork right onto the Shadow Lake Loop trail, and loop around Shadow Lake, naturally. (This junction is easily missed, so watch for it.)

Upon exiting the trail to the Jupiter Access Road (doubletrack), you have two choices: 1) Go right for 0.1 mile and fork left on Keystone Trail. Take Keystone for 1 mile to the junction with Apex, fork left, and retrace your tracks to the Five-way Junction, Steps Trail, etc. 2) Go left and to the base of Jupiter Lift. Descend the Thaynes Canyon jeep road, Comstock Mine Trail, and Powerline Trail; connect with the Thaynes Canyon jeep road; and then finally take Spiro Trail back to town. Burly ride!

**McConkey's Loop** (5.5 miles, strenuous, tech 3-5): McConkey's Loop ventures to PCMR's most remote areas; it requires strong legs for the hefty climb and razor sharp skills for the dicey descent.

From Town Lift, pedal up the doubletrack on the right side of the old angle station, pass MMT, and fork right onto Steps Trail to continue climbing. After rounding a switchback near a pair of old wooden water tanks, fork left on Second Steps Trail, which might not be signed. (If you top out on a doubletrack, you missed the turn.) Wind through the aspens and exit to the wide, dirt King Road. Go left, descend to a multiple junction of roads, turn right, and head to the base of McConkey's Lift.

Gear down, way down. Chug up the gravel lift road for 0.7 mile, and fork right on McConkey's Trail, which rises steeply up the aspen-lined ski runs (tech 3-4). Exit to the lift road and climb gradually to where the road bends to the right on the edge of a ski run. (You'll pass some tempting downhill trails along the way. Try them if you dare.) Hop onto a singletrack just before the road bends right, and cross the ski run past an "out of bounds" sign. Take the trail left along the edge of Daly Bowl, and fork left atop the knoll on Black Forest Trail to start the downhill.

The entrance to Black Forest is scary steep and rates high on the "pucker" scale (tech 4-5); the descent gets nastier before it gets easier, so pucker up! You'll skitter over loose tread, tire-swallowing ruts, and downed timber, some of which has been piled up into makeshift ramps. As you exit the conifers and enter the aspens, you'll pass TG2 Trail, which forks right. Stay left and ride straight off the small ridge to a T-junction with MMT. Go left onto MMT then immediately right onto Link. Turn sharply left onto John's '99 Trail, which traverses the hillsides on primo singletrack all the way back to the base of Bonanza Lift.

### ! Know Before You Go

- The resort's base activities, PayDay Lift, and Town Lift operate on weekends from late May to mid June and then again from early September to mid October. The resort base and lifts run daily from mid June to early September.
- Town Lift (recommended for bike access) and PayDay Lift operate Monday-Thursday, noon to 9 p.m.; Friday and Saturday, 10 a.m. to 10 p.m.; and Sunday, noon to 8 p.m. Early and late season weekend hours are noon to 8 p.m. Holiday hours may vary. Contact PCMR for details.
- A single lift ride is $11; all-day is $18.
- Mountain bike rentals are available at the resort base.
- A helmet must be worn at all times when mountain biking at the resort.
- Always yield to hikers, to horseback riders, and to mountain bikers riding uphill.
- Smoking is not allowed on the mountain.
- Be prepared for rapidly changing alpine weather, and carry adequate food and water.
- Know your limits and the limits of others in your group.
- Dogs are not allowed at the resort's base facilities.
- Trails are not regularly patrolled.

### ? Maps & More Information

- Contact Park City Mountain Resort for an Activities and Trail Guide: (435) 647-5408; www.parkcitymountain.com.
- *Park City Trail Map,* by Mountain Trails Foundation.

### Trailhead Access

Town Lift takes off from Park Avenue between 8th and 9th Streets. PayDay Lift runs from the resort base: From the intersection of Park Avenue (UT 224) and Deer Valley Drive, go west on Empire Avenue, turn right on Silver King Drive, and park in the resort's designated lots.

and contour across the face of PCMR through long patches of dense timber that separate the ski runs. The cushiony path clings to the 8,300-foot contour for about a mile. Pass the junction where upper Crescent Mine Grade Trail (CMG) forks right (see "Option"), and curve around the ski run to intersect the Claim Jumper road (**m4.2**). Go down the jeep road about 50 feet, and veer right onto lower CMG.

Though a bit choppy at first, CMG becomes a smooth-flowing one-laner that will have you whooping and hollering like a miner who just struck the motherlode. The tread is little more than tire width, so you have to shoot straight with your front wheel (tech 3). If you twitch-

Jenn and Joe wait for their slow-poke guidebook-author friend to catch up.

and-pitch, you'll "garage sale" down the steep runs like an out-of-control skier. After a mile of sweet singletrack, Eagle Trail intersects CMG from the right, and the two trails become one, but for only about 50 feet. Where the trail splits, fork left on Eagle Trail and drop quickly into the trees (tech 3⁺). (CMG, the right fork, is posted as "no bikes on horse trails until after 6 p.m.") Although your eyes will gravitate to the sweeping view of Park City Golf Course and Park Meadows far below, keep them glued to the rapidly descending trail in anticipation of several hairpin turns. Intersect Spiro Trail (**m6.0**), and let gravity draw you back to the trailhead. Old Spiro may have gone bust, but his trail is a real gem.

**Option:** Upper CMG-MMT Add-On

With a rebel yell, Billy Idol once sang that he wanted "more, more, more." Here's how. To add 3.6 miles and 400 vertical feet, ride as described above, but fork right on upper CMG just before MMT intersects the Claim Jumper road. Climb steadily on good tread (tech 2-3) for a mile, and then intersect the dirt Thaynes Lift road, which rises up from the base of Thaynes Lift. Go left, climb a tad more, and race your buddies to the yurt at the Five-way Junction on Crescent Ridge. Take the ridge-top doubletrack north just less than a mile (watch out for a steep gravelly descent past the top of Ski Team Lift), and turn left on MMT. MMT switchbacks downhill across ski runs on a high speed course for 0.9 mile before intersecting the Claim Jumper road. Go right on the jeep road for 50 feet to pick up lower CMG at **m4.2** in the main description above to finish off this extended loop. For still more miles, see "Beyond Spiro" and "Shadow Lake Loop."

Golf is for wimps. Go mountain biking instead.

### ! Know Before You Go
- Spiro Trail is a main thoroughfare for bikers and hikers, so use *extreme* caution when descending, and be prepared to yield the trail on a moment's notice, especially at switchbacks.
- Look for a new trail (built in 2006) accessing Spiro from the PCMR base area, thus eliminating part of the climb on lower Spiro.

### ? Maps & More Information
- USGS 1:24,000: Park City West, Utah (trails are not shown).
- *Park City Trail Map,* by Mountain Trails Foundation.

### Trailhead Access

From the intersection of Park Avenue (UT 224) and Deer Valley Drive (look for Jans and Cole Sport), go west past Cole Sport on Empire Avenue, turn right onto Silver King Drive, and park in the lower PCMR lot. On your bike, exit the parking lot, go left on Silver King, and then take an immediate right onto Three Kings Drive, which runs along the golf course. Go left onto Crescent Road and find the Spiro trailhead at the bend next to a dirt road. Alternatively, you can park near the Spiro trailhead on the edge of Three Kings Drive; but heed any parking restrictions. Parking is not allowed at the Spiro trailhead itself.

## 16 Beyond Spiro

**JUST THE FACTS**

| | |
|---|---|
| Length: | 15.6 miles, loop |
| Tread: | 13.5 miles singletrack, 1.6 miles doubletrack, 0.5 mile pavement |
| Physically: | Moderately strenuous (big climb at first then lots of rolling trail; hard to follow–not for the "navigationally challenged") |
| Technically: | 2-4+ (good trails throughout; roots and tight turns on Johns; rocky tread and tight switchbacks on Sweeney's) |
| Gain: | 2,000 feet |
| In a nutshell: | Spiro-Thaynes Canyon-MMT-Crescent Mine Grade-Thaynes Lift Road-Five way Junction-Steps-MMT-Link-John's '99-John's-Sweeney's |

**WHY SHOULD U RIDE THIS TRAIL**

Cross-country purists will love this ride because it expands upon Spiro Trail and takes you one step closer to singletrack heaven. Directions, however, are hellish because the route ties together nearly a dozen trails between Park City Mountain Resort (PCMR) and Daly (Empire) Canyon. You'll warm up on Spiro, Mid Mountain, and Crescent Mine Grade Trails with a near 2,000-foot climb, then embark on a cross-country circuit that is chock-full of diversity: Steps Trail is a fast switchbacking descent, MMT, Link, and John's '99 Trails contour through stands of lush timber, John's Trail (different from John's '99) slithers like a snake downhill through dense aspens, and Sweeney's Switchbacks culminates the loop with tight turns and rocky tread—right when you are most fatigued. But after you recover, you'll want to ride this loop over and over.

### Details

Gear down for the steep ramp that greets you on Spiro. You'll stay in your easiest gears as you climb in earnest for a mile up a dozen tight switchbacks (tech 3+), and pass the junctions with Eagle (**m1.1**) and Armstrong Bypass Trails. Break out across the ski runs under King Con Lift, and catch your breath on a short but welcomed descent. Shimmy up two tight turns and cross a doubletrack posted as "closed to bikes as per county ordinance 196." Continue climbing through pristine aspens and firs to the junction with the Thaynes Canyon jeep road (**m2.8**). Go left, and spin up the doubletrack to the junction with Mid Mountain Trail (MMT) (**m3.2**), just past Powerline Trail.

Go left on MMT (tech 3), and contour across the face of PCMR through long patches of timber that separate ski runs. The cushiony path clings to the 8,300-foot contour for about a mile before intersecting Crescent Mine Grade Trail (CMG) in the middle of a wide ski run (**m4.1**). Fork right and climb CMG (tech 3) for 1 mile to the Thaynes Lift road. Go left on the dirt road, climb a tad more, level out, and race your buddies to the yurt at the Five-way Junction on Crescent Ridge (**m6.1**).

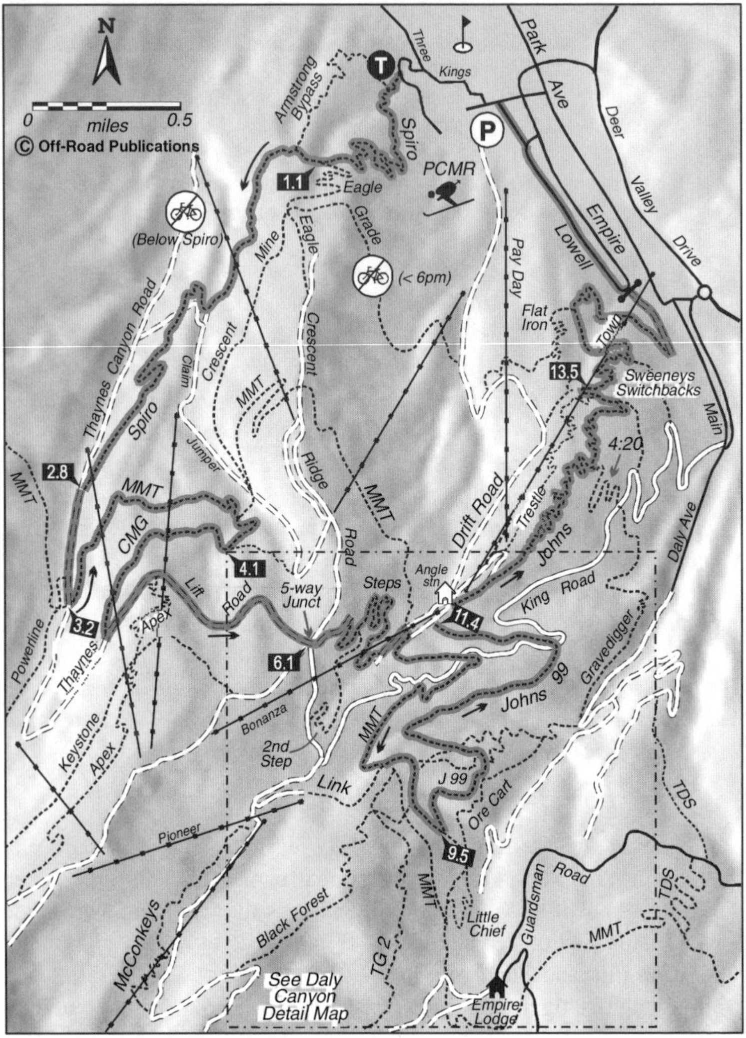

**100** Mountain Biking Park City & Beyond

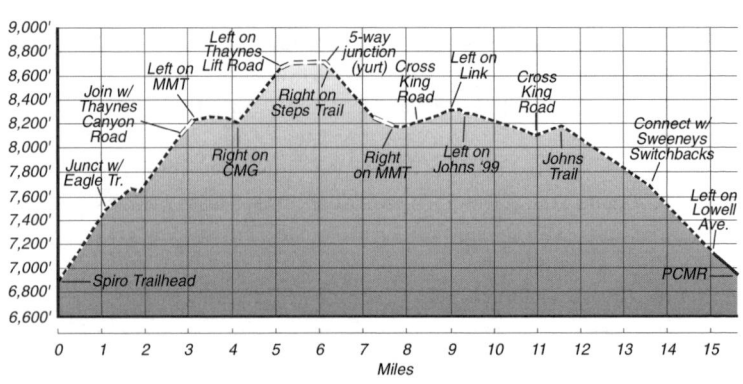

Beyond Spiro  101

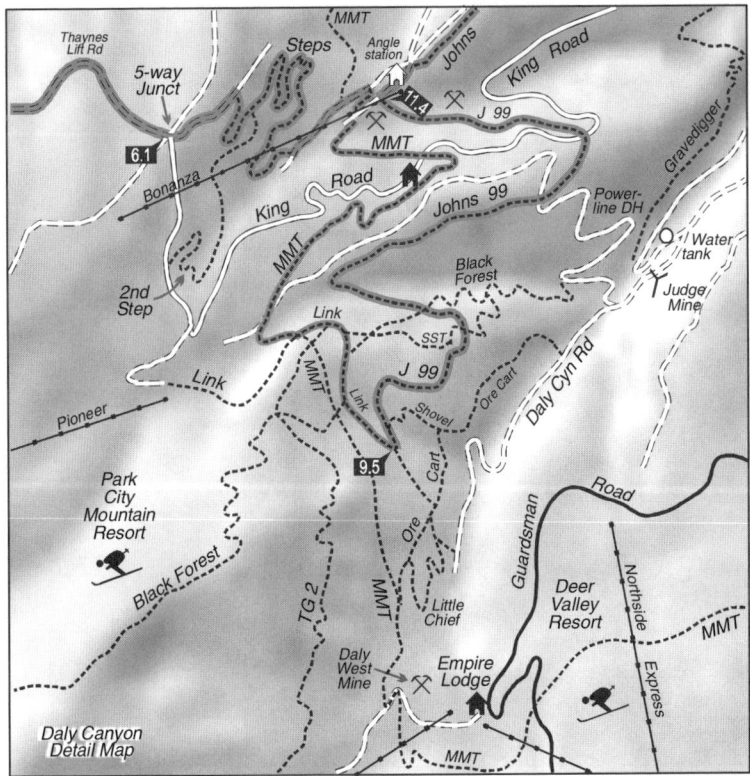

Daly Canyon Detail Map. You'll be tested later!

Go down the doubletrack to the right of and just below the prominent Crescent Ridge road, and turn sharply right in a few hundred yards onto Steps Trail. Steps takes you on a mile-long, switchbacking flight down a sunny, oak-brush hillside, passing the historic Silver Queen tanks along the way. Upon exiting the trail to a dirt road, fork left and freewheel downhill. Pass MMT forking left (see "Option: Return to Spiro" below), and watch closely for MMT forking right shortly thereafter. Take it. (If you descend to the old angle station, then turn sharply right to go around the building and take the doubletrack that is *above* the Bonanza Lift base.) Exit MMT to a doubletrack that is above the Bonanza Lift base, and take the track uphill/right for 0.1 mile; then fork left to resume on MMT. Phew! (MMT is well marked.)

MMT crosses a dirt service road and then the wider dirt King Road. After a sharp right-hand turn under the power lines, the trail passes behind PCMR's maintenance buildings and rises up two sharp, steep switchbacks in a patch of dense aspens. Climb gradually on buffed tread through stately aspens and firs to the junction with Link Trail. Fork left on Link, squeeze through a pair of handlebar-wide trees, and wiggle-and-jiggle on tight tread

John's '99 Trail.

through side-swiping aspens. Ignore several unsigned and less-traveled trails intersecting Link, and drop down a steep ramp on loose tread to the junction with John's '99 Trail (**m9.5**).

Fork sharply left and double back below Link and MMT across the same timbered slopes through which you just rode. Like Link, John's '99 is tight, threaded with roots, and slips through tightly packed aspens that nip at your tires and bar ends (tech 3-4). It's a hoot for those with deft skills, but it might be a nuisance for those who are tentative. After crossing a gulch, John's '99 narrows to barely tire width and crosses oak-brush slopes. Check your balance and watch your front wheel. Cross King Road, continue traversing on singletrack, and exit to the old Silver King Mine at the base of Bonanza Lift (**m11.4**).

If you cursed Link and John's '99, then skip the last leg of this loop and seek the easier way down to the base of PCMR on Drift Road and Billy's Bypass, or pursue the option below for "Return to Spiro." But if you're itching for more technical tree-riding, then chug up the gravel path to the right of Town Lift, and fork right onto John's Trail. Now the fun really begins. John's winds through the tightly spaced aspens like a slalom

So that's where my ski went.

course gone awry, taking 2.2 miles to cover 0.6 mile as the crow flies. Turns are innumerable, needless to say, and you'll need acute handling skills to manage the roots that swarm the trail (tech 3-4$^+$). The aspens are so thick that you'll feel like you've been sucked into a Bev Doolittle painting. Pass 4:20 Trail forking right, and continue down to the junction with Trestle Trail. (This junction can be confusing.) Go downhill a bit more and intersect a doubletrack; take it to the right a couple hundred feet, and then fork left on Sweeney's Switchbacks next to the old tram towers and under the modern-day Town Lift (**m13.5**).

Named appropriately, Sweeney's switches back and forth down the hillside, in and out of the woods and across ski runs. Go left where South Sweeney's forks right. Square up for a wicked section of jagged bedrock, cross Creole ski run, pass Flat Cable Trail forking left, and enter a grove of maples. Stop! Fork right just after you enter the maples to continue on Sweeney's (might not be signed). You should be heading back under Town Lift. Exit to a dirt road, take it left to the horseshoe bend where Empire Avenue becomes Lowell Avenue, and take Lowell to the base of PCMR.

**Option:** Shadow Lake Add-on

Add a couple miles and 500 feet more of climbing by combining "Shadow Lake Loop" with this route. Follow "Shadow Lake Loop" up to and around Shadow Lake and descend Keystone-Apex Trails to the Thaynes Lift road. Cruise over to the Five-way Junction at the yurt and hook into the description above at **m6.1**.

**Option:** Return to Spiro

If you got battered on Link and John's '99 Trails and dread the thought of the technical mayhem of John's and Sweeney's Switchbacks Trails, then you can return to Spiro via MMT and biker-friendly trails across PCMR. You won't feel short changed.

Upon exiting John's '99 Trail to the base of Bonanza Lift (**m11.4** above), go left and climb the doubletrack above Bonanza Lift to the familiar junction with MMT. Retrace your tracks to Steps Trail, but not all the way. Stay on MMT and cross the Crescent Ridge road; then descend across ski runs until you intersect the steeply rising Claim Jumper road. Either continue on MMT to the Thaynes Canyon road and retrace your original tracks down Spiro, or fork sharply right onto Crescent Mine Grade Trail. For the later, CMG is a freewheeling glide on a smooth but super tight one-laner. Watch your front wheel and be careful with your pedal stroke. If you twitch-and-pitch, you'll "garage sale" down the slopes like an out-of-control skier. Fork left onto Eagle Trail and descend its switchbacks to Spiro (**m1.1** above), which culminates the ride.

### ! Know Before You Go

- This loop requires trail knowledge and good route-following skills, as you will follow many trails and pass many junctions along the way. These trails are very popular with hikers so be cautious and courteous, especially when descending.
- Look for a new trail (built in 2006) accessing Spiro from the PCMR base area, thus eliminating part of the climb on lower Spiro.

### ? Maps & More Information

- USGS 1:24,000: Park City West, Utah.
- *Park City Trail Map,* by Mountain Trails Foundation.

### Trailhead Access

From the intersection of Park Avenue (UT 224) and Deer Valley Drive (look for Jans and Cole Sport), go west past Cole Sport, turn right onto Silver King Drive, and park in the lower PCMR lot. On your bike, go left on Silver King, then immediately right on Three Kings Drive, which runs alongside the golf course. Turn left onto Crescent Road and find the Spiro trailhead at the bend next to a dirt road. Alternatively, you can park near the Spiro trailhead on the edge of Three Kings Drive; but heed any parking restrictions. Parking is not allowed at the Spiro trailhead itself.

## 17 Shadow Lake

**JUST THE FACTS**

| | |
|---|---|
| Location: | Park City Mountain Resort |
| Length: | 14.7 miles, loop |
| Tread: | 2.5 miles doubletrack, 12.2 miles singletrack |
| Physically: | Strenuous (long climb to Shadow Lake, then lots of freewheeling) |
| Technically: | 2-3+ (good trails throughout; tight turns on Spiro, Apex, and Steps; narrow tread on Keystone, Crescent Mine Grade, and Eagle) |
| Gain: | 2,400 feet |
| In a nutshell: | Spiro-Thaynes Canyon Road-Powerline-Comstock-Shadow Lake-Keystone-Apex-Thaynes Lift Road-Steps-MMT-Crescent Mine Grade-Eagle-Spiro |

*This high-alpine loop is for bikers who have good knowledge of the local trails but need guidance putting it all together into a sensible route. You'll be out for the better part of the day piecing together a dozen trails, and while navigation may seem daunting, you'll agree that the loop fits together perfectly.*

*This cross-country trek starts with a steady, almost-eternal climb from town to Shadow Lake in Park City Mountain Resort's famed Jupiter Bowl. A host of prime-cut singletracks take you back to the base in a roundabout fashion. The interplay of high-speed straightaways, ever-present switchbacks, forest-draped paths, and panoramic views mean that this loop never has a dull moment. And as is always the case in the mountain biking world of Park City, you can add more trails and more miles.*

### Details

Shift into granny gear and attack Spiro Trail with vigor. The trail's moderately steep grade and dozen switchbacks (tech 3+) will have you huffing and puffing the whole way. Despite the rigors, the aspen-, oak-, and maple-draped trail is a joy to climb. Pass Eagle Trail forking left (**m1.1**, your return trail) and Armstrong Bypass forking right. Keep spinning up across wooded slopes and enjoy a short but welcome descent after crossing under King Con Lift. Two quick turns precede a junction with a doubletrack that is posted as "closed to bikes as per county ordinance 196." Cross the road and climb steadily through stately aspens and firs to the Thaynes Canyon jeep road (**m2.8**).

Take the doubletrack uphill for 0.3 mile and fork right on Powerline Trail. There is no rest for the weary because Powerline rises directly, and you'll keep grinding away in your easiest gears (tech 2+). You'll find a slight respite where the singletrack exits to a doubletrack across from the huge mine tailings at the base of Thaynes Lift. Fork right on Comstock Trail and get back to work. Intersect the upper Thaynes Canyon jeep road and climb it to Shadow Lake in Jupiter Bowl (**m4.7**). Phew!

Don't dismount for a siesta just yet; there is still more climbing to do. Ugh! Go up the jeep road to the right and around a gate. The steep grade

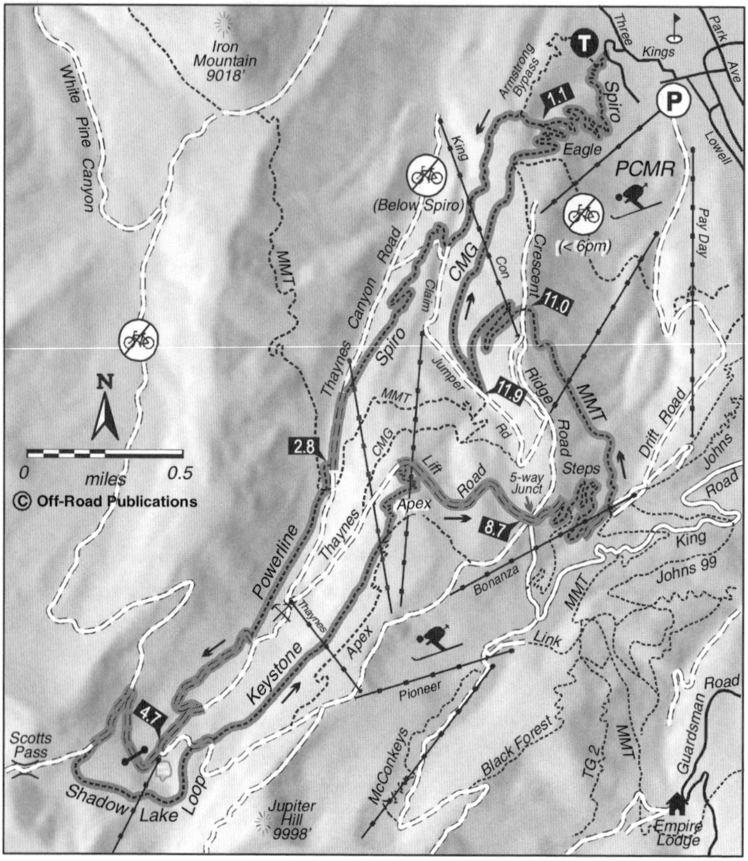

**106** Mountain Biking Park City & Beyond

and loose gravel might make your legs scream uncle; hang tough, you're almost there. Round a left-hand switchback, and fork left on the Shadow Lake Loop Trail, 0.7 mile up from Shadow Lake. (If you reach Scott's Pass, you missed the turn.) Zoom across a meadow and into the timber on

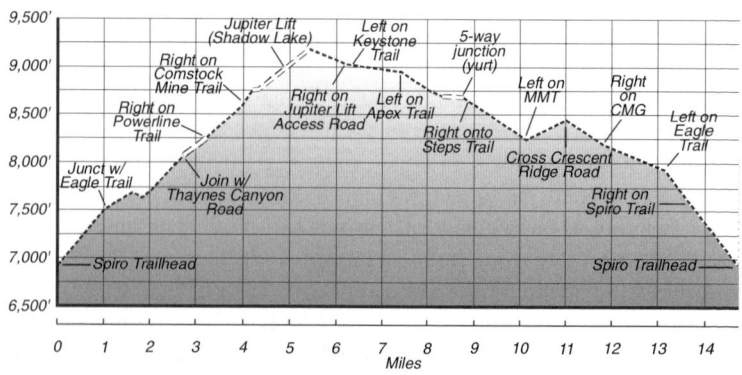

the narrowing trail, pass a scenic view of Shadow Lake, and glide down sweet singletrack back to the lake. Now you can chug-a-lug and chow some grub. Good job.

Upon exiting the Shadow Lake Loop Trail to the Jupiter Access Road (doubletrack), take the road right for 0.1 mile to the bend, and fork left on Keystone Trail. This old doubletrack has healed over into a tight singletrack with high-speed straightaways, passing through a canopy of timber and crossing ski runs (tech 2-3). It rates high on the fun-o-meter. You need to fork left on Apex Trail 1 mile down Keystone, so keep your eyes peeled for the easily missed junction. Descend around tight turns on Apex (tech 3-4), in and out of the trees, and to the Thaynes Lift road. Go right on the flat doubletrack and race your buddies the Five-way Junction on Crescent Ridge (**m8.7**).

Aspen leaves sprinkle the Comstock Mine Trail.

To continue, take the doubletrack signed for Steps Trail to the right of the main ridge road. (To bail out, head straight down the Crescent Ridge road and veer left down Eagle Trail [tech 4] to shortcut the loop back to Spiro.) Steps Trail (tech 3) switchbacks down the oak brush slopes without much fanfare, but don't get complacent because there is a short "sucker" climb near the bottom that will suck your momentum if you're in the wrong gear. Exit to a doubletrack, and take it downhill. Don't let your blazing speed make you miss the left turn onto MMT, which takes you back up to Crescent Ridge (**m11.0**).

After crossing the ridge, MMT takes you on a fast descending traverse high above Thaynes Canyon to the Claim Jumper road (**m11.9**). Don't cross the road and continue on MMT, although there is no harm in doing so; instead, fork sharply right and double back on Crescent Mine Grade Trail. The trail is choppy at first; then it smooths out, and makes a beeline traverse across grassy ski slopes (tech 3$^+$). Be sure to stay on the straight and narrow because the trail is super tight; if you twitch-and-pitch, then you'll "garage sale" like an out-of-control skier.

Eagle Trail enters from the right and both trails merge as one for about 50 feet. Where the combined trails splits, go left on the continued Eagle Trail. (Crescent Mine Grade forks right and is posted as "no bikes

Left: Keystone Trail; right: Shadow Lake Loop Trail.

on horse trails until after 6 p.m.) Descend rapidly around five tight switchbacks (tech 3⁺) to the familiar junction with Spiro Trail. Revenge is sweet and so is descending Spiro back to the trailhead.

**Option:** Beyond Spiro

If you're keen to the trails on PCMR, then you know that MMT, Link Trail, and John's '99 Trail are ultra-sweet. Add a few more miles by veering right onto MMT from the bottom of Steps Trail and adding on part of the chapter "Beyond Spiro." This side loop takes you to Daly Canyon and back to Bonanza Lift, where you can finish off the Shadow Lake Loop on MMT, CMG, Eagle, and Spiro as described above.

### ! Know Before You Go

- Spiro Trail is a main thoroughfare for bikers and hikers, so use *extreme* caution when descending, especially when rounding the switchbacks.
- Stay on designated trails; some resort roads are closed to public use.
- Look for a new trail (built in 2006) accessing Spiro from the PCMR base area, thus eliminating part of the climb on lower Spiro.

### ? Maps & More Information

- USGS 1:24,000: Park City West, Utah (trails are not shown).
- *Park City Trail Map,* by Mountain Trails Foundation.

### Trailhead Access

From the intersection of Park Avenue (UT 224) and Deer Valley Drive (Jans and Cole Sport), go past Cole Sport on Empire Avenue, turn right onto Silver King Drive, and park at PCMR's lower lot. On your bike, exit the parking lot, go left on Silver King Drive, right on Three Kings Drive alongside the golf course, and left on Crescent Road. The Spiro trailhead is next to a dirt road where Crescent bends left. Alternatively, you can park near the Spiro trailhead on the edge of Three Kings Drive, but heed any parking restrictions. Parking is not allowed at the Spiro trailhead.

caveat: MMT is incomplete. Until a usable trail easement is established between Pinebrook Peak and Ecker Hill Middle School, riding MMT out-and-back is recommended. (See chapter "Mid Mountain Trail [North]).

Here's the ticket for a sweet ride: take MMT-North of Red Pine Lodge to the scenic saddle (6.2 miles from Red Pine Lodge and 2.3 miles north of Ambush Trail); then return partway and descend Ambush and lower Holly's Trails to the base for another ride up the gondola. Total distance is about 12.5 miles, and the ride is rated moderate.

Lower Holly's Trail.

**Holly Flander's Trail** (4.4 miles, moderately easy, tech $2^+$-$3^+$): If you just want to do laps, then Holly's and Ambush Trails are the best routes down to the resort base, where you can catch the gondola again. Holly's is the quickest way down and requires the least amount of cross-country effort. To find Holly's Trail, take MMT 1 mile north of Red Pine Lodge to where it intersects a dirt service road on a small ridge. Go right then immediately left. Upper Holly's zigzags across a ski run then enters the timber on a long descending traverse, which can be choppy with small rocks (tech $3^+$). Pass the bottom of Ambush Trail in 1.7 miles and take lower Holly's to the base in another 1.7 miles. There are some tricky bits along the way (tech $3^+$), so watch your front wheel.

Look for a new trail forking from lower Holly's. This trail will offer an alternate route to the base that more closely follows the hills' natural contours. From the resort base, this trail will also offer a more biker-friendly climb to the Ambush-Holly's junction.

**Ambush Trail** (7.8 miles, moderate, tech $2^+$-$3^+$): Ambush Trail begins 3.9 miles from Red Pine Lodge via MMT, so it takes a bit more effort to reach than Holly's. It's worth it. (See chapter "Mid Mountain Trail [North].") Ambush initially drops through a dense grove of bleach-white aspens then ducks into dark conifers beyond the junction with Rob's/Sunpeak Connector Trail. The trail is fun and fast. After crossing a dirt road, you'll have to gear down for a gradual half-mile climb. Intersect another dirt road, and take it uphill and around the right side of Sun Lodge, where you'll connect with Holly's Trail. Take Holly's Trail to the base for a 7.8 mile ride from Red Pine Lodge.

The Canyons' gondola puts you right on the famed Mid Mountain Trail.

**Ricochet Trail** (4 miles, easy, tech 4-5): This downhill-only trail is geared for downhillers only! It begins at the second switchback on upper Holly's Trail and drops 500 feet in 0.75 mile with tight switchbacks and steep, rough drops. Needless to say, compared to Holly's Trail, it takes a fall-line approach to getting down the mountain. It reconnects with Holly's just above the junction with Ambush Trail. Long-travel suspension and expert skills are recommended.

**Holly's-Ambush Loop** (10.2 miles, strenuous, tech $2^+$-$4^+$): If you're short on cash, training for the NORBA circuit, or just one of those cross-country diehards who insists that downhills must be earned, then this loop is for you. You'll climb 3.4 miles and gain 1,200 feet on Holly's Trail, traverse on MMT, and then descend Ambush-Holly's back to the resort base. The climb is tough, but the downhill is a thrill a minute.

Go around Sundial Hotel at the resort base to the old cement amphitheater, and pick up Holly's Trail under the gondola. Three wide switchbacks take you up across open ski runs and into the timber. Portions of lower Holly's are buffed (tech $2^+$); others are wickedly steep, rocky, and may require hike-a-biking (tech 4-5). Take either Holly's (preferred) or Holly's Bypass across a doubletrack in a hollow, and keep chugging uphill through woodlands and across ski runs. Near Sun Lodge, fork left on upper Holly's Trail at the junction with Ambush Trail. The remaining climb is a low-gear grind on both smooth and choppy tread (tech 3).

Aspen leaves bedeck the Mid Mountain Trail.

Top out on a small ridge overlooking the entire resort, go right on the service road, and fork right on MMT in about 100 feet. Take MMT past the maintenance buildings, fork right, and duck back into the woods. Exit to a horseshoe bend on another dirt road, and take the road uphill for 0.3 mile; then fork right on the continued MMT. Past the junction with Ridge Connector Trail, MMT angles downhill on an all-out bombing run through dense conifers. Only two switchbacks slow your speed before you come to the junction with Ambush Trail. Ambush drops quickly into fluttering aspens (tech 3), then forks right at the junction with Rob's/Sun Peak Connector Trail before darting into the conifers. After crossing a dirt road, Ambush bends right, and you'll have to climb moderately for one-half mile. Intersect another dirt road, and take it uphill and around the right/south side of Sun Lodge. There, you'll return to the familiar junction with Holly's to complete the loop. You can seek vengeance on lower Holly's as you return to the resort base (tech $3^+$).

**Mid Mountain-Wasatch Crest Loop** (23-25 miles, strenuous, tech $2^+$-5): Go big! Use the gondola as a stepping stone for this epic loop on the Wasatch Crest. Although the lift saves you 1,000 feet of vertical, you'll still gain 2,200 feet and reach a top elevation of 9,900 feet, so this route may not be the best choice for unacclimated "flatlanders." Follow the chapter "Mid Mountain-Wasatch Crest Loop," but start your ride at Red Pine Lodge, **m16.8** in the description. (Adjust your mileage accordingly.)

In a nutshell, you'll take MMT south to Iron Mountain Pass and descend to Thaynes Canyon at Park City Mountain Resort. From there, you'll climb Powerline Trail, Comstock Mine Trail, and the upper Thaynes Canyon road to Shadow Lake. Then you'll chug up to Scott's Pass and battle the infamous "Vomit Hill" to the top of Scott's Hill. Take the Wasatch Crest Trail northward as it rolls along the ridge top past Lake Desolation and to the Mill Creek Canyon divide. Reenter The Canyons Resort on the Ridge Connector Trail and descend to MMT. There, you have two choices: fork left on MMT and descend Ambush Trail-Holly's Trail to the resort base (25 miles total), or fork right on MMT and take it back to Red Pine Lodge (23 miles total). Whoa, what a ride!

## ⚠ Know Before You Go

- Flight of the Canyons Gondola operates Wednesday through Sunday, 9:30 a.m. to 4 p.m., late June through Labor Day, and weekends only after Labor Day, weather permitting. Lift prices are $12 for adults, $8 for seniors (over 65), $6 for kids (7-12), and free for children 6 and under. Down-lift rides from Red Pine Lodge to the base are free.
- Gondola tickets can be purchased at All Seasons Adventures, located in the lobby of The Canyons Grand Summit Hotel, and at Canyon Mountain Sports, located in The Canyons Resort Village: (435) 615-3440.
- Helmets must be worn at all times when bicycling at The Canyons Resort.
- Respect public and private property, and stay on trails designated as open to bicycles.
- Yield to all other trail users, and yield to ascending bikers.
- Red Pine Lodge is open for lunch Wednesday through Sunday.
- Bicycle rentals are available at Canyon Mountain Sports: (435) 615-3440
- The Canyons hosts many events throughout the summer, including concerts and a farmers' market. Visit www.thecanyons.com for more information.
- Sheep are herded in the resort between Red Pine Lodge and Ambush Trail. Use caution when encountering sheep. Ride slowly through the herd, and don't threaten sheep dogs. In a calm but firm voice, tell the sheep dog to "go home." If your own dog is with you, the safest course of action is to leash your dog and turn around. Call The Canyons for seasonal sheep herding information.

## ❓ Maps & More Information

- USGS 1:24,000: Park City West, Utah.
- *Park City Trail Map,* by Mountain Trails Foundation.
- The Canyons Resort: (435) 649-5400, www.thecanyons.com.
- Canyon Mountain Sports: (435) 615-3440

## Trailhead Access

The Canyons Resort is located 4 miles north of Park City and 2.7 miles south of I-80 (Exit 145). Take Canyons Resort Drive past the resort facilities, turn right on High Mountain Road, and park in the gravel lot next to Sundial Hotel.

# Mid Mountain Trail (North)

**JUST THE FACTS**

| | |
|---|---|
| **Location:** | North of The Canyons Resort |
| **Length:** | 7.4 miles, out-and-back (about 8.5 miles one-way when completed to Ecker Hill Middle School trailhead) |
| **Tread:** | 7.4 miles singletrack |
| **Physically:** | Moderate (steady, moderate climbs on the return) |
| **Technically:** | 2-3+ (smooth tread with a few choppy spots) |
| **Gain:** | 400 feet |
| **In a nutshell:** | Hunter's Trail of the Mid Mountain Trail |

**Why Should U Ride This Trail**

When completed, the visionary Mid Mountain Trail will be a near-30-mile trail from Deer Valley Resort through Park City Mountain Resort and The Canyons Resort to I-80 near Pinebrook. The Hunter's Trail section of the MMT takes you from The Canyons Resort to within a few miles of the northern trailhead. You can't get all the way to the trail's proposed end at Ecker Hill Middle School because trail easements across private lands in that area have not been secured. Therefore, it is recommended that you turn around at Pinebrook Peak. No problem. The resulting 7.4-mile scamper is mighty fine. Like other sections of the MMT, Hunter's Trail stays close to the 8,000-foot mark and darts into pristine timber; however, it is unique in that it runs a short distance along an open ridge that affords sweeping views of deep canyons and towering mountains both near and far. On the way out, you'll freewheel generously on well-crafted tread. The return entails several miles of steady, moderate grades that are easily managed by those with good fitness.

## Details

First some fine print: At the time of publication, riding the MMT to its designated trailhead at Ecker Hill Middle School was not recommended because the connector trail had not been completed, and the majority of the Pinebrook trails were closed to public use. "Public" means anyone who is not a member of the Pinebrook Master Association. The future looks bright, however, because Synderville Basin Special Recreation District and Mountain Trails Foundations are working closely with the Pinebrook Master Association and other land owners to develop a usable trail easement that will address the concerns of land owners and satisfy the needs of trail users. It's difficult to swim in rough water, so keep the seas calm for those who are trying to keep trail negotiations afloat by riding the Hunter's Trail section of MMT out-and-back and not poaching the Pinebrook trails.

Next, to say the Hunter's Trail of the MMT is a moderately easy, 7.4-mile ride is misleading. Why? First you have to get up to the MMT, which begins 1,000 feet above The Canyons Resort base. Whoa! Currently, there

**116** Mountain Biking Park City & Beyond

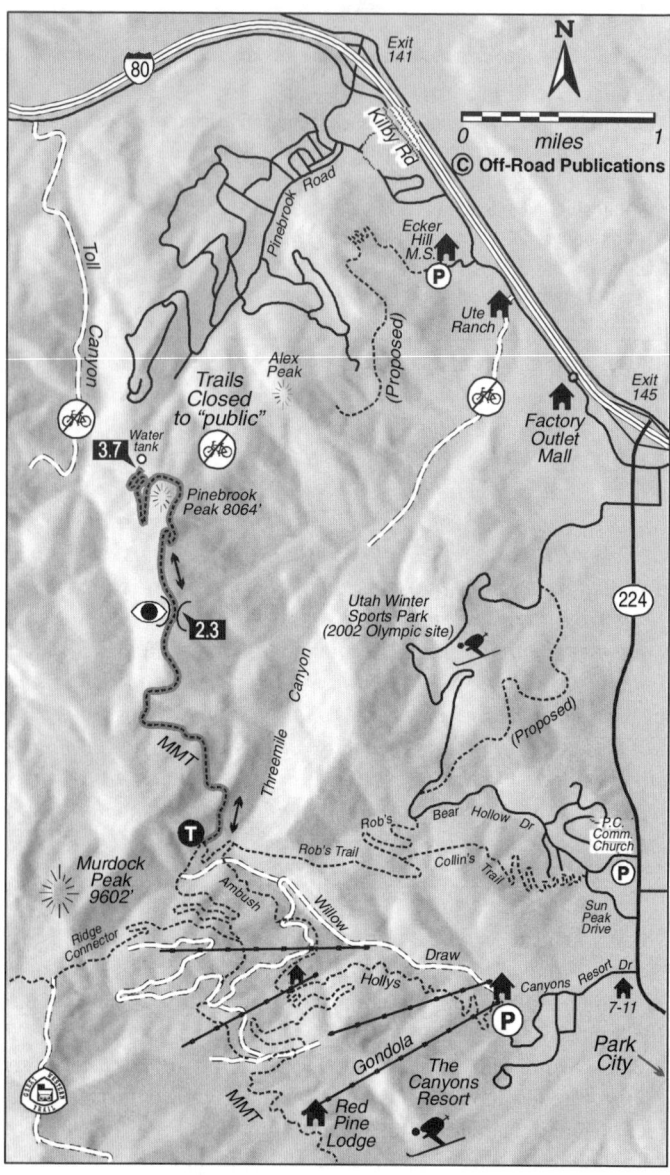

are three ways to get there. The first and easiest way is to ride the Flight of the Canyons Gondola (for a fee) and pedal 3.9 miles on MMT to the Ambush Trail/Hunter's Trail (MMT) junction. The second and third ways forego the lift and require you to pedal to the top. One option is to climb through The Canyon's Resort on Holly's and Ambush Trails to the Hunter's Trail (MMT) junction. (Watch for a new trail, which will make the climb to the Holly's/Ambush junction easier.) The second option is to climb from

# Mid Mountain Trail (North)  117

Heading across The Canyons to the Hunter's Trail section of the MMT.

the Sun Peak development just north of the Canyons on Collin's and Rob's Trails then on upper Ambush Trail to the Hunter's Trail (MMT) junction. See "Options" below for a discussion of all three ways.

Regardless of how you get to the Ambush Trail/Hunter's Trail (MMT) junction, here's what you'll find. Hunter's Trail (MMT) rolls gradually downhill across the steep, timbered headwater slopes of Threemile Canyon (tech 3). A few "kickers" along the way add excitement to the otherwise tame trail. The trail drops a couple hundred feet over one-half mile, so keep in mind that you'll have to climb this on the return. Thereafter, the trail catches the 8,000-foot contour, dodges in and out of the thick woods, and rolls northward just below the crest of the ridge. Take five at a breezy

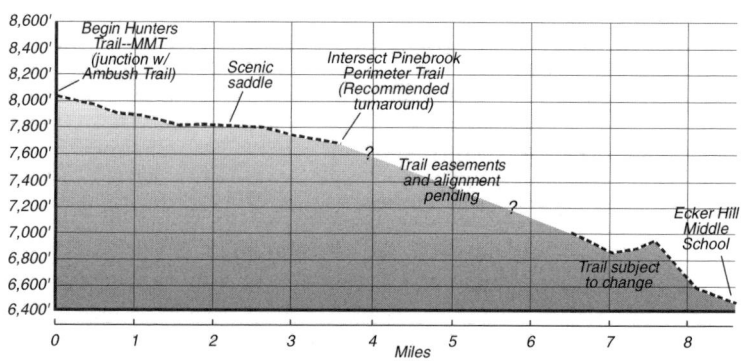

Ride out-and-back on Hunter's Trail until MMT is complete.

clearing on the ridge top (**m2.3**), where biker's congregate to enjoy the circumambient view of Murdock Peak to the southwest, Toll Canyon to the west, and Snyderville Basin and distant Uinta Mountains to the east.

Continuing on, the trail descends quickly around Pinebrook Peak, drops through a right-hand switchback, and comes to the junction with the Pinebrook South and West Perimeter Trails (**m3.7**). Hunter's Trail (MMT) ends here presently. Turning around and retracing your tracks is recommended. Climb steadily back to Ambush Trail, and consider your options for descending.

If you pedaled up to MMT from the Canyon's Resort base or from Sun Peak, then you know how to get home. If you started at Red Pine Lodge, then you can reach the resort's base by descending Ambush and Lower Holly's Trails. They're a blast. (See "Mid Mountain Trail [Middle]" for details.)

**Option:** Access to Hunter's Trail from Red Pine Lodge

If you caught a ride on the gondola, then head north on MMT. Duck into the timber, and then climb for 1 mile across ski runs to a doubletrack on a small ridge. Here you can sight back to Red Pine Lodge and across many of the resort's famous ski bowls that drop from the Wasatch Crest. Go left onto the dirt road for about 50 feet (Holly's Trail goes to the right on the road), fork right onto singletrack, and cross more service roads. Pass the resort's maintenance sheds on the left, and fork right one hundred yards farther onto MMT. Roll through the woods and exit to another service road where the road makes a sharp bend (2 miles from Red Pine Lodge). Climb the dirt road 0.3 mile, and fork right onto MMT.

## Mid Mountain Trail (North)

Pass through a grove of leaning aspens, and fork right at the junction with Ridge Connector Trail. A fast, mile-long descent on smooth trail and through the shadow-filled conifers takes you to the junction of Hunter's Trail (MMT) and Ambush Trail (3.9 miles from Red Pine Lodge). Ride out-and-back on Hunter's and descend Ambush and lower Holly's Trails to the resort's base or Rob's and Collin's Trails to Sun Peak.

**Option:** Climbing Holly's and Ambush Trails to Hunter's Trail (3.8 miles, tech 2-4+, 1,100-foot gain)
Unwilling to cough up the bucks for the gondola, or do you *like* to climb? If so, then this is one way up to Hunter's Trail (MMT). Keep in mind that it entails a 1,100-foot warm-up climb.

Go around Sundial Hotel at The Canyons Resort to the old cement amphitheater. There, pick up Holly's Trail under the gondola. Three big switchbacks take you up across a wide ski run and into the timber (trail may be rerouted due to resort construction). Portions of lower Holly's are sweet (tech 2), others are wickedly steep and may require hike-a-biking (tech 4+). (Watch for a new trail to the right/north of lower Holly's, which will offer a more biker-friendly climb to the junction with Ambush Trail.)

Fork right on Ambush Trail near Sun Lodge, and go down a dirt road to where it bends right; then fork left onto the continued Ambush Trail. Cross the Willow Draw dirt road, and resume climbing Ambush through thick conifers and then into dense aspens. Go left at the junction with Rob's Trail (formerly the Sun Peak Connector Trail), and climb to the junction with Hunter's Trail (MMT). After riding out-and-back on Hunter's Trail (MMT), try descending Rob's and Collin's Trails for variety.

**Option:** Climbing Collin's and Rob's Trails to Hunter's Trail (3 miles, tech 2-4, 1,450-foot gain)
Built in 2004, Collin's Trail and Rob's Trail offer an alternate way up to Hunter's Trail. Bikers with billy goat genes will love this approach.

Collin's Trail starts a couple hundred yards down Sun Peak Drive from its junction with Bear Hollow Drive. You'll climb aggressively up nearly a dozen switchbacks right from the start. Then the trail makes an ascending traverse up to the junction with Rob's Trail. (Alternatively, you can skip Collin's Trail and access Rob's Trail by pedaling 1.2 miles up Bear Hollow Drive from its junction with Sun Peak Drive to the big right-hand bend.)

Rob's makes one switchback to the right, and then curves around the shady side of one knoll and the sunny side of a second knoll before intersecting Ambush Trail. A quick 0.4-mile climb on Ambush takes you to Hunter's Trail. After riding out-and-back on Hunter's Trail (MMT), try descending Ambush and Holly's Trails for variety.

When driving to these Sun Peak trails, you are asked to park at the Park City Community Church near the intersection of Bear Hollow Drive and UT 224.

## ! Know Before You Go

- At the time of publication, all Pinebrook trails were closed to the "public," so plan on riding out-and-back on Hunter's Trail (MMT). Pick up *Park City Trail Map*, by Mountain Trails Foundation, for trail updates.
- Sheep are herded in The Canyons Resort between Red Pine Lodge and Willow Draw, and northward toward Pinebrook Peak. Use caution when encountering sheep. Ride slowly through the herd, and don't spook or threaten sheep dogs. In a calm but firm voice, tell the sheep dogs to "go home."

## ? Maps & More Information

- USGS 1:24,000: Park City West, Utah (trails are not shown).
- *Park City Trail Map,* by Mountain Trails Foundation.
- Snyderville Basin Special Recreation District: (435) 649-1564, www.basinrecreation.org

## Trailhead Access

To reach The Canyons Resort, drive 4 miles north of Park City on UT 224. From I-80, take Exit 145 and drive 2.7 miles south on UT 224. Take Canyons Resort Drive past the base facilities, turn right on High Mountain Road, and park in the dirt lot on the south side of Sundial Hotel.

To access Collin's and Rob's Trails, drive one-half mile north of Canyons Resort Drive on UT 224, and turn left on Bear Hollow Drive. Park at the Park City Community Church.

When MMT becomes a through trail to Ecker Hill Middle School, you'll want to set up a shuttle between the school and The Canyons Resort. From Park City, drive north on UT 224 to Kimball Junction on I-80, and turn left onto Kilby Road at the stop light before the interchange. Drive 1.3 miles, passing the Park City Outlet Stores along the way, and turn left for Ecker Hill Middle School. Park behind the school.

You can never get enough of the MMT.

in aspens, as the trail traverses westward and curves through several dark hollows. Cross the doubletrack in White Pine Canyon and continue on MMT (**m9.5**). (See "Option" for the proposed White Pine Canyon Trail.)

The next 3 miles to Red Pine Lodge are certainly the sweetest, as you'll enjoy boatloads of buffed trail (tech 2⁺). Climbs are brief, if not trivial, and the trail strives to follow the 8,000-foot contour, for after all, MMT was originally called the "8,000-foot Trail." Pass a cement building on the left—it's a public restroom—and cross the paved Colony road where it makes a bend (**m10.6**). One-half mile farther, intersect a doubletrack and take it left/uphill for a few hundred feet; then fork right on the signed MMT. Cross another paved road and arrive at Red Pine Lodge. Before you continue, take an all-but-mandatory lap around the mini "freeride" park near the bridge. It's perilous . . . Not!

From the lodge, cut across the field at the top of the gondola to continue on MMT. The trail contours initially; then it rises gradually across a slope of oak brush before intersecting a dirt road on a small ridge (**m13.3**). If you need to get down the mountain quickly, then take the road to the right and hop on Holly's Trail; otherwise, go left on the dirt road for 50 feet and fork right on MMT (singletrack). The singletrack crosses several dirt roads, and then the route follows a service road west past some maintenance sheds. Fork right 100 yards past the sheds to continue on MMT (singletrack). It contours again and then intersects another dirt service road where the road makes a switchback (**m14.4**). Chug up the road for 0.3 mile and fork right on the signed MMT (singletrack). Pass through a grove of leaning aspens, and cross more ski runs before forking right at the junction with Ridge Connector Trail. The long canyon below you, Willow Draw, is the grand finale, which begins now.

A fast, mile-long descent through the shadow-filled conifers is a sample of more downhills to come (tech 2⁺), and you'll feel like a Jedi warrior scooting through the Forests of Endor in *Return of the Jedi,* except you'll be wearing a mile-wide grin instead of your war face. Exit the timber, cut

Towering aspens enclose the MMT.

across a ski run, and fork sharply right on Ambush Trail (**m16.3**). (Hunter's Trail of the Mid Mountain Trail goes straight/north and leads to Pinebrook Southeast Perimeter Trail. See the chapter "Mid Mountain Trail [North].")

A 1,000-foot descent awaits you, so be off. Ambush Trail (tech 3) drops into a dazzling grove of aspens, forks right at the junction with Sun Peak Connector Trail, a.k.a. Rob's Trail, and then darts into the conifers. After crossing the Willow Draw dirt road, you'll have to climb for about one-half mile. The uphill is easy, on a relative scale, but the miles you have logged so far make it doubly difficult. Exit the trail to another dirt road, and take the road uphill to the right and around the right/south side of Sun Lodge. There, you'll connect with Holly Flander's Trail (**m18.5**). (Watch for a new trail that will run below Holly's and offer an alternate route to the resort base.)

Holly's crosses ski runs and wooded islands on both buffed and rough tread (tech $2^+$-$3^+$). Ignore or explore Holly Flander's Lower Bypass Trail, as both trails merge on the other side of the doubletrack in a hollow/ski run. Finally, exit the trees to the resort's lowest slopes and zigzag down three wide switchbacks to the base (**m20.2**). Go right on the paved service road past Sundial Hotel to the gravel parking area.

**Option:** Making it a loop
In about the time it takes to set up a shuttle between The Canyons and Spiro Trail, you can ride the extra 4.2 miles. Here's how: From The Canyons' base at Sundial Hotel, go left on High Mountain Road and left again on Canyon Resort Drive and coast to UT 224. Go right on UT 224 for 0.6 mile to the intersection with White Pine Canyon Road, and hop on the paved Farm Trail. The path curves behind the historic McPolin Farm and then follows along the edge of UT 224, past the Park City Golf Course. Turn right on Thaynes Canyon Drive, left on Three Kings Drive, and right on Crescent Road to reach the Spiro trailhead. To reach Park City Mountain Resort's parking lot, stay on Three Kings Drive, and go left on Silver King Drive.

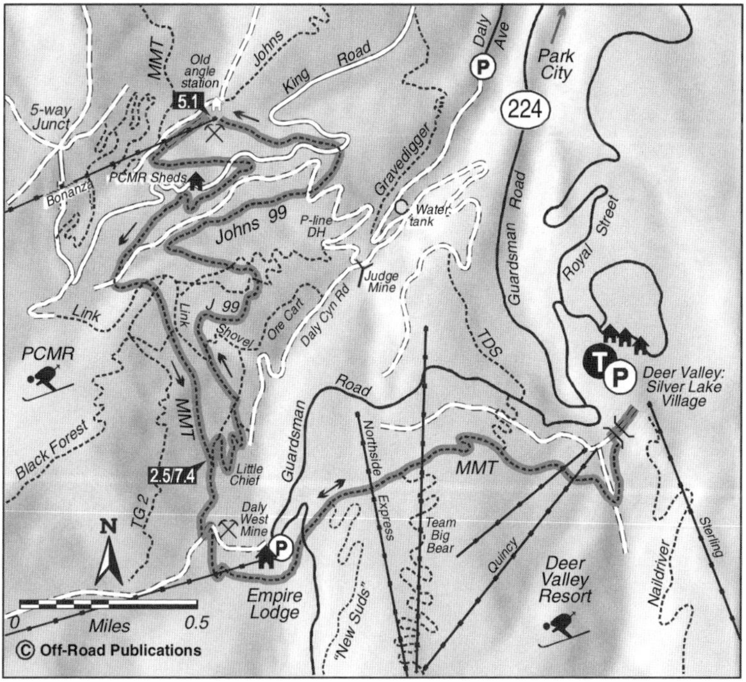

## Mid Mountain Trail (South) 127

MMT rises uphill and affords views into Daly (Empire) Canyon and across the canyon to the condo-lined slopes of DVR. Fork right onto Little Chief Trail (**m2.5/7.4**) to begin the more challenging section of the upcoming loop. (For a more mellow ride, just stay on MMT until you reach Bonanza Lift at Park City Mountain Resort and turn around to retrace your tracks back to DVR.) Just down the trail, fork right again to stay on Little Chief (Ore Cart Trail goes straight downhill), drop through a few switchbacks over a half mile, and pass a faint trail forking sharply right.

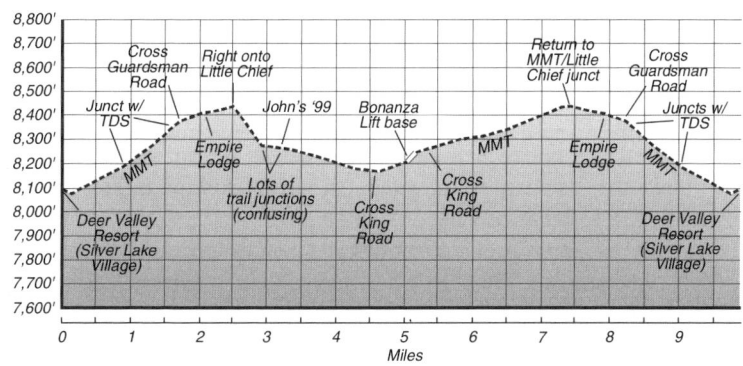

Left: The Daly West Mine hoist is a Park City landmark. Right: Riders take part in the IMBA Epic Ride on MMT (2004).

Intersect Ore Cart and go right; then fork left immediately onto Link Trail toward PCMR. You should be traversing the hillside on a contour. Squeeze through tightly spaced aspens and stay straight on John's '99, where Link forks left/uphill and Shovel Trail forks right/downhill. Are you with me? You should be still be contouring on a level keel across the hillside.

John's '99 is a real hoot. Unlike the wide and forgiving MMT, which was cut by machine, J '99 is a tight one-laner that was built by hand. Nary a tree was sacrificed in the process. Inasmuch, the aspens brush by your shoulders like slalom gates and their roots nip at your tires like a rabid dog (tech 3+). You must have keen reflexes to keep on course and not dab a foot. After a stretch through a patch of dark conifers, J '99 crosses a gulch and angles across a slope of bristly oak brush. Again, you must concentrate to stay on the straight and narrow. Cross Powerline Downhill Trail and then King Road. Another half mile of singletrack takes you to the historic Silver King Mine and the base of Bonanza Lift (**m5.1**). The interpretive plaque at the mine is a must read.

To continue the loop, go around the lift base and chug up the dirt service road that is between the lift and the old gondola angle station. Don't take the road next to the mine. Pass MMT forking right (it heads across PCMR to Thaynes Canyon), and then fork left onto MMT shortly thereafter. After crossing a doubletrack and then King Road, MMT banks sharply right and runs behind PCMR's maintenance buildings. Gear down in anticipation of two sharp steep switchbacks tucked amidst a dazzling grove of aspens. MMT rises at a steady leg-friendly grade from the aspens into the conifers. Return to the familiar junction with Little Chief Trail (**m7.4**), and retrace your tracks around Empire Lodge back to DVR.

**Option:** Empire Lodge trailhead
If you start from Empire Lodge, then you can skip the out-and-back section on MMT between Silver Lake Village and Empire Lodge and shorten the ride by about 4 miles. In doing so, the physical difficulty drops to moderately easy, which is about as easy as singletracks get in this neck of the woods.

**Option:** Lower Tour des Suds Add-on
Pedaling from town to Silver Lake Village on Marsac Avenue/Guardsman Road is a bear, so if you're heading out from town by bike try accessing MMT via Tour des Suds in Daly Canyon instead. If you park and embark from the top of Daly Avenue, then you will avoid pavement altogether and ride entirely on dirt.

### Know Before You Go

- Trail junctions can be confusing around Daly Canyon, even though most are signed.
- Do not enter any mine structures because they might be unstable and collapse.

### Maps & More Information

- USGS 1:24,000: Brighton, Heber City, Park City East, and Park City West, Utah.
- *Park City Trail Map,* by Mountain Trails Foundation.

### Trailhead Access

From Old Town Park City, go to the roundabout at the intersection of Heber Avenue and Deer Valley Drive, and turn right onto Marsac Avenue, which becomes Guardsman Road (UT 224). (Alternatively, go up Main Street, turn left on Hillsdale, and then turn right onto Marsac/Guardsman Road.) Pass the Ontario Mine, and turn left onto Guardsman Pass Connection then right at the junction with Royal Street West to reach Silver Lake Village. Alternatively, from Snow Park Lodge, drive up Royal Street and Royal Street West.

## 22

# Mid Mountain Trail (The Full Monty)

**JUST THE FACTS**

**Location:** Deer Valley Resort to Pinebrook
**Length:** 32.2 miles, one-way w/ out-and-back (about 28 miles one-way when MMT is completed to Ecker Hill M. S.) (0.5 mile doubletrack, 31.7 miles singletrack)
**Physically:** Strenuous (long miles, rolling terrain; many easier options)
**Technically:** 2+-3+ (excellent trails with intermittent choppy sections)
**Gain:** 2,500-3,000 feet (pending completion of MMT)
**In a nutshell:** MMT (Deer Valley Resort-Park City Mountain Resort-Canyons Resort-Pinebrook Peak-Canyons Resort; route will eventually end at Ecker Hill M. S.)

### Why Should U Ride This Trail?

In 1994, Troy Duffin, former executive director of Mountain Trails Foundation, envisioned a trail that would connect all three of Park City's ski areas. While mapping and planning, he realized that the 8,000-foot contour was the perfect elevation for linking together lodges and ski lifts and for all around access. With that, the trail was originally dubbed the "8,000-foot Trail." Following a snap line across hill and dale for nearly 30 miles proved impossible, but remarkably, the end result stayed within about 300 feet of the center line and avoided any significant climbs.

Mid Mountain Trail offers superb cross-country-style singletrack riding with lots of pedaling in the middle chain ring. Views are sporadic, as thick woodlands enclose much of the trail, but when the forest parts, you'll get an eyeful of Park City's environs. You can access the trail from numerous locations (see the three other Mid Mountain Trail chapters), but to truly appreciate MMT you have to ride the whole thing from Deer Valley Resort through Park City Mountain Resort and The Canyons Resort to Ecker Hill Middle School near I-80. Whoa! It's a long haul, but by the ride's end you'll agree that the trail "surpasses the ordinary." Perhaps that's why in 2004 the International Mountain Bike Association (IMBA) named Mid Mountain Trail as one of its "epic" rides.

### Details

First some fine print: At the time of publication, riding the MMT to its designated trailhead at Ecker Hill Middle School was not recommended because the connector trail from Pinebrook Peak had not been completed, and the majority of the Pinebrook trails were closed to public use. "Public" means anyone who is not a member of the Pinebrook Master Association. The future looks bright, however, because Synderville Basin Special Recreation District and Mountain Trails Foundations are working closely with the Pinebrook Master Association and other land owners to develop a usable trail easement that will address the concerns of land owners and satisfy the needs of trail users. It's difficult to swim in rough water, so keep the seas calm for those who are trying to keep trail negotiations afloat by turning around at Pinebrook Peak—not poaching

## Mid Mountain Trail (The Full Monty) 131

Mid Mountain Trail was dedicated an IMBA "Epic" Ride in 2004.

Pinebrook's trails—and descending through The Canyons Resort, for now.

From Silver Lake Village at Deer Valley Resort, head down the dirt service road to the right of Sterling Lift. Immediately after going under the skiers' bridge, fork left on MMT, and stay on it for the next 28-30 miles! Although the trail starts out chunky and choppy (tech 3+), it improves quickly. Cross a doubletrack rising up from the base of Quincy and Red Cloud Lifts, and gradually roll uphill across ski runs (tech 2+). Pass Tour de Suds/Ontario Bypass Trail, which forks right, and wobble around some tight switchbacks. The trail can get booted around here because of ski resort development, so keep an eye out for directional markers. Ride through a tranquil stand of timber, pass the junction with Tour des Suds, and cross Guardsman Road to the guardrail on the other side. Here, you'll pick up the combined MMT/Little Chief Trail and curve around Empire Lodge (**m2.5**). The colossal hoist of the nearby Daly West Mine stands as a tribute to Park City's historic mining days. Where the trail exits to a dirt road, go left around the horseshoe bend for about 50 feet, and fork right on the continued MMT.

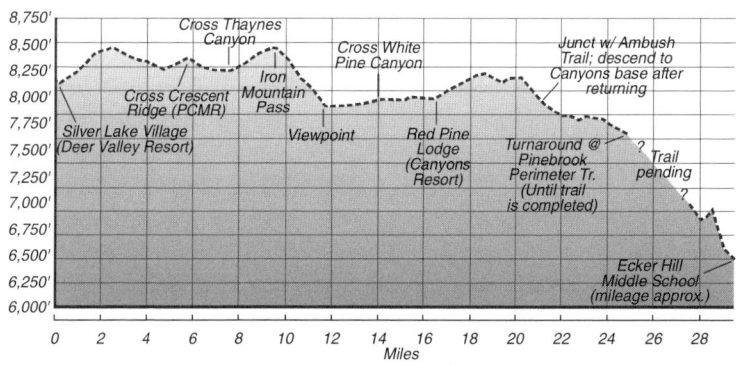

# 132  Mountain Biking Park City & Beyond

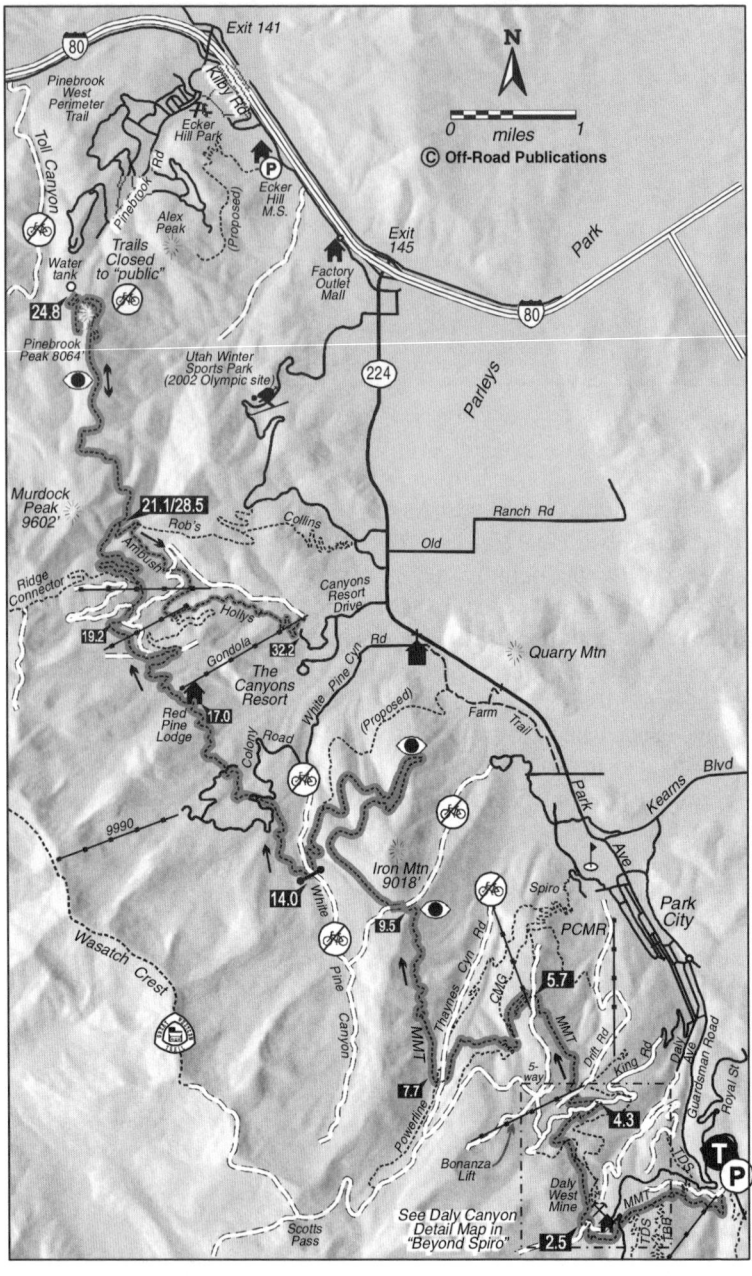

MMT rises around a rocky outcrop and affords a view across Daly (Empire) Canyon to the condo-lined slopes of Deer Valley Resort. Beyond the junction with Little Chief Trail (**m2.5**), MMT smooths (tech $2^+$) and penetrates darkened conifers followed by dense aspens. Bank down two sharp turns and ride behind the maintenance sheds for Park City Mountain Resort; then turn sharply left, and cross the dirt King Road (**m4.3**). Cross another dirt road, and enter a ski run uphill from Bonanza Lift. Go right and descend the doubletrack but not to the lift's base: watch for MMT forking left immediately. Intersect another doubletrack, which rises up from the old angle station, go left, uphill, and then fork right immediately on MMT. A gentle climb takes you up to Crescent Ridge (**m5.7**). Cross the ridge-top doubletrack and zoom down across ski runs high above Thaynes Canyon. Cross the Claim Jumper jeep road and pass the junction with Crescent Mine Grade. A free-flowing descent through timber and across ski runs takes you to the Thaynes Canyon doubletrack (**m7.7**). Climb gradually for almost 2 miles to Iron Mountain Pass, take a break, and absorb the sublime view of Park City's northern environs (**m9.5**).

Iron Mountain Pass is a point of commitment because there is no public access to MMT until you reach The Canyons Resort 7 miles later, and from there it's another 4.5 miles to the resort base. If you're feeling fresh, then press on. Go left on the doubletrack at the pass; then fork right immediately on the continued MMT. Whip through the aspens like a skier on a slalom course, and descend gradually across the thickly timbered flank of Iron Mountain. Full suspension is a godsend on this stretch because small jagged rocks can make the tread quite choppy (tech $3^+$). Where the trail exits the timber at a left-hand hairpin turn, you can survey your upcoming route as it crosses the wooded backside of the Wasatch Crest to The Canyons. The trail darts into a stand of spindly, close-in aspens and winds through several hollows forested with shadow-filled conifers. Cross the doubletrack in White Pine Canyon (**m14.0**) and continue on MMT. (Plans are on the drawing board for a trail that will descend the south side of White Pine Canyon and link to the paved Farm Trail near McPolin Farm. When this trail is completed, it will provide public access to MMT. Keep your ears tuned to local happenings.)

The next 3 miles to Red Pine Lodge are among the sweetest, as you'll float along boatloads of buffed trail (tech $2^+$) and pass through tall fluttering aspens. Pass a cement building, which is a public restroom, and cross the paved Colony Road. One-half mile farther, intersect a doubletrack and take it left/uphill for a few hundred feet; then fork right on the signed MMT. Cross another paved road and arrive at Red Pine Lodge (**m17.0**). If your timing is right, then you can fill your belly with delectables at the lodge's café.

From the lodge, pick up MMT on the northwest side of the clearing, and climb gradually for a mile to a doubletrack on a small ridge. The next mile can be confusing because MMT crosses and follows several dirt roads,

Long Live Long Rides!

but the route is well signed. Go left on the dirt road for 50 feet and fork right on MMT. (Holly Flander's Trail is accessed by going right on the dirt road.) Pedal up a service road for about 100 yards past the resort's maintenance sheds, and fork right on MMT. The trail contours briefly through the woods and intersects another dirt service road where the road makes a horseshoe bend (**m19.2**). Chug up the road for 0.3 mile and fork right on the signed MMT. The remaining MMT is entirely singletrack. Pass through a grove of leaning aspens, and fork right at the junction with Ridge Connector Trail. You'll feel like a Jedi warrior scooting through the Forests of Endor in *Return of the Jedi* on a fast, mile-long descent through the cool conifers (tech 2⁺).

Go straight at the junction with Ambush Trail (**m21.1/28.5**) onto Hunter's Trail section of the Mid Mountain Trail (tech 3), and contour across the steep headwater slopes of Threemile Canyon. MMT latches onto the 8,000-foot mark one last time, as it rolls along the ridge and then across a breezy meadow. Bikers tend to congregate here to enjoy the close-up views of Murdock Peak and Toll Canyon and distant sights of Snyderville Basin and the Uinta Mountains.

## Mid Mountain Trail (The Full Monty)

Continuing on, the trail descends quickly around Pinebrook Peak, drops through a right-hand switchback, and comes to the junction with the Pinebrook South and West Perimeter Trails (**m24.8**). Hunter's Trail (MMT) ends here until the remainder is completed. Turning around and retracing your tracks to Ambush Trail is recommended. Climb steadily back to Ambush Trail for the culminating descent. (If you rode through to Pinebrook in years past then you know about the hideous climb up "33-silly switchbacks." That section will likely be abandoned for a more logical trail that will contour from Pinebrook Peak over toward Alex Peak. There, MMT will connect with the Ecker Hill Middle School Trailhead. For now, Pinebrook Trails are off limits! Consult the latest edition of *Park City Trails Map* by Mountain Trails Foundation for trail updates.)

Ambush Trail initially drops through a dense grove of bleach-white aspens then ducks into dark conifers beyond the junction with Rob's/Sunpeak Connector Trail. The trail is fun and fast. After crossing a dirt road, you'll have to gear down for a gradual half-mile climb. Intersect another dirt road, and take it uphill and around the right side of Sun Lodge, where you'll connect with Holly's Trail. Descending Holly's to The Canyons Resort base (**m32.2**) is an exciting way to end an epic ride.

**Option:** MMT Loop
If shuttling between the endpoints is not an option, then you'll have to ride the Full Monty as a 40-mile loop. Instead of pedaling up the heavily traveled Guardsman Road to Silver Lake Village, simply follow Tour des Suds up Daly Canyon to MMT. You'll miss only a mile of trail, but spend more time on dirt rather than on paved roads.

**Option:** MMT one section at a time
You don't have to ride the entire Mid Mountain Trail; that's part of its allure. To experience a section at a time, consult the chapters "Mid Mountain Trail (North), (Middle), and (South)."

### ! Know Before You Go

- Again, riding Pinebrook's trails is not recommended for now, so you can't "legally" reach the trailhead at Ecker Hill Middle School.
- This is a big ride, stock up with water, food, tools, and appropriate clothing. Your only contact point is Red Pine Lodge in The Canyons Resort, when it's open.
- MMT is signed throughout with carsonite posts.
- There are many ways to exit MMT between Deer Valley Resort and Park City Mountain Resort, but no public access exits between Thaynes Canyon and The Canyons Resort, that is, at least until the proposed trail on the south side of White Pine Canyon is built. Likewise, there is no access from MMT between The Canyons Resort (Ambush Trail) and Pinebrook.

- Sheep are herded in The Canyons Resort. Use caution when encountering sheep. Ride slowly through the herd, and don't spook or threaten sheep dogs. In a calm but firm voice, tell the sheep dog to "go home." Call The Canyons for seasonal sheep herding information.
- Down-lift service is free on The Canyons' gondola from Red Pine Lodge to the resort base, should you need a quick way down. See the chapter "The Canyons Resort" for hours of operation.

### Maps & More Information

- USGS 1:24,000: Brighton, Heber City, Park City East, and Park City West, Utah.
- *Park City Trail Map,* by Mountain Trails Foundation.

### Trailhead Access

When the MMT is completed, you'll want to shuttle a pick-up vehicle to Ecker Hill Middle School. From Park City, drive north on UT 224 and turn left onto Kilby Road at the stop light just before the I-80 interchange. Pass the Park City Outlet Stores, and park behind Ecker Hill Middle School. Alternatively, take Exit 141 from I-80 (Jeremy Ranch). Turn left onto Kilby Road and drive 1.2 miles to Ecker Hill Middle School. In the meantime, however, park at The Canyons Resort, located 4 miles north of Park City and 2.7 miles south of Exit 145 from I-80. Take Canyons Resort Drive past the resort base facilities, turn right onto High Mountain Road, and park in the gravel lot next to Sundial Hotel.

To reach the trailhead at Deer Valley Resort, drive into Park City on Park Avenue (UT 224), turn left onto Deer Valley Drive (at Jans and Cole Sport), and fork right onto Marsac Avenue/Guardsman Road at the roundabout. (Alternatively, go up Main Street, turn left onto Hillsdale, and then turn right on Marsac Avenue/Guardsman Road.) Pass the Ontario Mine, and turn left onto Guardsman Pass Connection then right at the junction with Royal Street West to reach Deer Valley Resort's Silver Lake Village.

## Mid Mountain Trail-Wasatch Crest

**JUST THE FACTS**

| | |
|---|---|
| **Location:** | PCMR to The Canyons and back—the long way |
| **Length:** | 29.2 miles, loop |
| **Tread:** | 4 miles doubletrack, 25.2 miles singletrack |
| **Physically:** | Strenuous (long climb from town to the Wasatch Crest, then rolling terrain at high elevation; White Pine Canyon to Iron Mountain Pass is a gradual but deceptively difficult climb) |
| **Technically:** | 2⁺-5 (excellent trails throughout but a few dicey spots; one short hike-a-bike on Wasatch Crest) |
| **Gain:** | 3,800 feet |
| **In a nutshell:** | Spiro-Thaynes Canyon-Powerline-Scotts Pass Road-Wasatch Crest-Ridge Connector-MMT-Thaynes Canyon-Spiro |

**WHY SHOULD U RIDE THIS TRAIL**

*Destined to become a Utah classic, this monster loop is reserved for singletrack purists and endurance junkies. You'll climb for what seems to be an eternity from the word go, top out at tree line, blaze down sinuous tracks, log long miles, and walk away with memories that will last a lifetime—that is if you can still walk after all is said and done. In an age when lift-served freeriding is becoming ever more popular, this ride puts the "mountain" back into mountain biking because you'll climb, traverse, and descend an entire mountain range. But this route is more than a ride of attrition because the trails are among the sweetest around. And the views from the top, of lofty mountains and deep canyons, beg for your camera. Mid Mountain Trail-Wasatch Crest Loop vies for top position on northern Utah's mountain biking "hit list."*

### Details

Settle into granny gear and pace yourself up Spiro Trail because there is a whole lot of climbing ahead of you. Spiro's steep grade, tight turns, and all-to-brief respites will have you huffing (tech 3⁺). Pass Eagle Trail, forking left after 1.1 miles, and pass Armstrong Bypass, forking right immediately thereafter. Break out across the ski runs under King Con Lift, and catch your breath on a short but welcomed descent. Continue climbing through pristine aspens and firs to the junction with the Thaynes Canyon doubletrack (**m2.8**). Head up the doubletrack for 0.3 mile, fork right on Powerline Trail, and pass Mid Mountain Trail (MMT), which will be your return route from the upcoming loop. Like Spiro, Powerline (tech 3) is a low gear grind, but it's a straight shot without a single turn (or breather). Near the base of Thaynes Lift and across from the big mine dump, veer right on Comstock Mine Trail (tech 3⁺), and keep whittling away at the mountain. After Comstock bends left and levels, it rejoins the Thaynes Canyon jeep road. Shadow Lake is 0.2 mile uphill (**m4.8**).

Slurp down a pack of gooey carbo fuel, but don't take a siesta or chow down because the climb continues, and the "best" is yet to come.

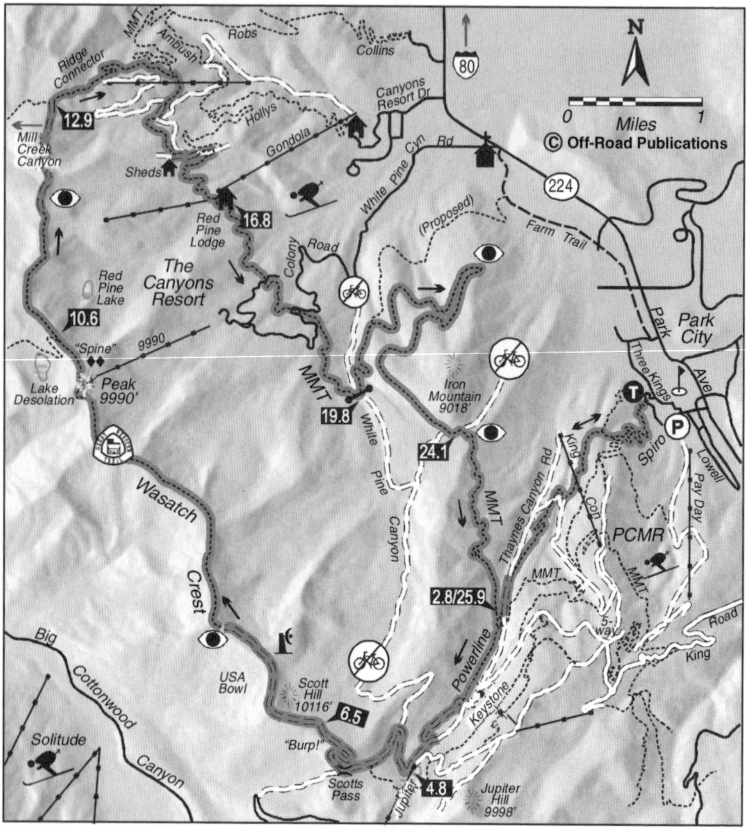

**138** Mountain Biking Park City & Beyond

Take the Scott's Pass jeep road past Jupiter Lift, and go around a gate. The gravelly doubletrack (tech 3+) switchbacks left and rises steeply to a multiple junction at Scott's Pass, where you might meet bikers who are accessing the Wasatch Crest/Great Western Trail from the Salt Lake side. Go right and climb past another gate, round two turns, and get ready to

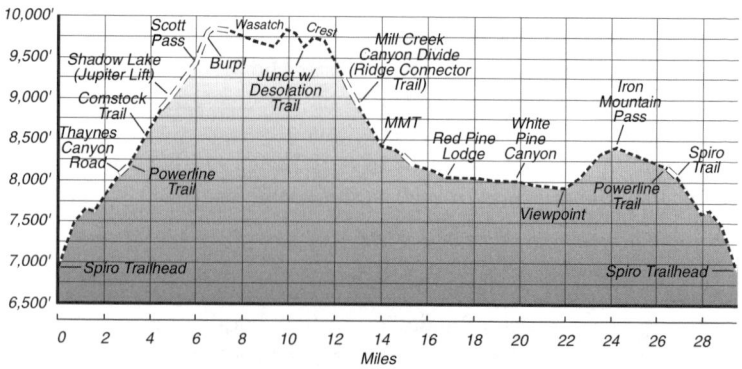

# Mid Mountain Trail-Wasatch Crest

Everyone's happy on the Wasatch Crest, now that Vomit Hill is behind them.

battle the infamous "Vomit Hill"(tech 3⁺). If you did chow heavily at Shadow Lake, then Vomit Hill might live up to its name. Burp! The last one hundred yards are the toughest (**m6.5**).

Rejoice! You're at the three-quarters mark in the ride: three quarters of the climbing is done, but three quarters of the distance remains. If you're pooped, then turn around and resolve to conquer this route another time; otherwise, press on.

Take the ridge-top doubletrack (tech 2) past the communications towers (stay on the low road) and along the top of what backcountry skiers call USA Bowl. Although you'll be clipping right along, don't pass up the stellar views of upper Big Cottonwood Canyon. Solitude and Brighton Ski Resorts lie at your feet, and the canyon's tallest peaks are at eye level. Westward, Mount Raymond and Gobblers Knob separate Big Cottonwood Canyon from Mill Creek Canyon.

The two-track turns to singletrack at the National Forest boundary, and now you'll have to steer your attention from the surrounding countryside to the trail beneath your tires (tech 3⁺). Singletracks don't come much better than this, as the trail rolls up and down along the ridge through crook-neck aspens and across wildflower slopes. Tackle a stiff 0.4-mile climb, curve high above Lake Desolation, and get ready to dismount when the trail descends abruptly and crosses the "spine" (tech 5). Competing glaciers gnawed away at the divide eons ago and left behind a backbone of jagged rock.

Fork right on the Great Western Trail at the junction with Desolation Trail (**m10.6**), and ride up past the watershed boundary. Singletrack reverts to doubletrack after a short, nasty descent (tech 4+), and you'll freewheel speedily past viewpoints of The Canyons Resort to a grassy meadow at the Mill Creek Canyon divide (**m12.9**).

Veer right onto a wide path that narrows quickly and hangs precariously above steep ski slopes. Hop onto the Ridge Connector Trail near the top of Super Condor Lift, glide downhill, and go right on MMT. (If you're toasted, then you can go left on MMT, descend Ambush and lower Holly's Trail to the resort base, and limp back to Park City on paved roads.) Exit the trail to a dirt road, descend the road 0.3 mile to where it makes a horseshoe bend left, and fork right on MMT. After a short section of contouring, MMT exits to another dirt service road. Take the road left and past the maintenance sheds on your right. Trail signs will direct you onto a singletrack, which crosses more dirt roads and passes trail signs for upper Holly's Trail on a small ridge. Here, you can survey your remaining miles, as MMT crosses the timbered backside of the Wasatch Range. Red Pine Lodge (**m16.8**) is a good place to take a break, have a snack, and reload on water (check for hours of operation).

During autumn, aspen leaves sprinkle the MMT like gold doubloons.

Over the next 3 miles, MMT is buttery smooth and clings to the 8,000-foot contour for near effortless cruising (tech 2). Cross two paved roads and pass a public restroom on the right; then cross a doubletrack in White Pine Canyon (**m19.8**). Past White Pine, MMT angles uphill ever so slightly on a roundabout way to Iron Mountain Pass (**m24.1**). Although this climb would be rated as easy on a relative scale, the trail's choppy tread (tech 3+) combined with the miles you've logged so far make it doubly difficult. Halfway to the pass, you can catch your breath where the trail switchbacks right and affords a great view back towards The Canyons.

At the pass, jog left onto a doubletrack, and then fork right immediately on MMT and savor a sweet 2-mile glide to Powerline Trail to complete the loop (**m25.9**). Retrace your tracks down the Thaynes Canyon doubletrack and Spiro Trail to Park City. The brief climb midway along Spiro may make your legs scream "UNCLE!"

Joe angles down the "spine" on the Wasatch Crest with Lake Desolation below.

## ! Know Before You Go

- There are no quick and easy ways off this route once you're up on the Wasatch Crest, so be aware of your endurance, water and food rations, and weather conditions.
- Red Pine Lodge is open for lunch Wednesday to Sunday, 11 a.m. to 4 p.m., late June through September.
- Look for a new trail (built in 2006) accessing Spiro from the PCMR base area, thus eliminating part of the climb on lower Spiro.

## ? Maps & More Information

- USGS 1:24,000: Park City West, Utah.
- *Park City Trail Map*, by Mountain Trails Foundation.
- *Mountain Biking Utah's Wasatch Front*, by Gregg Bromka (Off-Road Publications).

## Trailhead Access

From the intersection of Park Avenue (UT 224) and Deer Valley Drive (Jans and Cole Sport), go west on Empire Avenue past Cole Sport, turn right on Silver King Drive, and park at Park City Mountain Resort's lower lot. On your bike, exit the parking lot, go left on Silver King Drive then immediately right on Three Kings Drive and along the golf course. Go left on Crescent Road, and you'll find the Spiro trailhead at the bend next to a dirt road. Parking is not allowed at the Spiro trailhead. Salt Lakers can access this route from Guardsman Road at the top of Big Cottonwood Canyon and can join in the fun from Scott's Pass.

## Park City to Salt Lake City

### JUST THE FACTS

**Location:** Park City Mountain Resort to Mill Creek Canyon
**Length:** 29 miles, one-way
**Tread:** 4.5 miles paved road, 5 miles doubletrack, 19.5 miles singletrack
**Physically:** Strenuous (long climb from PC to Wasatch Crest, rolling trail at high elevation, endless descent to SLC)
**Technically:** 2-5 (excellent trails with some rough spots)
**Gain:** 3,250 feet (loss: 5,000 feet. Yeah, baby!)
**In a nutshell:** Park City-Spiro-Thaynes Canyon-Powerline-Scotts Pass-Wasatch Crest-Great Western Trail-Mill Creek Canyon Road-Mill Creek Pipeline-Mill Creek Canyon Road-Salt Lake City

*This ride defines the term "mountain biking" because it takes you from Park City to Salt Lake City on trails that go over the Wasatch Range. "That's sick," you say? This is a tough ride, no doubt, but it follows some of the best singletracks in Utah, so "sick" means good—no, awesome! The initial 2,800-foot climb through Park City Mountain Resort to the Wasatch Crest is long-winded, and it concludes with a gut-wrenching grind up what locals affectionately call "Vomit Hill." The Wasatch Crest/Great Western Trail rolls along the top of the range between the tops of Big Cottonwood and Mill Creek Canyons, where the views of mountains, canyons, alpine bowls, and distant towns will blow the mind of any mountain biker who is new to this neck of the woods. Descending the entire length of Mill Creek Canyon from the ridge to Salt Lake City is the grand finale. The trail drops 4,000 feet over 16 miles, and three quarters of it is on prime singletracks. What more could you want?*

### Details

Settle into granny gear and grind slowly up Spiro Trail because there is a lot of climbing ahead of you. You'll stay in your granny gear the whole way up Spiro because of the trail's steep grade, tight turns, and all-too-brief respites (tech 3-4). Pass Eagle Trail, forking left after 1.1 miles, and pass Armstrong Bypass, forking right immediately thereafter. Break out across the ski runs under King Con Lift, and catch your breath on a short but welcomed descent. Continue climbing through pristine aspens and firs to the junction with the Thaynes Canyon doubletrack (**m2.8**). Head up the doubletrack for 0.3 mile, fork right on Powerline Trail, and pass Mid Mountain Trail (MMT). Like Spiro, Powerline is a low gear grind (tech 3), but it's a straight shot without a single turn or breather. Near the base of Thaynes Lift and across from the big mine dump, veer right on Comstock Mine Trail (tech 3+), and keep whittling away at the mountain. After Comstock bends left and levels, it rejoins the Thaynes Canyon jeep road. Shadow Lake is 0.2 mile uphill (**m4.8**).

Slurp down a pack of gooey carbo fuel, but don't take a siesta or chow down because the climb continues, and the "best" is yet to come.

Left: Solitude's Honeycomb Cliffs backdrop the Wasatch Crest. Right: Bob slips through a grove of crook-neck aspens.

Take the Scott's Pass jeep road past Jupiter Lift, and go around a gate. The gravelly doubletrack (tech 3$^+$) switchbacks left and rises steeply to a multiple junction at Scott's Pass, where you might meet bikers who are accessing the Wasatch Crest/Great Western Trail from the Salt Lake side. Go right and climb past another gate, round two turns, and get ready to battle the infamous "Vomit Hill"(tech 3$^+$). If you did chow heavily at Shadow Lake, then Vomit Hill might live up to its name. Burp! The last one hundred yards are the toughest (**m6.5**).

Take the ridge-top doubletrack (tech 2) past the communications towers (stay on the low road) and along the top of what backcountry skiers call USA Bowl. Although you'll be clipping right along, don't miss the stellar views of upper Big Cottonwood Canyon. Solitude and Brighton Ski Resorts lie at your feet, and canyon's tallest peaks are at eye level. Westward, Mount Raymond and Gobblers Knob separate Big Cottonwood Canyon from Mill Creek Canyon.

The two-track turns to singletrack at the National Forest boundary, which means that you'll have to steer your attention from the surrounding countryside to the trail beneath your tires (tech 3$^+$). Singletrack doesn't come much better than this, as the trail rolls up and down along the ridge through crook-neck aspens and across wildflower slopes. Tackle a stiff 0.4-mile climb, curve high above Lake Desolation, and get ready to dismount when the trail descends abruptly and crosses the "spine" (tech 5). Competing glaciers gnawed away at the divide eons ago and left behind a backbone of jagged rock.

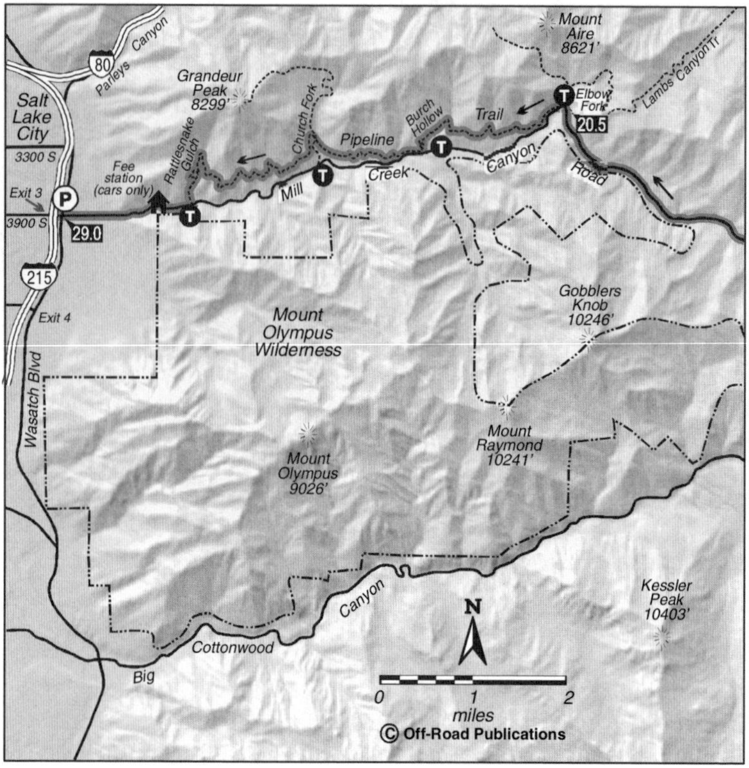

# 144 Mountain Biking Park City & Beyond

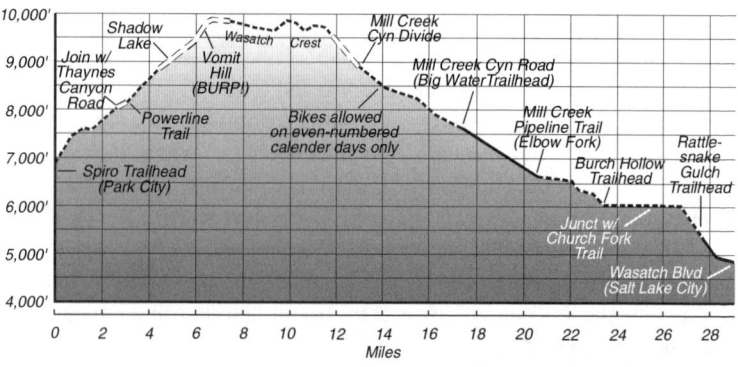

Fork right on the Great Western Trail at the junction with Desolation Trail, and ride up past the watershed boundary. Singletrack reverts to doubletrack after a short nasty descent (tech 4+), and you'll freewheel speedily past viewpoints of The Canyons Resort to a grassy meadow at the Mill Creek Canyon divide (**m12.9**).

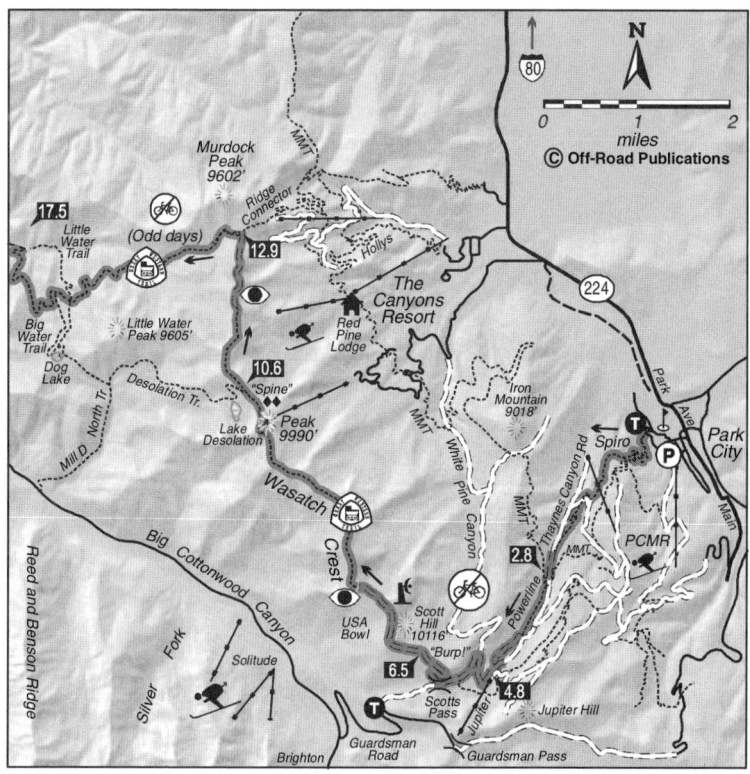

You're just past the halfway point, and the rest of the ride is a lesson in physics because you've built up a ton of potential energy and gravity is a powerful force. Go left at the divide onto the doubletrack-turned singletrack, and descend like hellfire. But be ready to hit the brakes at a moment's notice because the trail harbors some hidden tricky bits (tech 4). Cut across pretty meadows, hop a couple of tiny creeks, and veer into the dark cover of the conifers. Trim your speed on the curves, and keep your eyes forward in anticipation of approaching bikers and hikers. (Always yield to hikers and to ascending bikers.) Roll through the four-way junction with Little Water Trail and turn right at the T-junction with Big Water Trail. Another mile and a half of buffed trail winds through the thick woods (tech 2+) down to the paved Mill Creek Canyon Road (**m17.5**).

Tuck and glide down the road for 3 miles to Elbow Fork, and hop onto the Mill Creek Pipeline Trail (**m20.5**). (Be cautious when descending the road because the lane is narrow, and motorists might not anticipate bicyclists going full-tilt around the blind curves.)

After an initially rough section (tech 3), Pipeline Trail smooths to hard-packed dirt (tech 2). Still, you must concentrate on your front wheel because the trail is narrow and edged with steep slopes. Eyes forward; don't look down! The trail becomes more comforting farther on. After

Mill Creek Pipeline Trail is a sweet way to finish this epic ride.

dropping across Burch Hollow, the trail descends quickly around six tight switchbacks (tech 4) to a junction near the Burch Hollow trailhead. Be cool, not lame—ride it, don't slide it!

Stay right/west on Pipeline Trail and contour across the canyon's steep slopes once more (tech 2). Portions of the trail are sunny and treeless; others are enveloped by a wooded canopy. The trail splits without warning a mile from the Burch Hollow trailhead; stay right and scamper up a sharp ramp, dubbed "sucker hill." You need to be quick with the shifters, or you'll get suckered into walking. (Straight is a dead end.) Play through the junction with Church Fork, and continue weaving into the forested hollows and out across the treeless slopes, where views are incredible. Fork left at the junction in Rattlesnake Gulch and square up for the sharp, rough descent to the trailhead (tech 4$^+$). Again, do your best to save the trail by not skidding.

Pop out to the paved Mill Creek Canyon Road, and tuck and glide past the fee station (no fee for bicycles, so you don't have to stop) and to Wasatch Boulevard (**m29.0**).

## ! Know Before You Go

- Bicycles are allowed on Upper Mill Creek Canyon Trails on *even-numbered* calender days only from July 1 to November 1. This includes Upper Mill Creek/Great Western Trail, Big Water Trail, and Little Water Trail. Mill Creek Pipeline Trail is excluded from this restriction. Thus, you can only ride this route on even-numbered calender days.
- All trails are popular with pedestrians, especially those in Mill Creek Canyon, so ride cautiously and courteously. Yield the trail to hikers and to ascending bikers.
- Be prepared for rapidly changing alpine weather.
- Dogs are not allowed on this ride because it enters the Big Cottonwood Canyon Watershed.

## ? Maps & More Information

- USGS 1:24,000: Brighton, Mount Aire, and Park City West, Utah.
- *Mountain Biking Utah's Wasatch Front,* by Gregg Bromka (Off-Road Publications).
- Wasatch-Cache National Forest (Salt Lake Ranger District): (801) 943-1794.
- Public Lands Information Center, c/o R.E.I. (Recreational Equipment Incorporated): (801) 466-6411.

## Trailhead Access

First shuttle a pick-up vehicle to Salt Lake. From I-80 at the mouth of Parley's Canyon, go south on I-215, and take Exit 3 for 3900 South. Park at the park-and-ride lot at the intersection of Wasatch Boulevard, or take Wasatch one block north to 3800 South/Mill Creek Canyon Road. (Heed parking restrictions along Mill Creek Canyon Road). If you are traveling northbound on I-215, take Exit 4 for 3900 South/3300 South to access Wasatch Boulevard and Mill Creek Canyon Road.

The ride starts on Spiro Trail in Park City. From I-80, take Exit 145 and drive into Park City. From the intersection of Park Avenue (UT 224) and Deer Valley Drive (Jans and Cole Sport), go west on Empire Avenue past Cole Sport, turn right onto Silver King Drive, and park in the lower lot of Park City Mountain Resort. On your bike, go left onto Silver King, and then take an immediate right onto Three Kings Drive, which runs alongside the golf course. Go left onto Crescent Road and find the Spiro trailhead at the bend next to a dirt road. (Parking is not allowed at the Spiro Trailhead.)

## 25

## Park City to Provo

| | |
|---|---|
| **Location:** | Park City (Canyons Resort) to Provo Canyon (Canyon Glen Park) |
| **Length:** | 47.5 miles, one-way |
| **Tread:** | 7 miles paved road, 3.5 miles paved trail, 4.6 miles doubletrack, 32.4 miles singletrack. |
| **Physically:** | Extreme (Can you say death march?) |
| **Technically:** | 3-5 (Good trails throughout with several extended hike-a-bike sections; some dicey descents, too) |
| **Gain:** | 7,500 feet—Ouch! |
| **In a nutshell:** | Holly's-Ambush-MMT-Ridge Connector-GWT (Mill Creek Canyon divide to Alpine Loop Highway Summit)-Aspen Grove Trail-UT 92-US 189-Provo/Jordan River Parkway |

*This ride is a "G.A.S."—Gonzo, Abusive, and Sick! But it's awesome! Whereas most rides in Park City go around in circles and never take you more than a couple miles from town, this trek follows the Great Western Trail (GWT) across a big chunk of the Wasatch Range. The facts above don't lie: the miles are long, the vertical gain is huge, the physical difficulty is off the charts, and the bulk of the ride takes place at elevations where the air is lean and clean. You'll encounter several hike-a-bike sections, but overall the Great Western Trail is biker friendly, if not sensational. As you can imagine, you'll take in some magnificent sights along the way: chiseled mountain peaks, glacial canyons, distant towns, and a half dozen ski resorts. You must plan this ride when the weather is forecasted to be high and dry and your fitness level is at its peak, or this heavenly ride will be hell. If you succeed, then this ride will become an indelible memory and one you can brag about for a lifetime.*

### Details

A decision must be made from the get-go. Do you want to knock off the initial 2,000-foot climb through The Canyons Resort to the Wasatch Crest on singletrack or on doubletrack? Singletrack is the correct answer, naturally.

Start at the old cement amphitheater at the resort base, and head up lower Holly Flander's Trail under the gondola. (Don't even think about cheating and taking the lift.) You'll settle into granny gear right away and encounter a few short hike-a-bike sections along the climb (tech 3-4⁺). After 1.7 miles, and near Sun Lodge, fork right on Ambush Trail, and chug up to Mid Mountain Trail (MMT). Go left on MMT, and climb moderately on smooth tread (tech 2⁺) and through dark conifers to Ridge Connector Trail, which, not surprisingly, connects with the Wasatch Crest at the Mill Creek Canyon divide (**m6.0**). (The doubletrack option, although tedious, is about a mile shorter and a bit faster because you'll just spin, spin, spin. Catch the doubletrack on the right side of the gondola and

On route to Big Cottonwood Canyon along the Wasatch Crest.

head up Willow Draw. Fork right up Willow Draw at the base of Super Condor Lift; then curve left across the hollow and climb across the open slopes. About 3.3 miles from the base, round a switchback to the right, and cross MMT. Bend left after crossing under Super Condor Lift and pump up the choppy road to the top of the lift, where a trail takes you to the Mill Creek Canyon divide.)

Now that we're all together, and our legs are warmed up, take the Wasatch Crest Trail/GWT south, climbing initially on a doubletrack (tech 2-3+). A short, nasty climb on loose rocks announces the start of singletrack (tech 5), which then smooths (tech 3). Stay left at the junction with Desolation Trail (**m8.5**) and hoof it up the "spine." Competing glaciers once gnawed at this ridge, leaving vertebrae of jagged rocks exposed in the trail (tech 5). The rest of the Wasatch Crest is gravy, as it undulates along the ridge top (tech 3). Look south and you'll spy a sea of mountain peaks sitting on the horizon; soon your route will go over them.

Singletrack reverts to doubletrack at the National Forest boundary and passes the communication towers on Scott Hill. On a sunny weekend, you'll likely find bikers congregating atop "Vomit Hill," trying to recoup after struggling up the gut-wrenching climb. Luckily, you'll freewheel down it. Turn right at Scott's Pass (**m13.1**) and descend on the doubletrack; lift your bike over a locked gate, and pop out to paved Guardsman Road. (Scott's Pass is your official bailout to Park City through Park City Mountain Resort, if your ride goes awry.) If you're playing through, then glide down Guardsman Road to Big Cottonwood Canyon Road, and

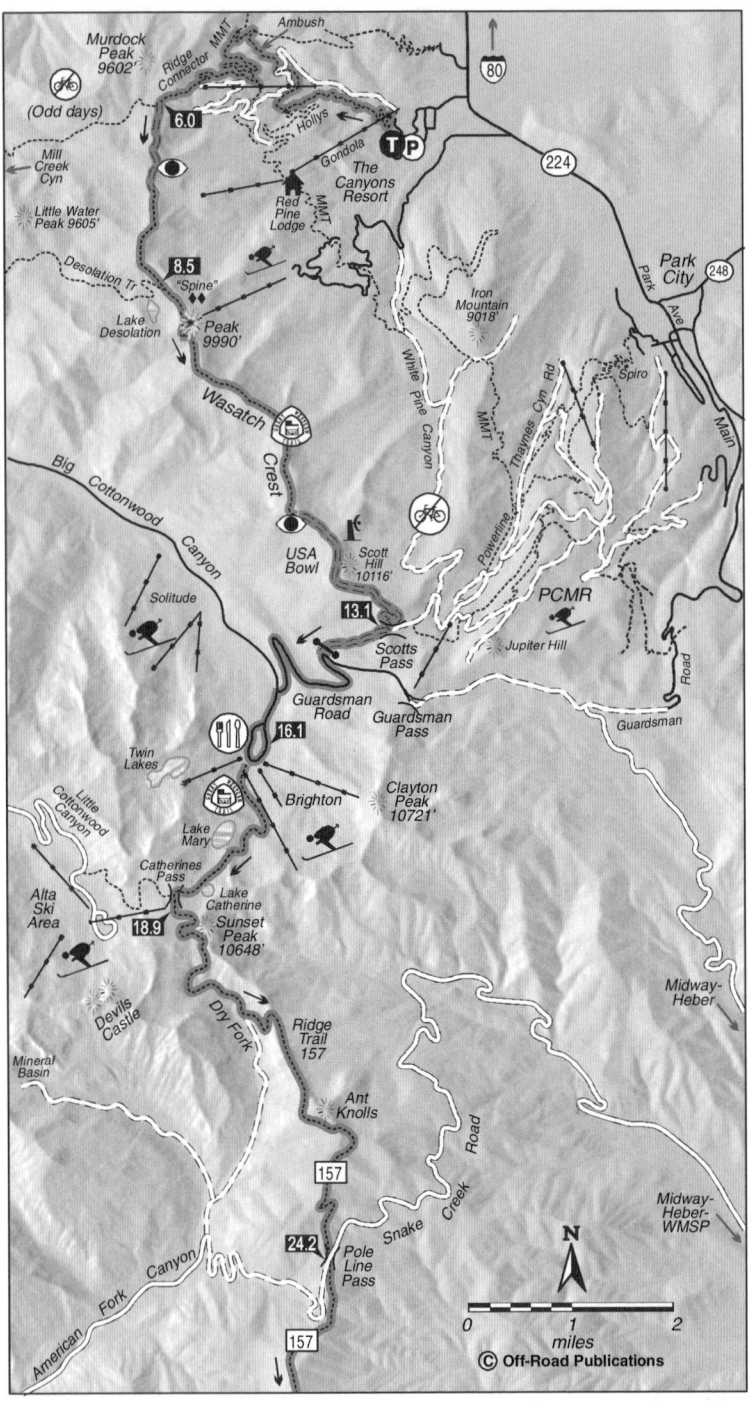

# Park City to Provo 151

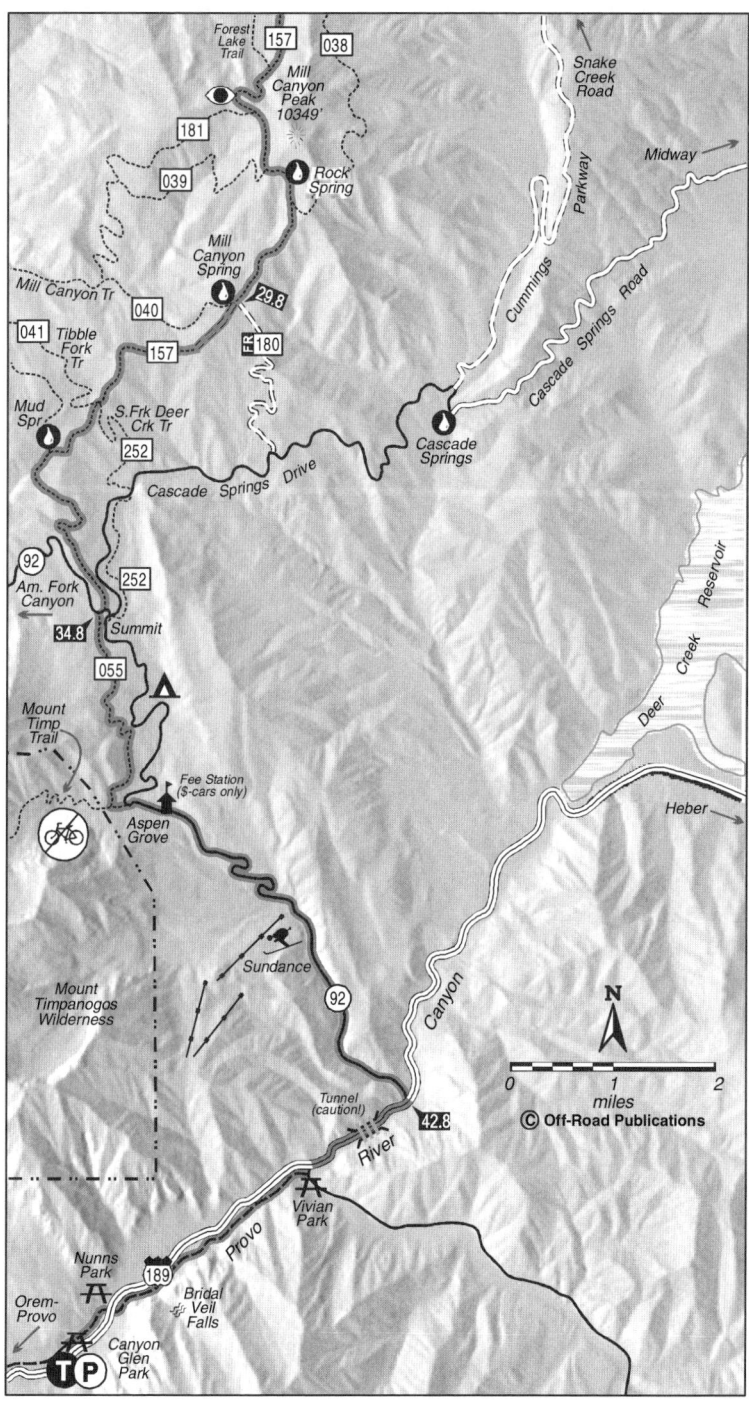

Left: Where it's ridable, Lake Mary Trail is sweet! Right: When the going gets tough, even the tough have to hoof it!

pump up the pavement to Brighton. You've burned some serious calories so far, so have lunch at the Brighton General Store and reload on water (**m16.1**).

Now the "fun" begins. The steep, rooted, bouldery Mary Lake Trail is geared more for bipeds than bicycles, and you'll ride-walk-ride-walk the whole thing (tech 3-5). Past Lake Catherine, the only way to reach Catherine's Pass (**m18.9**) is to thrown your rig over your shoulder and bike-pack. If not for the beauty of these mountains, walking barefoot on hot coals would be more enjoyable. Grin and bear it.

Surprise! You'll keep hoofing past Catherine's Pass, too. Sometimes "life's a beach," and you'll have to slog through thick, soft beach sand, which has eroded from a sandstone layer underground. When you reach a

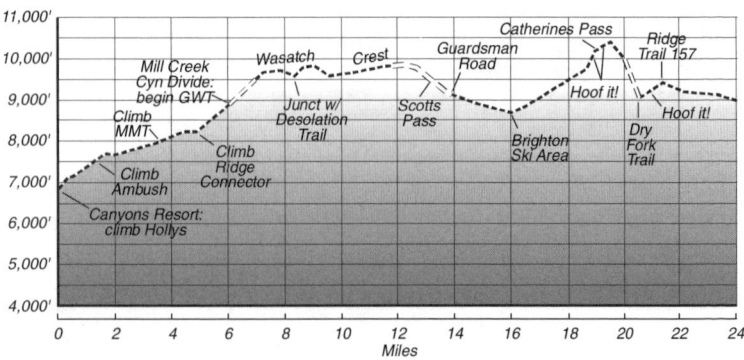

divide where you can view Alta, Brighton, American Fork Canyon, and Mount Timpanogos in one full spin, go left/east toward Sunset Peak, following signs for GWT, and take the trail just below the ridge. This is your "Last Chance Texaco" to turn around and limp home because once you descend into Dry Fork (upper American Fork Canyon), you're committed to finishing the ride come hell or high water. Ready?

Anxiety will only compound the wickedness of the descent into Dry Fork, so stay calm in your head and loose on your saddle. After all, it's only a bike ride. Still, watch out for risky stunts on the top section of singletrack and loose rubble on the lower section of doubletrack (tech 4+). There is no shame in dismounting. Besides, you'll have a better chance to admire the stunning glacial architecture that surrounds you. Do not descend the doubletrack all the way into American Fork Canyon. Watch carefully for the Dry Fork Trail/Great Western Trail forking left near a log barrier, which closes the upper basin to vehicles; then with practiced proficiency, push, drag, and haul your bike up the eroded trail (tech 4-5) to the ridge. There, Ridge Trail 157 traverses kindly around Ant Knolls (tech 3-4) and drops through aspens and grassy fields to Pole Line Pass (**m24.2**).

Leaving the Alpine Ridge behind on Ridge Trail 157.

Legs still feeling fresh? If not, then you're in trouble. Although most of the climbing is behind, you won't be out of the woods until you reach the Alpine Loop Highway Summit, which is 10.6 miles away. Onward. Battle the sand and rocks to Sandy Baker Pass, veer right on Trail 157

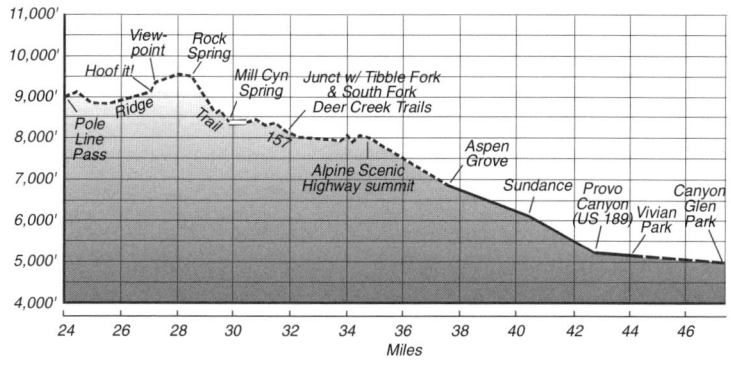

(tech 3⁺), and enjoy excellent singletrack, which curves around Mill Canyon Peak. The Alpine Ridge, marked by the backsides of Snowbird and Alta, slowly fades to the north while Box Elder Peak looms to the west. You'll climb steadily past the junction with Forest Lake Trail and then hike-a-bike yet again to a small divide where Mount Timpanogos declares its majestic presence. Timp will be your constant companion from here on. Pass Rock Springs, which can be used in a pinch to reload your water, and square up for the notoriously nasty descent over loose dirt and rubble to Mill Canyon Spring (tech 4⁺, **m29.8**).

Head due south from Mill Canyon Spring on Ridge Trail 157, which is doubletrack for one-half mile and then narrows to singletrack. Short rocky climbs balanced by longer descents (tech 3-4) take you along the undulating ridge past the four-way junction with Tibble Fork Trail-South Fork Deer Creek Trail and then past Mud Spring. Thereafter, smoother, faster trail (tech 3) provides a welcomed relief, but there are two short stinging climbs (tech 4⁺) between the junction with Pine Hollow Trail and the Alpine Loop Highway Summit (**m34.8**).

If you are still of sound mind and body, then more singletrack waits to be conquered, but if you're cooked, then just coast down the Alpine Loop Highway to Provo Canyon. It's a tough call because the highway's fast curvy course is a thrill a minute. Still, singletrack rules, so pick up the Summit-Aspen Grove Trail, No. 055, behind the outhouse at the parking area. Head-high wildflowers and fluttering aspens crowd the trail, and you'll feel like you won the bonus round in a game show, but there are choppy sections, too, so don't let your guard down (tech 3-4). Go left when you intersect the Mount Timpanogos Trail, and exit to the highway at Aspen Grove.

You'll break the speed limit easily if you let gravity have its way, so be prudent; you're too close to the end to blow it by crashing. Pass Sundance, go right on US 189 in Provo Canyon (**m42.8**), and ride the highway's shoulder for 1 mile to Vivian Park. (Use caution going through the tunnel: Wait for traffic to clear behind you, and then sprint like mad.) Finally, hop on the paved Provo-Jordan River Parkway, and cool down with an idle coast past Bridal Veil Falls, through Nunns Park, and to Canyon Glen Park; then dive headlong into your cooler for celebratory refreshments. You did stock the cooler, didn't you?

If you're wondering, "Hey, we're not in Provo yet," then you're right. Just limp 6 more miles down the Provo-Jordan River Parkway. But enough is enough!

**Option:** Mill Creek Canyon Trailhead
Salt Lake bikers can access the ride from the top of Mill Creek Canyon Road by heading up Big Water Trail and GWT to the Mill Creek Canyon divide. Doing so will shorten the ride by about 2 miles and lessen the elevation gain by 1,000 feet, but it doesn't make the entire ride any easier.

## ! Know Before You Go

- This ride is *huge*, so be prepared. Know your ability and that of others in your group. Carry a ton of food and a gallon of water. Take along appropriate tools, a cell phone, and foul weather clothing. Bring maps if you are not familiar with these trails. In all, the extra weight of these items offsets the disasters that may arise without them.
- If you are riding with others, then stay together or regroup often so riders don't stray off-course or get stranded.
- Food and beverages are available at Brighton General Store. Call ahead for store hours. Spring water is *generally* reliable, and potable, at Rock Spring and Mill Canyon Spring.
- Many sections are remote and not easily accessed in the event of an emergency, so always err on the side of caution to avoid a mishap.

## ? Maps & More Information

- USGS 1:24,000: Aspen Grove, Bridal Veil Falls, Brighton, and Park City West, Utah.
- Wasatch-Cache National Forest (Salt Lake Ranger District): (801) 943-1794.
- Uinta National Forest (Pleasant Grove Ranger District): (801) 377-5780.
- Public Lands Information Center, c/o R.E.I. (Recreational Equipment Incorporated): (801) 466-6411.
- Brighton General Store: (435) 649-9156.

## Trailhead Access

The route starts at The Canyons Resort, but first you must shuttle a return vehicle to Provo Canyon. From The Canyons, drive into Park City on UT 224 and go left on Kearns Boulevard (UT 248) and take it to US 40. Drive south on US 40 for 9 miles to Heber and fork right on US 189 for Provo Canyon. Canyon Glen Park is about 20 miles from Heber (4 miles past the junction with UT 92 to Sundance). To cut the ride short, park at Vivian Park (1.2 miles past UT 92).

If accessing this ride from Mill Creek Canyon in Salt Lake, then first shuttle a return vehicle to Provo Canyon by taking Exit 272 from I-15 for UT 52/8th North Street (Orem). Canyon Glen Park is 2.6 miles up Provo Canyon on US 189.

# KAMAS RIDES

# Hoyt Peak

**JUST THE FACTS**

**Location:** Mountains immediately northeast of Kamas
**Length:** 22.6 miles, loop
**Tread:** 7.3 miles paved roads, 15.3 miles dirt roads and doubletracks
**Physically:** Strenuous (one big hillclimb ending with hike to summit of Hoyt Peak)
**Technically:** 2-4+ (dirt and rock doubletracks; Wide Hollow descent is steep, rocky, and rutted)
**Gain:** 3,500 feet
**In a nutshell:** UT 32-FR 080-FR 408-UT 150

*WHY SHOULD U RIDE THIS TRAIL If you have a penchant for climbing hills, then Hoyt Peak is your ride. You'll grind your gears up dirt roads and doubletracks for nearly 8 miles, rising above the agrarian Kamas Valley to the windswept summit of Hoyt Peak. Naturally, this much climbing is rewarded with an equal amount of descending. Some sections flow as freely as surfing on gentle waves; others are as punishing as riding a two-wheeled jackhammer. So, put your nose to the handlebar and hammer at race pace, or spin your granny gears and enjoy the intimacy of the encompassing forests.*

## Details

Head north out of Kamas on UT 32. (Stay to the far right side of the road and ride in single file to give motorists plenty of room.) After 3.2 miles, turn right onto Upper Loop Road (3200 North) next to Kamas Valley Co-Op. Climb gradually for 1 mile to where the paved road bends south (at Weller Service), and turn left/east onto a good dirt road signed for Piute Creek and FR 080 (**m4.2**). The tedium of the day's task unfolds as you grind up Hoyt Canyon and pass Camp Aerie (tech 2+). You're crossing private property, so stay on the main road, which is public access. The road bends right near a brown storage shack and rises more steeply. Now, tedium becomes a full-on workout. Ignore all side roads branching from the main track. As you climb, the roadside forest parts to reveal a panoramic view of Kamas Valley and the distant "Wasatch Back." Fork left at a Y-junction ahead, and grind up a despairingly steep, rock-studded hill (**m7.1**). About 1 mile farther, you'll reach a cattle guard and gated fence, signed "Leaving Camp Aerie property." The road is now posted as FR 080 (tech 2+-3+), and you are entering the Wasatch-Cache National Forest. The climb continues.

Fork left at an unsigned but obvious split in the road 0.4 mile from the gate. A series of short ascents leads to another junction where Wide Hollow (FR 408) forks right (**m9.0/16.0**). Remember this junction upon returning from Hoyt Peak because Wide Hollow is your route down. Go left on FR 080, but fork right in 1 mile to avoid climbing a steep, rocky

<< The Bluffs Overlook (Soapstone Basin)

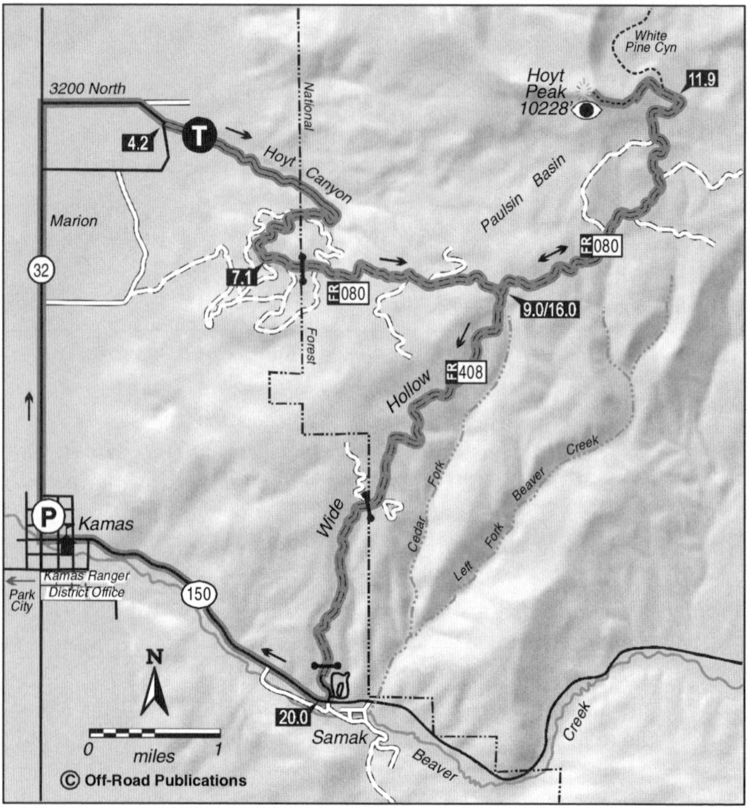

**158** Mountain Biking Park City & Beyond

doubletrack. Pass a spring and a log fence, and then stay left at two upcoming junctions. You'll be pedaling uphill—steeply at times—through mixed timber with a rolling basin to the right/southeast.

Finally, your objective comes into view: the treeless summit of Hoyt Peak. Angle up the rutted jeep road to a wire fence in a saddle (**m11.9**). *Now*, the going gets tough. (As if it hadn't already?) Turn left/west and keep chugging uphill. The road's steepness combined with the high alti-

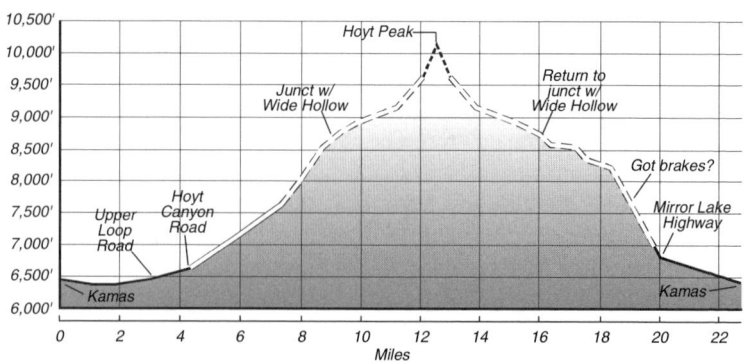

tude make this stretch grueling. Fork left on a faint jeep road when you reach the rim of upper White Pine Canyon. Beyond a wire fence, the path fades to an ATV trail then to a singletrack then to a game trail; then it ultimately fades away. Ride what you can, and hike the rest to the summit. From the top, you

Old photo but still a great ride with great views.

can see the Wasatch Range stretching over 50 miles from Provo Peak to Francis Peak. A small wedge of Utah Lake can be seen through the deep, V-shaped slash of Provo Canyon. Kamas Valley sprawls out below Hoyt Peak while the Uinta Mountains mold the eastern skyline.

You've paid your dues; get ready for a wild descent. Be sure you don't miss the turnoff for Wide Hollow (**m9.0/m16.0**). Ride cautiously because a number of wickedly rocky sections in upper Wide Hollow can take you by surprise (tech 4), especially if you've built up a head of steam. Beyond the first steel gate, the road descends more steeply and becomes increasingly rocky. Some portions are downright brutal, even with dual suspension. Go around a second gate, posted "Kamas Wildlife Management Area," and coast past private homes to Mirror Lake Highway/UT 150 (**m20.0**). Enjoy smooth pavement and a gentle downhill all the way back to Kamas, unless the wind is blowing up canyon; then it's as tedious as the climb.

## ! Know Before You Go

- Lower Hoyt Canyon and lower Wide Hollow cross private lands, so stay on the main dirt roads and heed all signs restricting travel.
- You may encounter off-road vehicles near Hoyt Peak and equestrians in Wide Hollow; ride attentively.
- This area is a prime big game hunting ground during autumn.

## ? Maps & More Information

- USGS 1:24,000: Hoyt Peak and Kamas, Utah.
- Wasatch-Cache Nat'l Forest (Kamas Ranger District): (435) 783-4338

## Trailhead Access

This loop begins and ends in Kamas. You can park at the town hall one block north of the intersection of UT 32 (Main Street) and UT 150 (Center Street/Mirror Lake Highway).

# Upper Setting Road

## JUST THE FACTS

**Location:** 9 miles east of Kamas
**Length:** 14 miles, out-and-back
**Tread:** Light-duty dirt road then rocky doubletrack
**Physically:** Moderately strenuous (one long climb with some rocky stretches)
**Technically:** 2+-4 (washboards give way to loose rocks and bedrock higher up)
**Gain:** 2,260 feet
**In a nutshell:** FR 034 (up-and-back)

*Upper Setting Road rises from the fertile Beaver Creek valley to cool, moist meadows surrounded by fir and spruce trees. Although the route is mostly a woodland tour, you'll find occasional views of the valley below and of treeless peaks above. Typical of the many backcountry roads in the Uinta Mountains, portions of Upper Setting Road are infested with rocks. You'll have to pump at full power to clear the rough stuff on the way up, and you'll have to pick your line carefully on the way down, even with today's cushy full suspension bikes. From the road's end, you can ride to East Shingle Creek Lake on a technical singletrack. Go for it; it's worth the effort.*

### Details

The road begins as hard-packed dirt with scattered rocks and some washboards (tech 2+). Although the road rises only moderately at first, it lifts you quickly above the Beaver Creek valley. Two miles into the ride, you round a prominent right-hand turn and pass through dispersed aspens. One mile farther, the road makes a dogleg bend across the left fork of Coop Creek, and then hugs steep talus slopes high above the Coop Creek valley. From these slopes, you have a good view of Pine Valley, where the Provo River slips between Taylor Fork ridge (middle ground) and Duchesne Ridge (distant south).

Farther on, the road is strewn with angular, embedded rocks (tech 3-4). Dodging these golf ball- to bowling ball-size rocks will be a novelty to some and a nuisance to others. When the conditions are at their worst, try shifting to a harder

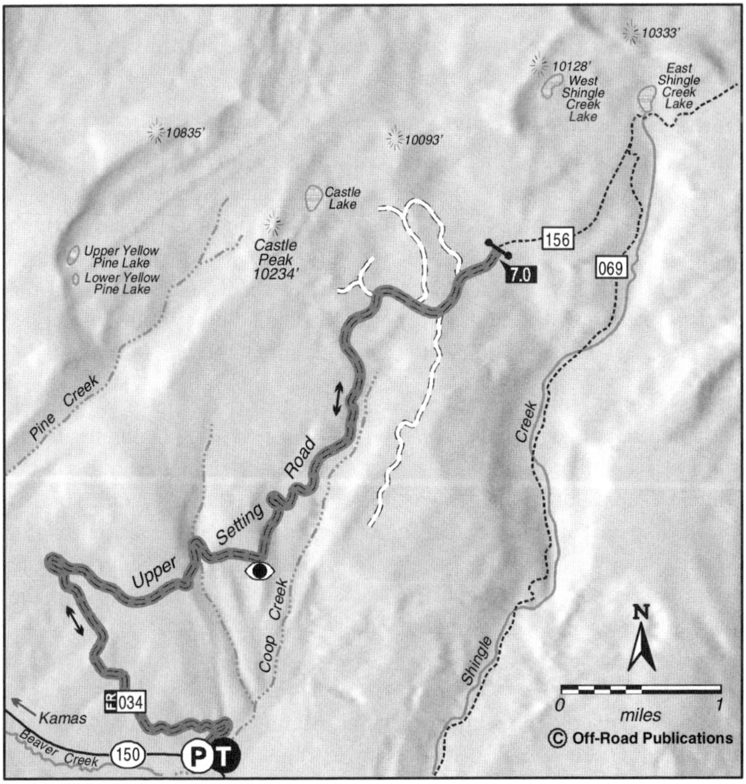

## Upper Setting Road        161

gear and pedaling while standing up to give your posterior a needed rest.

Nearly 6 miles into the ride, the road levels briefly and weaves through stands of spruce surrounded by marshy meadows. Numerous doubletracks branch from the main road. Many are closed to motor vehicles to improve watershed and wildlife habitat; some might be worth exploring by bike.

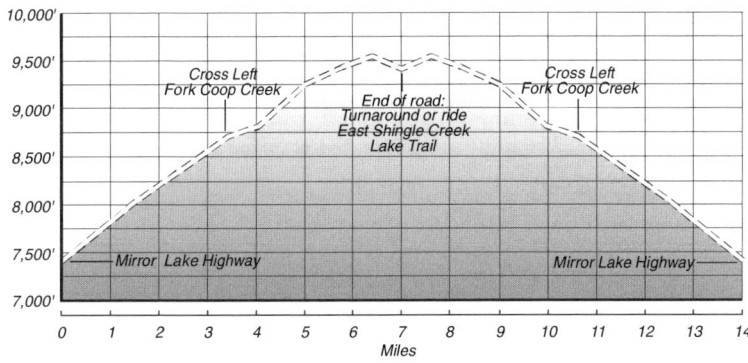

From the route's highest point, you can spy on some of the western Uintas' treeless peaks. Thereafter, a bumpy half-mile descent brings you to the road's end and to the turnaround point (**m7.0**).

**Option:** East Shingle Creek Lake Trail
While you're up here, tackle the trail to East Shingle Creek Lake. Although it's only 2.7 miles round trip, the technical singletrack is pretty burly because you must bunny hop over roots, cant-and-ratchet through boulders, balance delicately around tight turns, and power up abrupt slopes (tech 3-5). When you're not dancing on two wheels, the stillness of the forest will charm you and its rich, earthy bouquet will revitalize you. East Shingle Creek Lake is one of thousands that dot the Uinta Mountains.

**Option:** Upper Shingle Creek Trail
Look before you leap; rather, *read* before you descend. If you pursue the trail to East Shingle Creek Lake, then you'll pass the upper junction for Shingle Creek Trail along the way. Be forewarned, the first 3 miles of this semi-primitive path are steep, technical, and at times torturous (tech 4-5). Lower Shingle Creek Trail is mighty fine. (See the chapter "Shingle Creek Trail.") Freeriders with long travel suspension bikes (and a shuttle up the road), however, just might dig the whole descent!

### Know Before You Go

- You may encounter vehicles on Upper Setting Road and hikers on East Shingle Creek Lake Trail. Upper Shingle Creek Trail attracts equestrians plus a few hearty hikers.
- Don't forget the insect repellant.
- A recreation use fee is required for all vehicles parked along UT 150 (Mirror Lake Highway) and at any trailhead or recreation site. The fee is $3.00 per day per vehicle or $6.00 per week per vehicle (if you plan to stay overnight). There are many self-service fee stations along the highway, or you can pay at the Kamas Ranger District Office.

### Maps & More Information

- USGS 1:24,000: Erickson Basin and Soapstone Basin, Utah.
- Wasatch-Cache Nat'l Forest (Kamas Ranger District): (435) 783-4338

### Trailhead Access

From Kamas, travel 8.3 miles east on UT 150 (Mirror Lake Highway). Turn left on Upper Setting Road (FR 034) shortly past Beaver Creek campground and park near the junction.

## 28 Shingle Creek Trail

### Just the Facts

**Location:** 10 miles east of Kamas
**Length:** 5 miles, out-and-back
**Tread:** Singletrack
**Physically:** Moderate (alternating short, steep, rocky climbs and smooth, flat sections)
**Technically:** 2-5 (alternating short, steep, rocky climbs and smooth, flat sections; chainring-bashing water bars)
**Gain:** 460 feet
**In a nutshell:** Shingle Creek Trail

### Why Should U Ride This Trail

Shingle Creek Trail is bitter-sweet. Where it's steep, it's a bitter pill to swallow because the tread gets excessively rough; where it's flat, it's as sweet as candy because the smooth tread gets matted with pine needles. If you're a pessimist with a "cup-is-half-empty" attitude, then the repeated dismounts will sour your ride; however, if you're an optimist and see the cup as "half full," then the brief runs on buffed trail will outshine any hardships encountered in between. And if you're into cyclocross, then the trail is the perfect test track to hone your dismount-remount skills. Regardless, everyone will appreciate the tranquil woods and the mottled shadows they cast upon the glistening creek.

### Details

Right from the start, you'll have to pump hard or walk briefly up a steep hill of loose rocks (tech 4⁺). The quick descent that follows is equally wicked. Cross the bridge over Shingle Creek and angle to the right. Another steep, rocky stretch greets you as the trail curves up the hillside. The trail levels and smooths briefly; then you face yet another hill. This one is as rough and rocky as a dry stream bed, and it will force you to hoof it once again (tech 5). Pass a small pond on the right, and watch out for two chainring-busting step-down drains that form an outlet for the water during "high tide."

Glide downhill to the stream's edge and relish a splendid stretch on buffed trail (tech 2-3); then rise away from the creek. A series of rock steps spaced tire width apart requires deftness, though some are just too much to handle (tech 4-5). Hop off and on your bike for more tall water bars (tech 4-5), and then angle down through a grove of aspens to a narrow footbridge over Shingle Creek (**m2.5**). The planks are too narrow to ride, so don't bother trying or you might end up in the drink. Besides, the trail on the other side is so steep and rough that it's off the charts of overall difficulty, so you might as well turn around.

**164** Mountain Biking Park City & Beyond

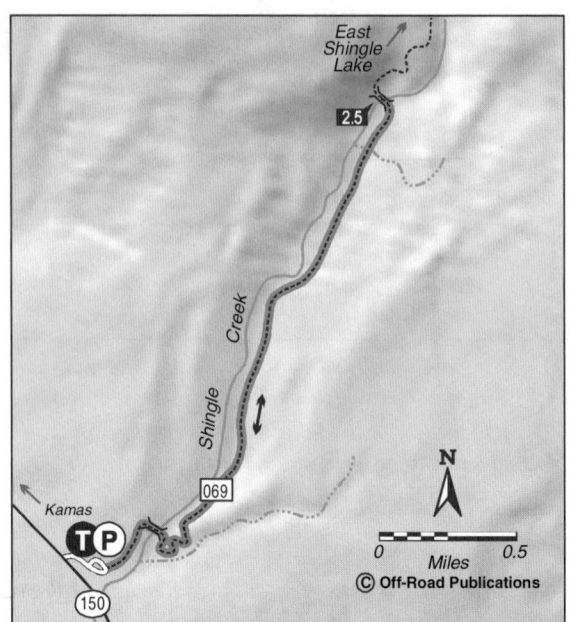

The return flight is full of freewheeling, but it's hardly a joyride because those blasted rock water bars test your patience. If you try to ride over them, you'll find out just how much ground clearance you have; if you get high centered, then you might "endo." Despite the trail's rigors, you should applaud the effort of the Kamas Ranger District to maintain it and keep it open to bicycles.

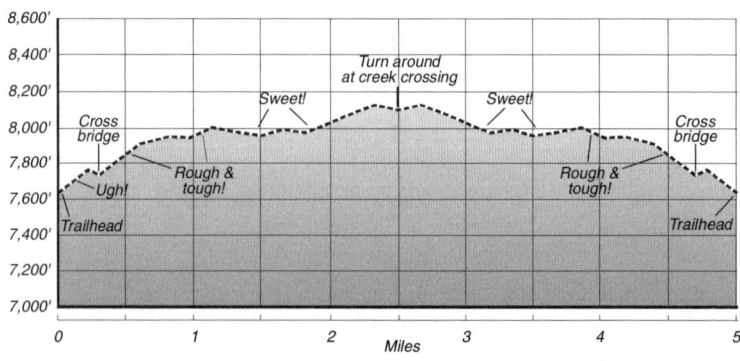

# Shingle Creek Trail

The sweeter side of Shingle Creek Trail.

## ! Know Before You Go

- Shingle Creek Trail is popular with hikers and equestrians, so ride cautiously and courteously.
- A recreation use fee is required for all vehicles parked along UT 150 (Mirror Lake Highway) and at any trailhead or recreation site. The fee is $3.00 per day per vehicle or $6.00 per week per vehicle (if you plan to stay overnight). There are many self-service fee stations along the highway, or you can pay at the Kamas Ranger District Office.

## ? Maps & More Information

- USGS 1:24,000: Erickson Basin and Soapstone Basin, Utah.
- Wasatch-Cache Nat'l Forest (Kamas Ranger District): (435) 783-4338

## Trailhead Access

The trailhead parking area is 9.5 miles east of Kamas on UT 150 (Mirror Lake Highway) and 0.3 mile east of the Shingle Creek Campground.

# Trial Lake

## JUST THE FACTS

**Location:** 18 miles east of Kamas
**Length:** 17 miles, loop
**Tread:** 8.1 miles paved roads, 2.7 miles dirt road, 6.2 miles doubletrack
**Physically:** Moderately strenuous (long climb on rocky jeep road; paved road descent)
**Technically:** 2-4+ (Spring Canyon Road is very rocky in spots; then it smooths but might have washboards; narrow shoulder on paved road)
**Gain:** 1,750 feet
**In a nutshell:** Spring Canyon Road (FR 041)-Trial Lake-Mirror Lake Hwy

## WHY SHOULD U RIDE THIS TRAIL

*Diversity highlights the Trial Lake loop. You'll climb a rugged jeep road, cruise along smooth dirt roads, and blaze down a paved Scenic Byway. Along the way, you'll wind through pristine forests, pass a multitude of alpine ponds, view majestic mountaintops, and peer at a river-cut gorge and a thundering waterfall. Pack along a rod and reel because the Uinta Mountains' lakes and streams are an angler's delight.*

### Details

You can ride this loop in either direction. Clockwise, the climb up Spring Canyon road is strenuous, and you may have to walk the roughest sections. But the payoff comes when you get to zoom down the highway back to the trailhead. Counterclockwise, the climb up UT 150 (Mirror Lake Highway) is aerobically easier, but the Spring Canyon road is a jackhammer descent. Let's go clockwise.

At first, the Spring Canyon road (FR 041) rises moderately with smooth tread and only intermittent washboards, so enjoy it while you can (tech 2+). Fork right about 2 miles up from the highway at the junction for Lambert Meadow. The road deteriorates to a cobble-infested beast (tech 4), and although it levels 0.5 mile past the trailhead for Alexander Lake, the rocks remain incessant. You may think you're out of the weeds, er, rocks, when you reach the Buckeye Lake turnoff, but the upcoming stretch is as difficult as riding up a dry stream bed. Ugh! Atop this climb you'll enjoy your first downhill, albeit brief, and pass spacious meadows. The road smooths to dirt and gravel not far past the

Add more miles by heading up to Bald Mountain Pass to catch this killer view.

# Trial Lake 167

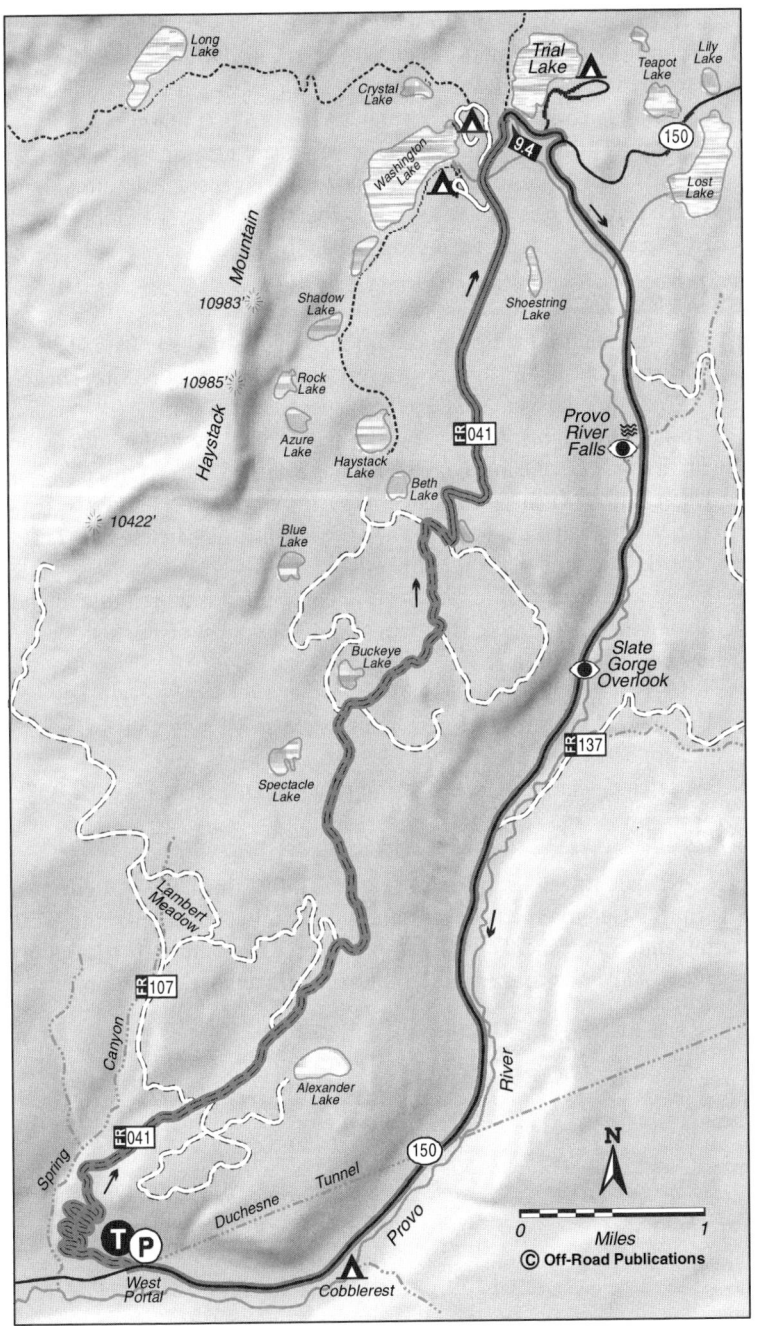

turnoff for Beth Lake, and you'll breathe a welcomed sigh of relief (tech 2). If you can forget the abuse endured so far, you'll find the remainder of loop to be quite pleasant. Pass the trailheads for Crystal and Washington Lakes, and then hop onto pavement near Trial Lake (**m9.4**).

Exit to UT 150 (Mirror Lake Highway), and tuck-and-glide back to your car. Don't let your quest for speed surpass the scenic attractions along the way: Be sure to stop at Provo River Falls and Slate Gorge Overlook to view the Provo River's erosive handiwork.

## ❗ Know Before You Go

- A recreation use fee is required for all vehicles parked along UT 150 (Mirror Lake Highway) and at any trailhead or recreation site. The fee is $3.00 per day per vehicle or $6.00 per week per vehicle (if you plan to stay overnight). There are many self-service fee stations along the highway, or you can pay at the Kamas Ranger District Office.
- Use caution when pedaling UT 150 (Mirror Lake Highway). It is heavily traveled by motorists and the shoulder is narrow. Stay far to the right and ride in single file.
- There are developed Forest Service campgrounds at Trial Lake and along the Mirror Lake Highway. Kamas has most visitor services.

## ❓ Maps & More Information

- USGS 1:24,000: Iron Mine Mountain, Mirror Lake, and Soapstone Basin, Utah.
- Wasatch-Cache Nat'l Forest (Kamas Ranger District): (435) 783-4338

## Trailhead Access

From Kamas, travel 18 miles east on UT 150 (Mirror Lake Highway). The Spring Canyon road is near milepost 18, immediately past the West Portal and Duchesne Tunnel camping area. It's signed for Lambert Meadow, Alexander Lake, and Trial Lake. Park at your discretion.

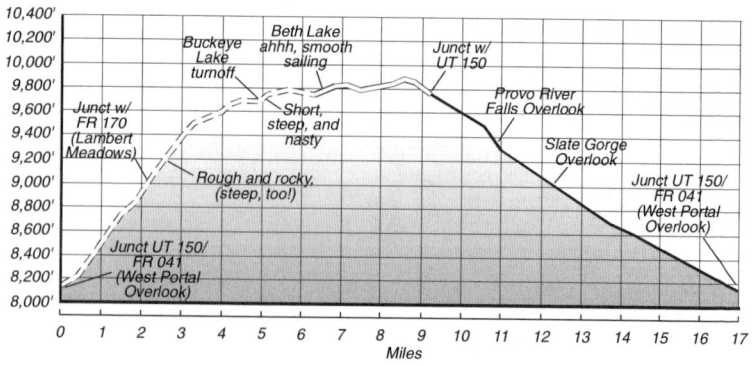

## 30 Beaver Creek Trail

**JUST THE FACTS**

| | |
|---|---|
| **Location:** | 6 miles east of Kamas |
| **Length:** | 18.8 miles, out-and-back |
| **Tread:** | Dirt roads, ATV trails, and singletracks |
| **Physically:** | Moderate (for the whole route); easy (shorter outings) |
| **Technically:** | 2-3+ (smooth trails with some rocky sections) |
| **Gain:** | 1,100 feet |
| **In a nutshell:** | Beaver Creek Trail to Soapstone Road and back |

**WHY SHOULD U RIDE THIS TRAIL?**

Although hucking it off sick drops makes for great video, and redlining your heart rate is the ultimate measure of fitness, there is a softer side to mountain biking, and you'll find it on the Beaver Creek Trail. Fledgling mountain bikers and families with children will enjoy rambling along the edge of a beaver-inhabited creek and through fragrant forests on a wide path that forms a part of the Taylor Fork-Cedar Hollow ATV trail system. Sure, gas-guzzling four-wheelers can be noisy and odorous, but they can also pack down a fine trail. A recent extension to the trail takes you all the way to Soapstone Basin Road, for an outing of respectful distance. Whether you bite off the whole trail or sample just a morsel, Beaver Creek Trail is a tasty treat.

### Details

Cross the highway from the Yellow Pine trailhead and pick up a singletrack that leads to a bridge over Beaver Creek. Gear down for a small hill. It's one of the toughest parts of the trail, and by the time you curse the climb, you'll have reached the top. After a mile, you'll pass through a gate and officially enter the ATV trail system. Go straight on Beaver Creek Trail. (Mine Trail forks right and rises steeply up the mountain.) One-half mile farther, the trail intersects and follows a gravel road for a few hundred yards, and then reverts to ATV trail. Most of the trail is smooth packed dirt (tech 2), but there are a few stretches of choppy rocks (tech 3). If the weather has been dry for a prolonged period, then the trail can be very dusty. Go through some fences, and pass an outhouse next to an ATV staging area; then join with another gravel road, which passes behind the Taylor Fork/Shingle Creek Campgrounds. An information kiosk gives directions for "Cedar Loop-Taylor Fork Trail, rocky and rough" (right) and "Beaver Creek, not so tough" (straight and reverse). Keep going straight (**m3.0**).

Stay right at intersections with numerous campground roads, and go past a picnic site and staging area for horses. The trail reverts to a wide, smooth dirt path passing through fir, aspen, and pines, and is closed to motorized use. A gentle but rocky descent may challenge kids and first-

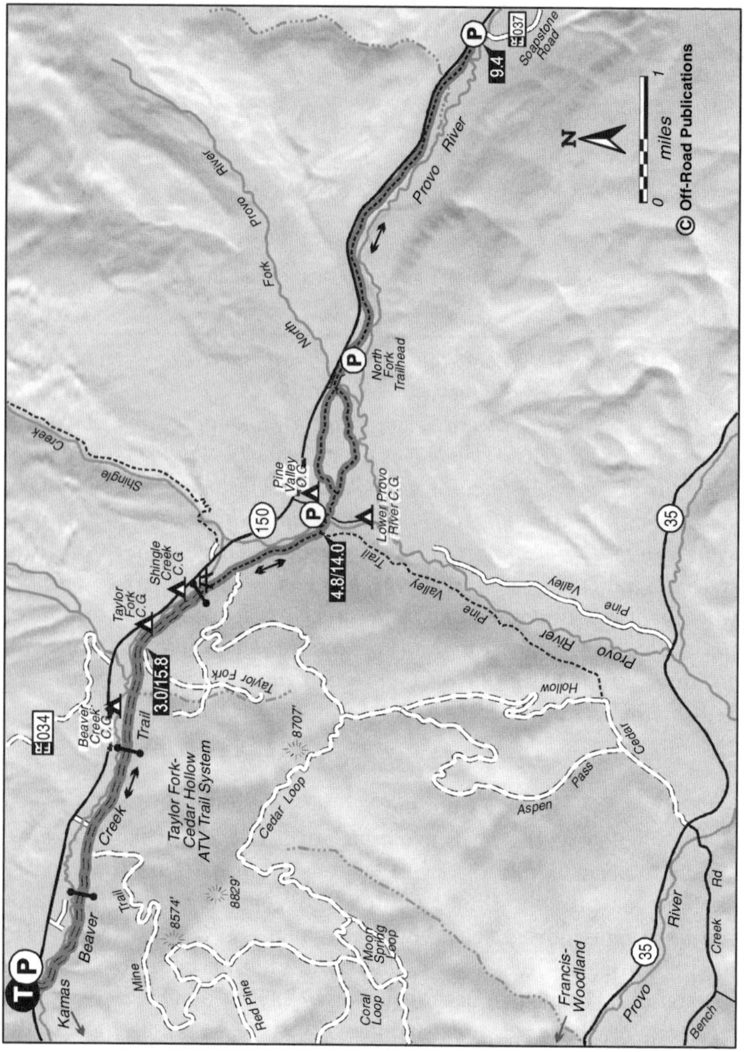

**170** Mountain Biking Park City & Beyond

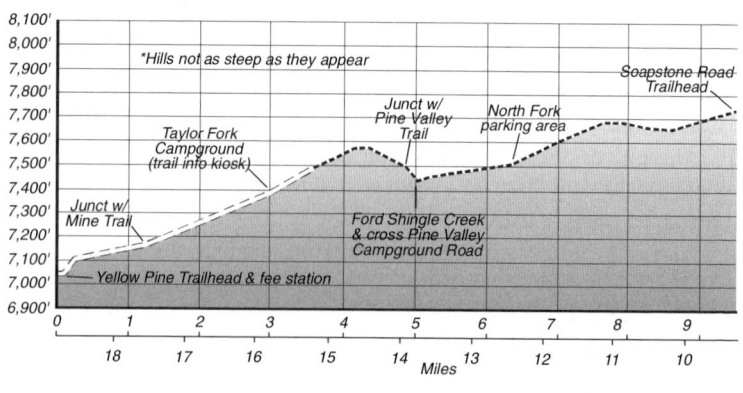

time riders, so you should decide if you want to climb this little hill on the return leg or turn around here. If you continue, you'll come to a junction one-half mile farther signed as "Pine Valley Trail" (right) and "UT 150/ North Fork" (straight/ left). (See "Option.") If you continue from here, then you'll descend a sharp rocky hill (tech 5) and have to ford Shingle Creek, which flows swiftly during spring runoff but becomes bone dry by late summer. This is another good place to turn around (**m4.8**).

Beaver Creek Trail is fun for the whole family.

Onward. Cross the paved access road to Pine Valley and Lower Provo Campgrounds and resume on the Beaver Creek Trail, which is a designated Scenic Byway Trail. The path splits after it exits the timber and enters a sage meadow; take either the gravel path to the right along the edge of the Provo River gorge or the dirt path to the left across the meadow. Both routes rejoin at a wooden footbridge that spans the North Fork of the Provo River, so for some variety take the other path on the return leg.

The "trail" widens to that of a one lane road past the North Fork trailhead and parking lot, and its thick, coarse gravel can bog down even the knobbiest of tires. The trail brushes the edge of the Provo River gorge then veers to within a stone's throw of the highway. Beyond the Provo River Overlook pullout, the path degrades to a rough, rocky lane, and you may have to dismount periodically (tech $3^+$-$4^+$); then the path all but fades away as it crosses a meadow. Just when you feel that the trail has abandoned you, you'll cross some small wood boardwalks, pass a rest bench, and pass numbered posts that mark interpretative stops. Exit to Soapstone Basin Road (**m9.4**), turn around, and retrace your tracks to the Yellow Pine trailhead.

**Option:** Taylor Fork/Cedar Hollow ATV Trail System
There are lots of miles to log on these ATV trails, but be forewarned, the trails are geared more for piston power than for muscle power. Pine Valley Trail (5.6 miles, out-and-back) is the most biker friendly of the bunch. It runs high on the west side of Pine Valley where the Provo River meanders across a wide fertile flood plain. Most of the trail has a good flow to it (tech 3), but it does contain a few tricky bits (tech $4^+$). It descends gradually from north to south, so you'll have to climb about 600 feet on the return leg. Go check it out; it's fun.

Beaver Creek Trail is just right for mountain bikes.

The rest of the ATV trail system is another story. Don't get duped into tackling it without the will to climb steep trails, battle menacing rocks, and subject yourself to physical and mental torture. To make an 18-mile loop, fork from Beaver Creek Trail and head down Pine Valley Trail to Cedar Hollow. "Sweet trail," you might think. Now for the bitter part. Climb steeply up the Cedar Hollow road to the ridge and to a junction for Cedar Loop. The right fork is a nasty, rocky descent on Cedar Loop-Taylor Fork, which will shortcut you back to Beaver Creek Trail in a pinch. Take the left fork and ride along the ridge, which is rather pleasant. Then the route turns south, descends off the ridge on a jackhammer trail laden with baby-head rocks (tech 4+), and comes to a junction with Moon Springs Loop. This is a point of no return because you must ride back over the ridge to get home. "Ride" is a generous term because Cedar Loop Trail is so steep, rutted, and rocky that you'll wish for a throttle. Without one, you'll hike-a-bike considerably. Stay right at the junction with Red Pine Trail, and pedal-and-push to the summit. The rocky and rutted descent on Mine Trail is thrilling, but is it worth the effort to get to it? Once was enough for this sucker.

## ! Know Before You Go

- A $3.00 recreation day-use fee ($6.00 per week) is required for all vehicles parked along UT 150 (Mirror Lake Highway) and at any trailhead or recreation site. Many self-service fee stations are along the highway, or you can pay at the Kamas Ranger District Office.
- Portions of the trail are open to motorized use.

## ? Maps & More Information

- USGS 1:24,000: Hoyt Peak and Woodland, Utah.
- Wasatch-Cache Nat'l Forest (Kamas Ranger District): (435) 783-4338
- "Taylor Fork/Cedar Hollow ATV Trail System" (Kamas R. D.)

## Trailhead Access

From Kamas, drive 6 miles east on UT 150 (Mirror Lake Highway), and park at the Yellow Pine trailhead. There is a self-service fee station across the highway.

# Soapstone Basin

**JUST THE FACTS**

| | |
|---|---|
| **Location:** | 19 miles southeast of Kamas |
| **Length:** | 15.4 miles, loop |
| **Tread:** | All dirt roads and doubletracks |
| **Physically:** | Moderate (solid climb then long, fast, gradual descent) |
| **Technically:** | 2-4 (rocky doubletrack for 5 miles then mostly smooth dirt roads) |
| **Gain:** | 1,400 feet |
| **In a nutshell:** | FR 304-FR 174-FR 089-FR 037 |

**WHY SHOULD U RIDE THIS TRAIL?**

Soapstone Basin is a fun, fast-paced tour that loops around a broad alpine valley pocketed with stands of aspen and fir trees. Dozens of wildflower species speckle the sunny meadows like paint spattered from an artist's brush. You won't find staggering views of mountain peaks along the main loop, although the Uinta Mountains do reveal themselves shyly once or twice. But you will find an eye-popping panorama of Utah's tallest peaks on the short optional spur to the Bluffs Overlook. There, you'll gaze into the Duchesne River Gorge and at peaks over 12,500 feet tall. The net vertical topography relief is over a mile. Needless to say, this cliff-edge perch is enough to make even non-acrophobes tremble.

## Details

You can ride Soapstone Basin in either direction. If you ride counterclockwise—the traditional direction in previous publications—then you'll embark with a stiff 1.5-mile climb. Nearly 8 miles of gradual climbing on mostly smooth dirt roads take you to the loop's highpoint. The loop concludes with a fast, furious, 5-mile descent on a rough doubletrack. Clockwise, you'll warm up gently for a mile and then climb in earnest for about 4 miles up a rocky doubletrack to the loop's highpoint. Thereafter, you'll race like the wind on smooth, gradually descending dirt roads for nearly 8 miles and then culminate the loop with a 1.5-mile freewheeling descent. Stronger riders might like going clockwise, climbing the rougher section first and then fast-tracking on the "back nine." Those with less gusto might like to go counter, tackling gentler hills and freewheeling down the rougher stuff. Here's the clockwise direction.

Start at the junction of FR 304 and FR 037, signed as "Wolf Creek, Piuta" (right) and "Cold Spring" (left), and take FR 304 east/left. It's flat and smooth for 0.7 mile to the crossing of Soapstone Creek. You may get your toes wet in early summer, but by midsummer the creek dries to a trickle. About 1.5 miles from the start, the road veers away from the creek and angles uphill on increasingly rocky tread (tech 3-4). Enjoy a slight respite before the doubletrack rises again, and then seek a clean line through a jumble of rocks (tech $3^+$-$4^+$). Hang tough; the rest of the loop is worth

**174** Mountain Biking Park City & Beyond

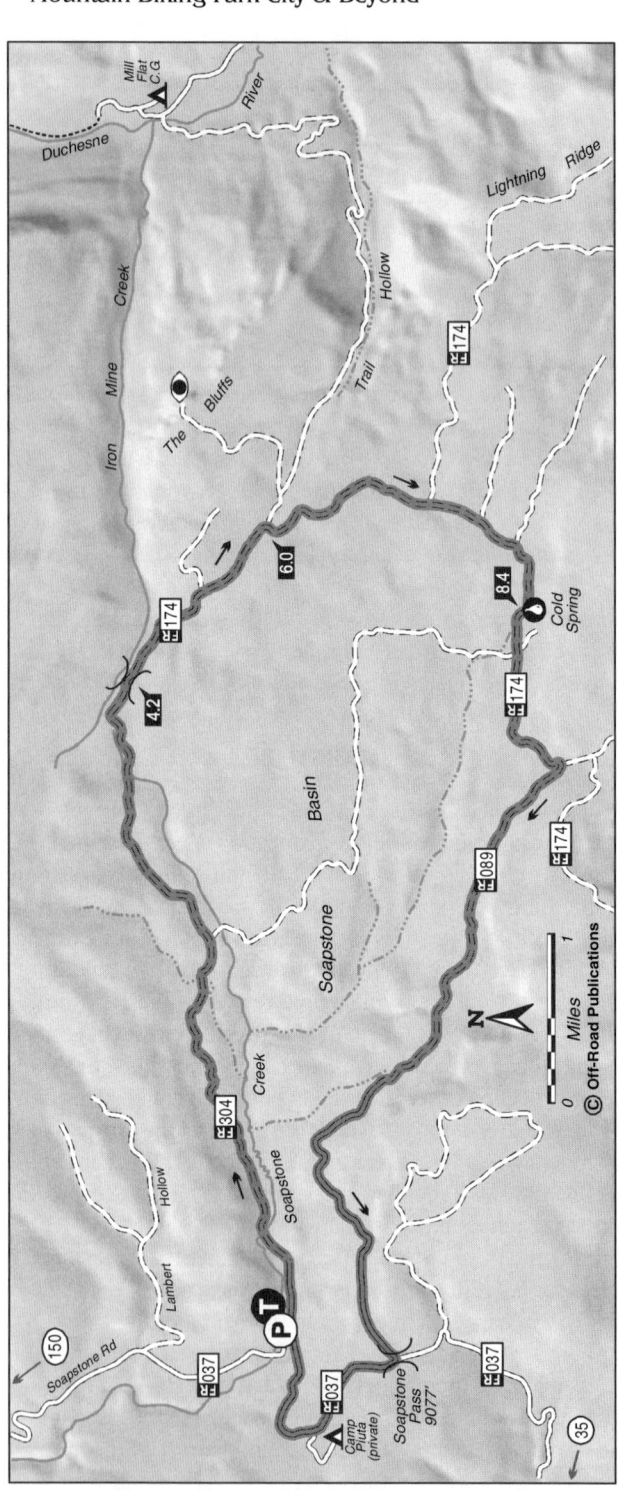

Don't pass up the killer views of the Duchesne River Gorge and Uinta Mountain peaks from The Bluffs.

the effort. The road levels at a small divide separating Soapstone Creek from Iron Mine Creek, and you can see Iron Mine Mountain to the north rising to nearly 10,500 feet (**m4.2**). Pump up one more short rise, and then cruise through patches of fir and around the east side of the basin to the junction with the Trail Hollow jeep road (**m6.0**). Trail Hollow provides access to the Bluffs (see "Option"), which offers a dizzying view of the sublime Uinta Mountains.

To continue on, stay on the main road (FR 174) as it bends west, and kick into high gear for fast cruising on the mostly smooth dirt road (tech 2⁺). Freshen up at Cold Spring (**m8.4**), and fork right on FR 089 1 mile farther. Here on the south side of the basin, you'll continue at a fevered pace down the long gradual hills and only have to pedal up a few short

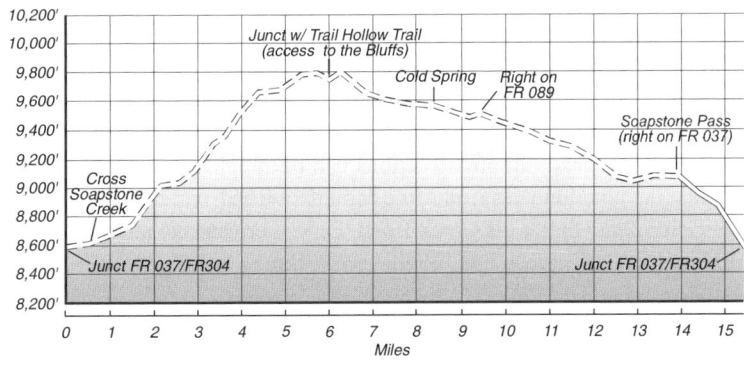

inclines. The bumps and grinds you endured earlier will be long forgotten. Turn right at Soapstone Pass onto FR 037, and descend the choppy road past Camp Piuta (tech 3) and back to the loop's starting point.

**Option:** The Bluffs Overlook
Although optional, you shouldn't pass up this 2.8-mile spur (out-and-back) because the views are spectacular. Head down the Trail Hollow jeep road about 0.2 mile, fork left, and climb out of the hollow, steeply at times, for about a mile to the viewpoint. You'll know when to stop! Without much warning, you'll toe the edge of a 2,500-foot gorge cut by the Duchesne River and you'll cast your eyes upon distant peaks that rise to over 12,500 feet. The combined negative and positive relief is over a vertical mile.

Although you might never guess it, the Uinta Mountains are the only major range in the nation to run east-west, which makes them a physiographic oddity. The Uinta crest forms the axis of a major anticline that bowed and lifted miles of the earth's crust from great depths. Subsequent erosion, most recently by glaciers, exposed the range's quartzite core at the tips of it's tallest peaks. These exposed metamorphic rocks date back over 1.5 billion years to the Precambrian Era.

### Know Before You Go

- Soapstone Basin is a designated ATV route, so you may encounter four-wheelers and other vehicles. Sheepherding occurs throughout the basin.
- Be cautious at the Bluffs Overlook because the cliff's blocky limestone rim might be unstable and crumble.
- Be prepared for rapidly changing alpine weather.
- The potability of Cold Spring is uncertain and all surface waters should be purified. Dispersed camping is plentiful around Soapstone Pass. There are Forest Service campgrounds along UT 150 (Mirror Lake Highway). Kamas offers most visitor services.

### Maps & More Information

- USGS 1:24,000: Iron Mine Mountain and Soapstone Basin, Utah.
- Uinta National Forest (Heber Ranger District): (435) 654-0470.

### Trailhead Access

From Kamas, travel 14.5 miles east on UT 150 (Mirror Lake Highway). Turn right/south on Soapstone Road (FR 037). The dirt road is suitable for passenger cars, although sections can be rough. After 2 miles, turn right at the junction with Iron Mine Mountain Road, and follow the signs for Camp Piuta and Wolf Creek Road. Park at or near the junction of FR 304 and FR 037, signed as "Wolf Creek, Piuta" (right), "Cold Spring" (left).

## 32 Bench Creek Trail

**JUST THE FACTS**

**Location:** 22 miles northeast of Heber; 24 miles southeast of Park City
**Length:** 18.0 miles, loop
**Tread:** 3.7 miles paved roads, 0.8 mile dirt road, 0.7 miles doubletrack, 12.8 miles singletrack
**Physically:** Strenuous (Bench Creek is a continual climb with steep sections and brief hike-a-biking; Camp Hollow is a semi-primitive singletrack; Little South Fork is very rocky at times, requires periodic hike-a-biking, and ends with a half-mile grunt up "agony hill")
**Technically:** 3-5 (variably maintained trails range from smooth to very choppy)
**Gain:** 2,400 feet
**In a nutshell:** FR 052-Bench Creek-Camp Hollow-Little South Fork-UT 35

**WHY SHOULD U RIDE THIS TRAIL**

Considered a secret stash among locals for years, the word is out about Bench Creek and an increasing number of bikers are making the long trip to Woodland. You won't find Bench Creek splashed across the covers of popular mountain bike magazines, but it's common to see cars topped with bike racks alongside trucks toting horse trailers at the parking area. What's the attraction? The Bench Creek loop links together prime singletracks across the pristine alpine hills flanking Duchesne Ridge/Heber Mountain. You'll climb continually on buffed and rough trail up Bench Creek Trail, careen down a tight cow path on Camp Hollow Trail, and then hike your bike through periodic rock gardens and endure "agony hill" on Little South Fork Trail. Sound ominous? Bench Creek is a tough ride, no doubt, but it represents backcountry trail riding at its best.

### Details

First some fine print. During the summer of 2005, the Heber Ranger District rerouted the upper portion of Bench Creek Trail away from the private lands of Wolf Creek Ranches and entirely onto the national forest. The description and mileages presented here are estimated to account for the new bypass route.

Secondly, many riders prefer to start at the Little South Fork trailhead and to knock off the 3.7 miles of paved roads first. If this is your first time on Bench Creek, then it may be wise to start from the Bench Creek trailhead. That way you can bail out easily if the initial climb proves overwhelming, and you'll be familiar with reaching the trailhead/parking area since you drove to it already.

From the Bench Creek trailhead/parking area, head up the rutted doubletrack for 0.6 mile to where the road crosses Bench Creek, fork right onto Bench Creek Trail, and go through a gate. Buffed, mellow trail greets you right away. "Sweet," you'll think. Then the trail rises sharply, but it mellows quickly thereafter. Shortly ahead, the trail repeats the theme but with a stiffer climb that may make you doubt the ride's appeal. In

<< Ridge Trail 157

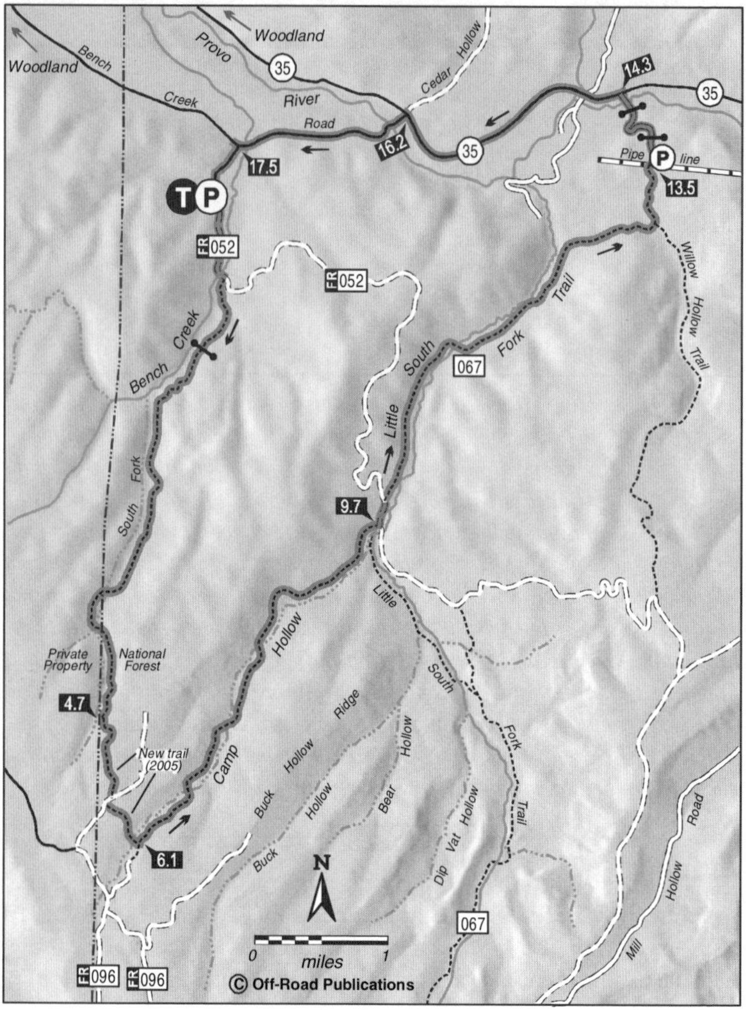

**180** Mountain Biking Park City & Beyond

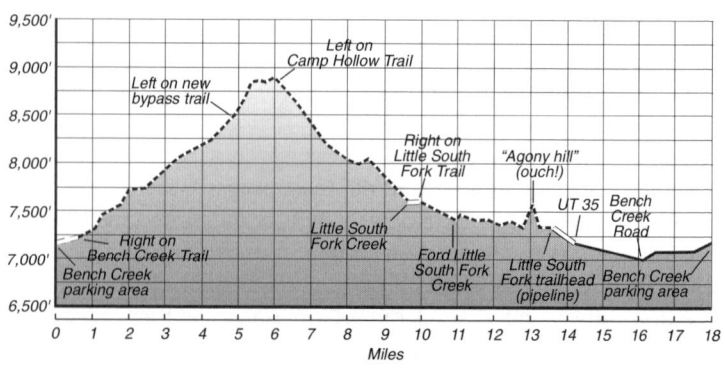

Get out of town, go to Woodland, and ride Bench Creek Trail.

seconds, however, another smooth, flat stretch will have you smiling from ear to ear. And that's how Bench Creek Trail goes: tough and buffed (tech $2^+$-$4^+$).

Cut across a small sage meadow and splash through several rivulets emanating from nearby springs. In Bench Creek to your right, beavers show off their craftsmanship in a series of log dams and huts. The trail crosses Bench Creek to its west side (ignore a trail forking right and uphill); then it crosses back again, and you'll face a rude little hill caked with soft sand and bedrock that will force all riders to hoof it briefly. True to form, the trail smooths again as it continues rising moderately up the hollow. An indestructible sign made of etched steel marks the boundary of national forest/private property and where the new bypass trail begins (**m4.7**). Built to government standards, you can be assured the new trail will not exceed an eight-percent grade. Cross a doubletrack in about a mile and descend to the junction with Camp Hollow Trail, No. 310 (**m6.1**).

Camp Hollow Trail begins as smooth singletrack and crosses a sage meadow with the distant Uinta Mountains in your sights. You'll cross the creek a few times, while banking down the twisting trail on buffed and choppy tread and through stands of fir and aspen (tech $2^+$-$3^+$). After the third creek crossing, the trail veers north away from the creek and rises

A thing of the past; Bench Creek "goes public" in 2005.

steeply for 0.2 mile up a side hollow to a small saddle; then it drops back to the stream's edge. This section may be overgrown, eroded, and dicey, so watch your front wheel (tech 3-4). Exit Camp Hollow Trail to a doubletrack next to Little South Fork creek (**m9.7**), and applaud the outstanding singletracks you've ridden so far.

Go left on the jeep road for a couple hundred yards, and then fork right on Little South Fork Trail, No. 067, which is marked with blue diamonds on a carsonite post. (You'll pass an unsigned trail forking right from the road before you reach the Little South Fork junction. It's a dead end.) Race through the sage and aspens for a mile on amazingly sweet trail (tech 3), and then ford Little South Fork creek. The ford can be deep and swift during early summer, but you should be able to hop across on rocks by midsummer.

Smooth trail continues for a short distance; then you encounter the first of several rock gardens. Some are ridable, if you possess adept skills; others are too rocky and even walking is a chore (tech 4-5). Nearly 2 miles from the creek crossing, the trail veers away from the stream, smooths, and comes to the base of "agony hill." The grade is miserably steep and the tread can be loose, but if you have the desire, the balance, and the power, then you'll find the hill ridable—barely. Collect yourself at the top, and hold on tight for a quick, nasty drop off the other side (tech 4$^+$). The trail flattens and smooths as it follows a wire fence across a wide brushy meadow, and you can breathe a sign of relief. Connect with a dirt road at the Little South Fork trailhead (**m13.5**), and take the road down to UT 35 (**m14.3**). (Close all gates behind you.)

Go left on the highway, pedal about 2 miles, and fork left on Bench Creek Road (**m16.2**). (It's at milepost 8 and across from the Cedar Hollow trailhead.) Cross over Provo River, climb a small hill, and turn left on the trailhead's paved access road (**m17.5**). (Look for where a chainlink fence ends on the left side of Bench Creek Road.) The parking area is a half mile farther.

**Option:** Loop without paved roads
If your dog is coming along, you can loop back to the trailhead without pedaling paved UT 35 and Bench Creek Road. When you exit Camp Hollow Trail to the doubletrack next to Little South Fork creek (**m9.7** above),

go left on the jeep road and return to Bench Creek. This "shortcut" is 4.3 miles long, entails a 400-foot climb, and is rough and rutted, especially the descent (tech 3-4). But, hey, it's dirt, right?

**Option:** Upper Little South Fork Loop
Add on 5.5 miles by skipping Camp Hollow Trail and targeting the entire length of Little South Fork Trail. In doing so, you'll traverse and climb on smooth jeep roads to Duchesne Ridge, and have the option of riding another 4 miles, out-and-back, to the very top of Heber Mountain.

Ride past Camp Hollow Trail (**m6.1** above), and take the left/east fork of FR 096 at a Y-junction. The smooth hard-packed dirt road rises moderately and traverses for 4 miles across Buck and Dip Vat Hollows to Duchesne Ridge. Fork right on FR 907 if you want to ride up to Heber Mountain for a panoramic view of the Uinta Basin and southern Wasatch Range; otherwise, continue on FR 096 for 0.4 mile to the upper Little South Fork Trail trailhead. (See the chapter "Little South Fork Trail.")

### Know Before You Go

- Bench Creek loop requires backcountry wits as some trails and junctions might not be marked.
- In 2005, upper Bench Creek Trail was rerouted onto the national forest, eliminating the need to trespassing on private property as in years past.
- Be prepared for rapidly changing alpine weather.
- Close all gates on trails and dirt roads.

### Maps & More Information

- USGS 1:24,000: Heber Mountain and Woodland, Utah.
- Uinta National Forest (Heber Ranger District): (435) 654-0470.

### Trailhead Access

From Heber, travel 4 miles north on US 40/189. Turn right onto US 189 for Kamas and wrap around Jordanelle Reservoir. Go east through Francis (flashing stop light) on Village Way (UT 35), and drive 4 miles to Woodland. Turn right onto Bench Creek Road, next to the church, and continue 3.3 miles. Turn right onto a paved road between two homes. (Look for a small valley making a notable break in the hills.) The trailhead is 0.5 mile farther, where pavement turns to dirt. To reach the Little South Fork trailhead, stay on UT 35 past the church and drive 5.9 miles to the junction signed "Little South Fork Cross Country Ski Trail."

From Park City, travel 15 miles on UT 248 to Kamas, and turn right/south onto UT 35/32. After 2 miles, turn left/east onto Village Way (UT 35) in Francis (flashing stop light). Drive 4 miles to Woodland and proceed as mentioned above.

## 33 Little South Fork Trail

### Just the Facts

**Location:** 28 miles southeast of Park City or 25 miles northeast of Heber
**Length:** 22.6 miles, loop (8.7 miles, one-way)
**Tread:** 5.2 miles paved road, 2.5 miles dirt road, 6.2 miles doubletrack, 8.7 miles singletrack
**Physically:** Strenuous as loop (long climb on dirt roads; trail requires strength, endurance, and sharp skills—even if shuttling to the top); moderate as one-way
**Technically:** 3-5 (semi-primitive trails, creek fords, notorious rock gardens)
**Gain:** 2,800 feet as loop (300 feet, one-way downhill)
**In a nutshell:** UT 35-FR 054-FR 122-FR 096-Little South Fork Trail

### Why Should U Ride This Trail

*If you've managed the impossible and have grown tired of Park City's singletracks, or if you're craving a real backcountry experience beyond the sight of condos and ski lifts, then head to Woodland and ride Little South Fork Trail. This trail is best ridden one-way—downhill—which is music to any freerider's ears; however, there is enough cross-country pedaling to keep this route off the radar of the armor-clad downhill crowd. In the real world of mountain biking, however, downhills are earned, so you should tackle the whole loop by climbing to the upper trailhead. Regardless of how you get to the top, Little South Fork is a blast to descend. The trail is no lollygagging, freewheeling coast because its semi-primitive tread requires aggressive riding. You'll encounter several water crossings and one bike-on-shoulders ford; near the end you'll have to endure menacing rock gardens and a short, gut-wrenching climb up "agony hill." It's all good because throughout the ride you'll penetrate pristine woods, traverse sunny meadows, and fill your soul with the nuances of nature.*

### Details

Mileage for this ride begins at the lower trailhead on the pipeline corridor, so adjust your distance depending on where you park. First things first: you have to get to the top. Don't cop out with a shuttle; make the 14-mile climb to justify cashing in on your downhill ticket. Return to UT 35 and pedal east on the highway for 5.2 miles alongside the South Fork of Provo River; then turn right onto the Mill Hollow road (FR 054). The dirt, gravel, and washboard road (tech 2+) rises steadily for 1.7 miles to the Mill Hollow Work Station. Immediately beyond, fork right onto FR 122, signed "Campbell Hollow, overflow camping" (**m7.8**). The Campbell Hollow jeep road is steeper and rockier (tech 3+) than the Mill Hollow road, but you'll avoid the incessant dust kicked up by passing motorists. Stay left at two junctions with FR 052, and cruise along the rolling ridge. Fork right onto FR 096, following signs for Heber Mountain and Camp Hollow (**m13.2**). Roll up and down along the ridge for 0.8 mile, and look for the signed trailhead on the right for Little South Fork Trail, No. 067.

Woodland
Cedar Hollow
35
Provo River
Pipe line
South Fork Provo River
Nobletts Creek
"Agony hill"
Willow Hollow Trail
Little South Fork Trail
FR 052
067
Wolf Creek Summit
Camp Hllw (Bench Crk Tr)
18.8
Road
FR 054
Campbell Hollow
FR 122
Mill Hollow
7.8
USFS Work Station (no services)
Mill Hollow Res.
Buck Hollow
Bear Hollow
Dip Vat Hollow
15.9
Granite Camp (private)
067
13.2
Duchesne Ridge
FR 096
FR 091
Upper Bench Creek Tr
FR 096
FR 054
Heber Mtn
Heber
N
0 miles 1
© Off-Road Publications

10,500'
10,000'
9,500'
9,000'
8,500'
8,000'
7,500'
7,000'
Right onto FR 096 for Heber Mountain, etc.
Right on FR 122 (Campbell Hollow)
Right on Little South Fork Trail
Old cabin
Right on FR 054 (Mill Hollow)
Little South Fork Trailhead (pipeline)
Ford Little South Fork Creek
"Agony hill"
UT 35
Little South Fork Trailhead (pipeline)
0 2 4 6 8 10 12 14 16 18 20 22
Miles

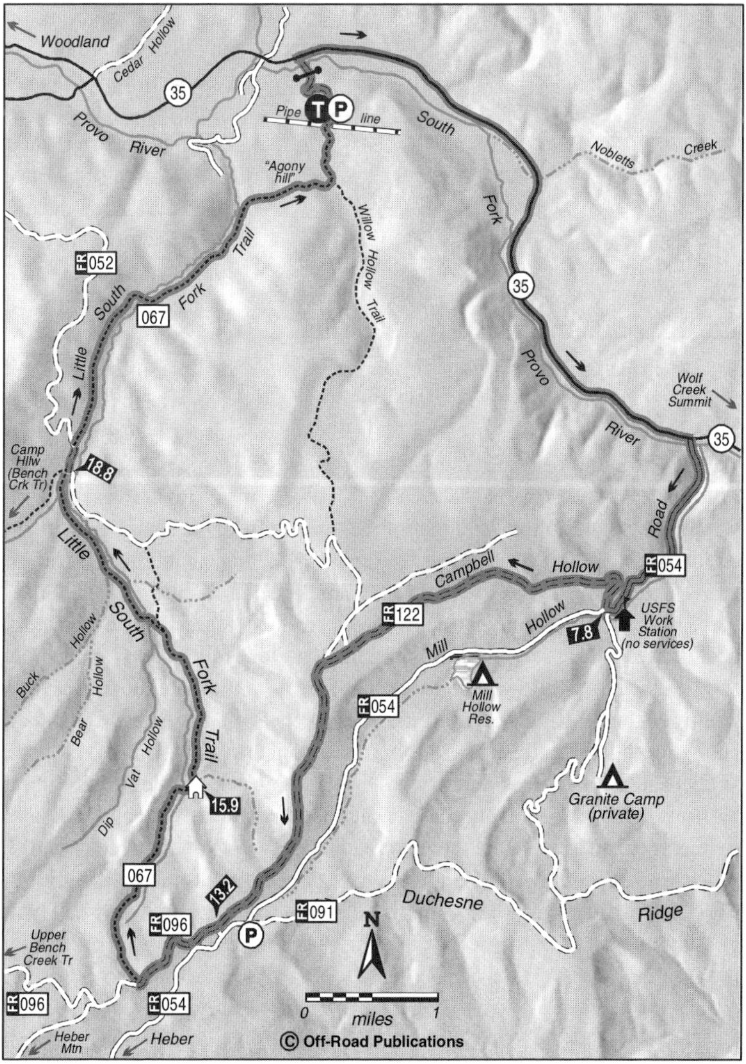

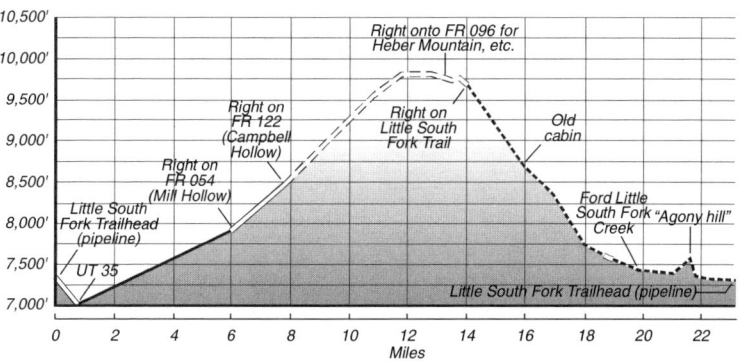

Little South Fork is a trickle at the top of the trail.

The trail begins on an old doubletrack that has been closed to vehicles with a dozen earthen berms. Many are worthy of a little "air time." After the last berm, watch for tree blazes directing you to the right and onto the singletrack. (Do not pedal uphill.)

Blaze across a meadow, drop down a sketchy hill, and dart into the dank woods (tech 3-4). Cross upper Little South Fork creek (just a trickle here), enter a meadow canvassed with wildflowers, and follow trail markers due north from the remains of an old cabin (**m15.9**). You'll cross a side drainage in doing so and then ride high above Little South Fork creek through small meadows and groves of timber. The trail splits about a mile from where you crossed Little South Fork near the old cabin; stay left following markers for Trail No. 067. (You may see "LSX" and "Willow Hollow" etched into aspens where the trail splits.) Continue the wild and serendipitous descent into the evergreens, and ford Little South Fork and Buck Hollow creeks. The trail stays on the left/west side of Little South Fork and weaves through sage and thickets. Pass Camp Hollow Trail entering from the left, and intersect a wide doubletrack next to the creek (**m18.8**). Take the jeep road left (away from the creek) for 0.1 mile, *not an inch farther*, and fork right on the continued Little South Fork Trail, which is marked with blue diamonds on a carsonite post. (There is another trail forking to the right just before Little South Fork. It's a dead end, so don't get duped.)

Farther down the trail, Little South Fork widens to a blue-ribbon stream.

You'll think you've hit the jackpot as the trail winds playfully for a mile across sage meadows and through aspen stands to the ford of Little South Fork creek. This ford can be dangerously deep and swift during early summer; by mid to late summer, you may be able to hop

Little South Fork Trail  **187**

across on rocks. Push your bike up a small, rough hill and resume your singletrack quest. All good things must come to an end, and the trail quickly turns to a rock-pocked hike-a-bike (tech 4-5). Fortunately, the path is on a near level keel—for now. Ahead, the trail veers far away from the stream and rises sharply up "agony hill, " which is downright painful. Push and pedal your bike for over one-half mile, but don't breathe a sigh of relief at the top because the drop off the other side, albeit half as long, is twice as evil (tech 4⁺). Finally, the trail mellows and follows a wire fence along the edge of a broad field to the trailhead at the pipeline corridor.

**Option:** One-way, downhill
Lack the gusto to pursue the loop? Here's how to get to the top. Take UT 35 to the Mill Hollow road (FR 054) as described above, but stay on the dirt road for 6 miles to the top of Duchesne Ridge and to the junction with FR 091. Park at or near the junction. On your bike, pedal west for one-quarter mile on FR 054 toward Heber and Lake Creek Summit, and fork right on a doubletrack signed "Campbell Hollow, Heber Mountain, etc." Turn left atop the small hill on FR 096 (**m13.2** above), and ride 0.8 mile to the upper Little South Fork trailhead.

### ! Know Before You Go

- Little South Fork Trail is popular with equestrians, so ride cautiously and courteously. Yield by stepping to the side of the trail.
- Be prepared for rapidly changing alpine weather.
- This area is popular with big game hunters during autumn.
- Close all gates on trails and dirt access roads.

### ? Maps & More Information

- USGS 1:24,000: Heber Mountain and Woodland, Utah.
- Uinta National Forest (Heber Ranger District): (435) 654-0470.

### ♪ Trailhead Access

From Heber, travel 3.7 miles north on US 40/189. Turn right onto US 189/UT 32 for Kamas and wrap around Jordanelle Reservoir. Go through Francis (flashing stop light) onto Village Way (UT 35), and drive 9.5 miles through Woodland to a gravel road signed "Little South Fork Cross Country Ski Trail." Park at your discretion at or near the highway, or take the dirt road uphill 0.8 mile to the trailhead at the gas pipeline corridor. The last 0.3 mile can be rough for passenger cars. Close all gates on the dirt road.

From Park City, travel 15 miles east on UT 248 to Kamas and turn right/south onto UT 35/32. After 2 miles, turn left/east in Francis (flashing stop light) onto Village Way (UT 35) for Woodland and proceed as mentioned above.

## 34 Mill Hollow-Duchesne Ridge

### Just the Facts

**Location:** 36 miles east of Heber, 39 miles southeast of Park City
**Length:** 12.1 miles, loop
**Tread:** 3 miles dirt road, 7.6 miles doubletrack, 1.5 miles singletrack
**Physically:** Moderate (steady climb on Mill Hollow Road, intermittent climbs on Duchesne Ridge, high elevation)
**Technically:** 2-3+ (gravel and washboards on Mill Hollow road, ruts on ridge road, choppy rocks on doubletrack descent and on singletrack)
**Gain:** 1,450 feet
**In a nutshell:** FR 054-FR 091-Yellow Lake jeep road-Reservoir Trail

### Why Should U Ride This Trail?

Pack up the camping gear, get out of town, and spend a weekend riding the dirt roads and trails on Duchesne Ridge. The Mill Hollow-Duchesne Ridge loop is a great introduction to this area. Unlike nearby Bench Creek and Little South Fork Trail, which require a "one-track" mind for all the singletrack you'll pedal, this loop follows good dirt roads throughout with just a touch of singletrack to whet your appetite. Technical difficulty is low, by and large, so all you need is good stamina. At nearly 10,000 feet in elevation, however, your stamina might diminish to that of a chain smoker due to the mighty thin air. Go slow, stop often, and enjoy the sights of distant mountains, deep valleys, and rolling highlands. If you make easy work of this loop, then you're ready to pursue the finer pleasures in life on Bench Creek and Little South Fork Trails.

### Details

Head out from Mill Hollow Reservoir, and climb steadily up the gravel and washboard road (tech 2) to Duchesne Ridge (**m3.0**). The climb is easy on a relative scale, but since it rises to nearly 10,000 feet, it's doubly hard and you'll be gasping for air if you're not acclimated. Fork left on FR 091, and roll out Duchesne Ridge's undulating jeep road. You'll cruise easily on hard-packed dirt with a few ruts (tech 2-3). There are great views along the way of the High Uintas to the far north, of the deep West Fork Duchesne River valley below, and of the Uinta Basin's expansive terrain elsewhere. Bend to the right around Mill Knoll and descend swiftly to Yellow Lake (**m6.8**). Watch out for gravel and rocks, which can slip under your tires like ball bearings. "Lake" is a generous term because by midsummer, it's little more than a murky puddle.

Go to the left/northwest side of the lake, and pick up a doubletrack that drops steeply into the woods (tech 4). Soon it mellows (tech 2+) and rolls across lush meadows surrounded by dense timber. Pass Skyline Trail forking left, bank around two switchbacks, and come to a steel gate near the Granite Education Mill Hollow Center (**m9.0**); then veer left onto the signed Reservoir Trail. "Whoa, where did this come from?" you might ask. Indeed, there *is* singletrack out here, if you know where to find it.

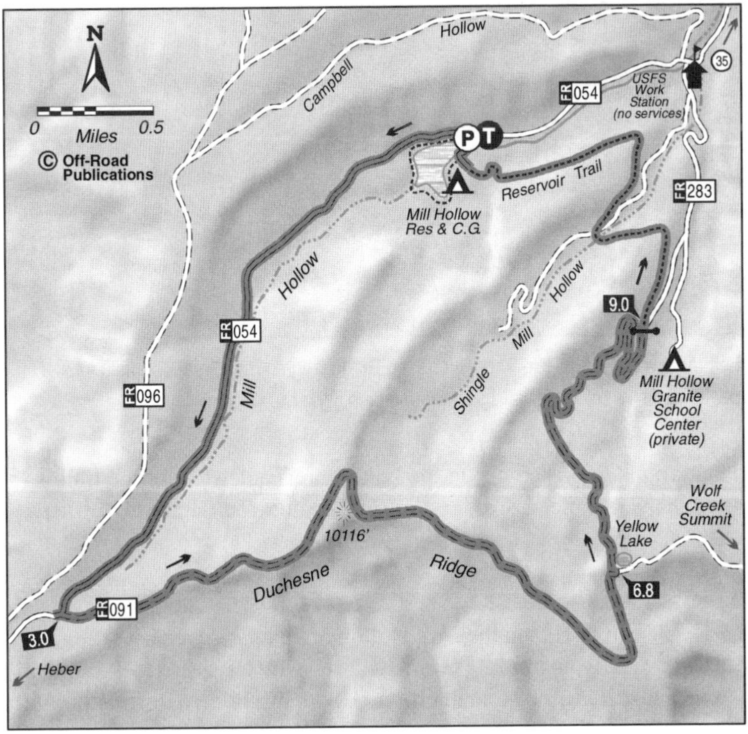

# Mill Hollow-Duchesne Ridge

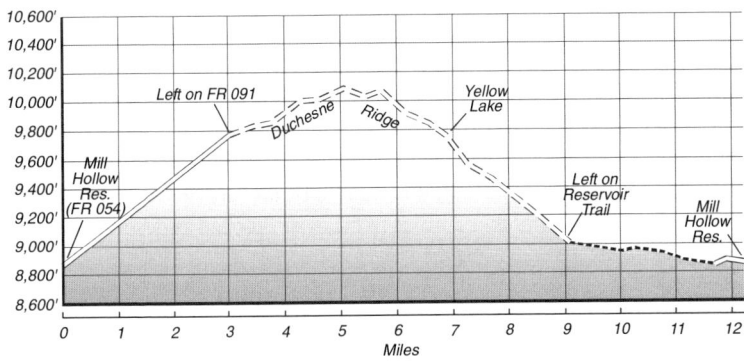

Reservoir Trail is smooth dirt with a smattering of rocks that compel you to watch where you put your front wheel (tech 2-3). Cross the footbridge over Shingle Mill Hollow Creek and cross a doubletrack, staying on singletrack. One-half mile farther, the trail widens to a pebbly doubletrack and enters Mill Hollow Campground at site No. 17. Follow the campground road back to the day-use parking area at the dam; otherwise, take

Left: A view of Heart Lake from Duchesne Ridge. Right: The Uinta Mountain's tallest peaks can be seen northward from the ride's highpoint.

a lap around the reservoir on the Lakeshore Trail. Most of the trail is in good shape, but the west side is off camber, and you'll have to step across the inlet creek.

### ! Know Before You Go

- Be alert to traffic on the Mill Hollow road up to Duchesne Ridge.
- Ride slowly, cautiously, and courteously on the Reservoir Trail because it is used as an interpretive path by children visiting the Mill Hollow Center.
- Mill Hollow Reservoir has a developed Forest Service campground ($12.00 per campsite or $4.00 for day use).
- Be prepared for rapidly changing alpine weather.

### ? Maps & More Information

- USGS 1:24,000: Heber City and Wolf Creek Summit, Utah.
- Uinta National Forest (Heber Ranger District): (435) 654-0470.

### Trailhead Access

From Heber, drive 3.7 miles north on US 40 and turn right onto UT 32 for Kamas and Francis. Go around Jordanelle Reservoir, and go straight through the stop light in Francis onto Village Way (UT 35) for Woodland. Drive 15.2 miles on UT 35, and turn right onto FR 054 for Mill Hollow Reservoir. Pavement turns to all-weather dirt and gravel. Take FR 054 for 2.9 miles to Mill Hollow Reservoir. You can park for free at the dam; otherwise, you must pay $4.00 to park at a campsite.

From Park City, take UT 248 (Kearns Boulevard) 15 miles to Kamas, turn right and drive another 2 miles to Francis. Proceed as described above.

## 35 Dock Flat

**JUST THE FACTS**

| | |
|---|---|
| **Location:** | 20 miles southeast of Heber |
| **Length:** | 12.6 miles, loop |
| **Tread:** | 2.4 miles paved roads, 4.5 miles gravel road, 5.7 miles doubletrack |
| **Physically:** | Moderate (moderately easy climb up Telephone Hollow, moderately strenuous climb to Dock Flat) |
| **Technically:** | 2-3 (rutted and rock-studded doubletracks, gravel and washboards on the Strawberry River road) |
| **Gain:** | 900 feet |
| **In a nutshell:** | US 40-FR 263-US 40-FR 143-FR 049 |

### WHY SHOULD U RIDE THIS TRAIL?

Dock Flat is a fun little outing that circles the rolling hills surrounding Strawberry River. Except for two short segments on busy US 40, the route passes through peaceful aspen groves that harbor deer and elk. You'll encounter two climbs on this ride. The first is a moderately gentle rise up Telephone Hollow. The second is a more strenuous pull up to Dock Flat. Each is offset by a fun-filled descent that will leave you wishing for more hills to climb. The remainder of the route is an idle cruise along the wide, dirt and gravel Strawberry River road and across sagebrush flats rimmed by timbered hills.

### Details

Start out by pedaling 1.4 miles west on US 40, and then turn right onto the doubletrack heading up Telephone Hollow (FR 263). It should be marked with a cross-country skier decal. Climb gradually for 1.5 miles to the hollow's shady summit. Along the way, thick groves of aspens with bleach-white trunks will captivate your eyes, and a fluttering melody of chirping crickets backed by warbling song birds will seduce your ears.

Stay on the main road, and descend one-half mile to a junction marked with blue trail diamonds tacked to a wooden post. You'll be whooping and a-hollering like a cowboy on a bucking bronco as you bound over the bumps and berms (tech 3+). Fork left and ride through Daniel Summit Estates to US 40 (**m3.9**). (This is a public access road, so you're not trespassing. Please close the gate.) Now you have to pedal along the highway's shoulder for 1 mile, so stay far to the right and ride in single file.

Fork right onto FR 143 opposite Lodgepole Campground and gear down. The hill ahead looks unbearably steep, but it's a bit of an illusion. The highway is still descending, so the grade of the dirt road looks nearly twice as steep as it really is. Even so, the mile-long, rock-studded climb (tech 3) will have you huffing in your granny gear, but motorists traveling the highway below might provide encouragement by honking their horns.

Flower-decked meadows blanket Dock Flat, which is the route's highest point. Cross the flat and descend swiftly through sweeping turns on a

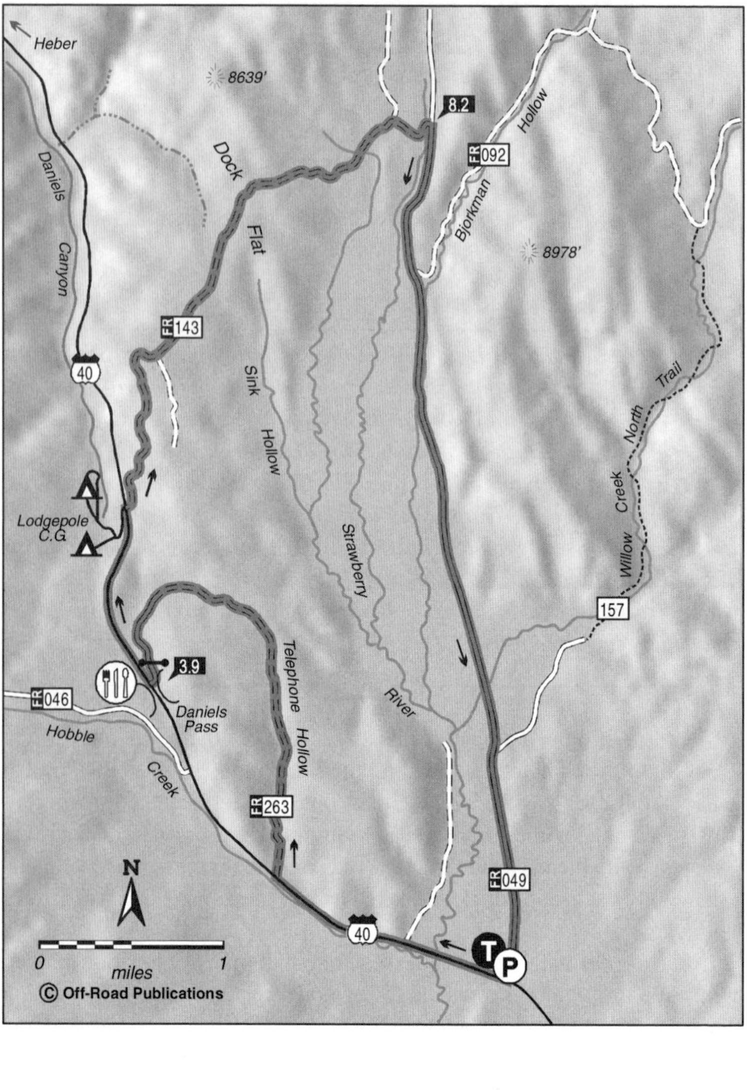

**192** Mountain Biking Park City & Beyond

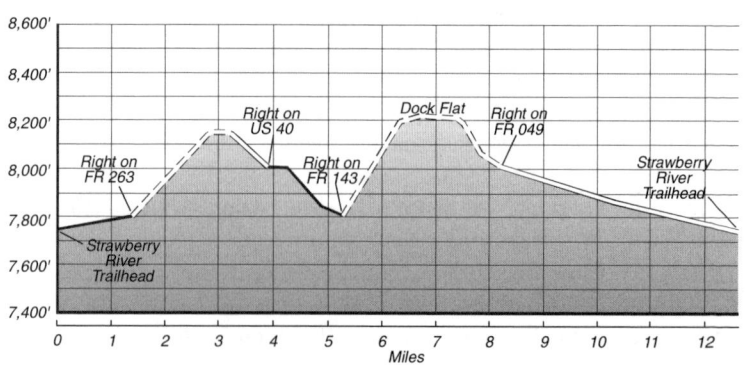

smooth dirt and gravel road (tech 2). Weave through vast aspen groves then cross Strawberry River, which is generally ridable, and join with the Strawberry River road (**m8.2**). Finish the loop by cruising 4.4 miles south on the level but gravel and washboarded road (tech 2). Let your eyes wander

After making the rugged climb to Dock Flat, you'll find smooth sailing through fragrant woodlands.

across the sage-covered valley to the nearby forest in search of deer and elk, but be alert to motorists driving the road.

**Option:** Willow Creek North Trail

This 5.5-mile side trip taps into one of the Uinta's best kept secrets—Willow Creek North Trail. The route begins with a moderate 2.5-mile climb up Bjorkman Hollow on a smooth, lightly rutted jeep road. Moose are know to inhabit the lush creek-fed hollow, and spying one is a real treat. Just beyond the road's summit, Willow Creek North Trail takes off to the right for a fast 3-mile descent on tight singletrack. Each of the seven creek crossings is ridable and unique: smooth, rocky, narrow, wide, shallow, deep, muddy. Your toes will get soaked at the very least. Adding on Willow Creek North Trail is worth the extra effort because singletrack beats dirt roads any day. (See the chapter "Willow Creek North Trail.")

### Know Before You Go

- The Strawberry River road receives moderate traffic, so ride attentively. Use caution when pedaling US 40. Stay to the far right and ride in single file.
- This route passes through private property; stay on designated roads.
- Daniels Summit General Store offers all sorts of munchies plus hearty burgers and juicy cuts of prime rib. Yum!

### Maps & More Information

- USGS 1:24,000: Co-op Creek and Twin Peaks, Utah.
- Uinta National Forest (Heber Ranger District): (435) 654-0470.
- Strawberry Visitor Center (at Strawberry Reservoir): (435) 548-2321.

### Trailhead Access

From Heber, drive 17.5 miles southeast on US 40 to Daniels Summit then another 2.8 miles to the Strawberry River road (FR 049) on the left/north. Park next to the highway at the snowmobile staging area.

## 36 Willow Creek North Trail

| | | |
|---|---|---|
| **Location:** | 21 miles southeast of Heber | |
| **Length:** | 8.8 miles, loop | |
| **Tread:** | 3.3 miles dirt road, 2.6 miles doubletrack, 2.9 miles singletrack | |
| **Physically:** | Moderately easy (steady climb up Bjorkman Hollow; seven wet crossings of Willow Creek) | |
| **Technically:** | 2-4 (gravel and washboards on Strawberry River Rd.; smooth doubletracks; good tread on singletrack; 7 rocky creek crossings) | |
| **Gain:** | 650 feet | |
| **In a nutshell:** | FR 049-FR 092-Willow Creek North Trail | |

*Whether you're a singletrack purist willing to go to the ends of the earth for a choice one-laner or a less devout biker looking for a fun, easy ride, Willow Creek North Trail is worth the drive, even though the loop has only 3 miles of singletrack. Once closed for rehabilitation in the early 1990s, Willow Creek North Trail reopened in 1994 for non-motorized use and has become one of the Uinta's best kept secrets. A decade of use by foot, horse, and bike traffic has morphed this once rough motorcycle trail into a smooth-flowing dirt path that is ideal for novice riders looking for a good workout or anyone needing to cool off from the summer's heat. You'll break a sweat climbing Bjorkman Hollow, but your toes, at the very least, will cool off as you splash through Willow Creek's seven water crossings.*

### Details

From the lower Willow Creek North trailhead, ride back to the Strawberry River road, and take it right/north for 2.4 miles. The road is flat as a pancake, but the gravel and washboards may wear your psyche thin (tech 2). Persevere. Fork right onto FR 092 for Bjorkman Hollow (**m3.3**), and climb gradually on packed gravel and then on smooth dirt (tech 2). After the road crosses over the creek and bends right, it rises moderately to the summit through stands of aspen and fir. Race down the other side to the left-hand bend and connect with Willow Creek North Trail (**m6.5**).

The trail is closed to motorized uses, so there will be no deafening, exhaust spewing, off-roaders to spoil the hollow's tranquility. If you listen closely, you might hear the bugling of distant elk. Glide down the aspen-lined hollow on the smooth dirt and rock-spattered trail and bounce across the first creek crossing. Each creek crossing has a different feel (tech 3-4). The second one has a tricky embankment, the third is smooth and you might be able to jump it with good speed, and the fourth can be hub deep during early summer. The fifth one hardly counts because it's a side tributary. The remaining two are wide, potentially deep (depending on sea-

Co-op Creek
Bjorkman Hollow
Dock Flat
Sink Hollow
Strawberry River
Telephone Hollow
Willow Creek North Trail
FR 092
FR 049
FR 263
157
40
3.3
6.5
8978'
8801'
N
0
1
miles
© Off-Road Publications

8,800'
8,600'
8,400'
8,200'
8,000'
7,800'
7,600'
7,400'
Right on FR 049
Right on FR 092
Right on Willow Creek North Trail
Got your rubber ducky?
Willow Creek North Trailhead
Willow Creek North Trailhead
0
1
2
3
4
5
6
7
8
Miles

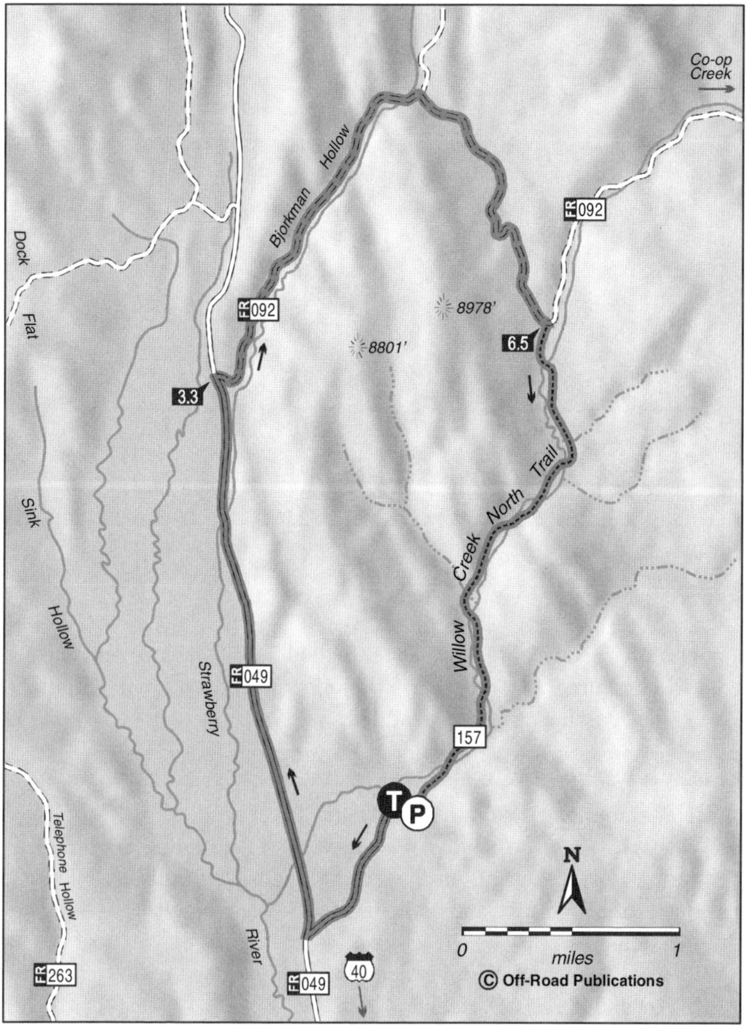

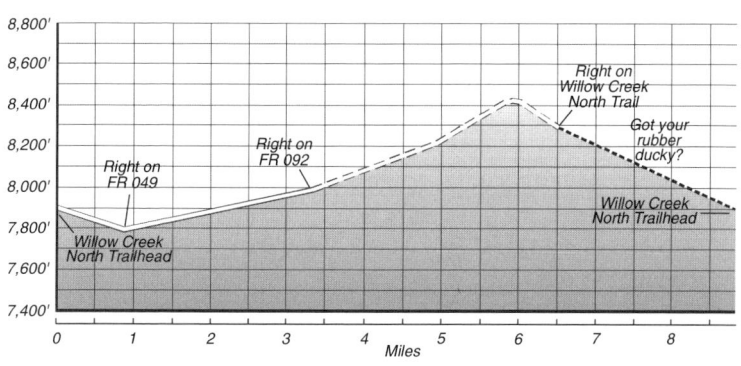

Don't forget your rubber ducky.

sonal runoff), and ridable if you carry a good head of steam. And if your head was steaming after the climb up Bjorkman Hollow, it will definitely have cooled down by the ride's end.

### Know Before You Go

- Be alert to motorists on the Strawberry River road.
- Water crossings on Willow Creek North Trail can be deep during spring runoff. During prolonged dry spells, the trail can get very dusty, and your bike and body will get slimed from the dust clinging to anything wet.
- Willow Creek North Trail is open to non-motorized uses, so yield to hikers and horseback riders.

### Maps & More Information

- USGS 1:24,000: Co-op Creek, Utah.
- Uinta National Forest (Heber Ranger District): (435) 654-0470.
- Strawberry Visitor Center (at Strawberry Reservoir): (435) 548-2321.

### Trailhead Access

From Heber, drive 17.5 miles southeast on US 40 to Daniel's Pass then another 2.8 miles to the Strawberry River road (FR 049). Drive 1.2 miles up FR 049, turn right for Willow Creek North Trail, and park at the end of the road in 0.8 mile.

## 37 Racetrack Peak

**JUST THE FACTS**

| | |
|---|---|
| **Location:** | 24 miles southeast of Heber |
| **Length:** | 30.4 miles, loop |
| **Tread:** | 2.1 miles paved road, 12.1 miles all-weather dirt roads, 16.2 miles doubletracks |
| **Physically:** | Strenuous (one moderate and one strenuous climb; long miles) |
| **Technically:** | 2-3+ (washboarded dirt and gravel road at first then choppy and rutted doubletracks) |
| **Gain:** | 4,000 feet |
| **In a nutshell:** | FR 082-FR 471-FR 084-US 40 |

**WHY SHOULD U RIDE THIS TRAIL?** This is a demanding, remote ride geared for strong riders with a penchant for exploring relatively unknown areas. The route ventures from Strawberry Reservoir to Currant Creek Reservoir and back again. There are two notable climbs along the way. First is a steady pull up the often-washboarded Co-op Creek dirt road. Second is a gut-wrenching, 2,000-foot ascent up the choppy Racetrack Creek jeep road. That the second climb is located half way into an already long ride makes it even tougher. Once you've made the grade, so to speak, you'll round out the day with miles of rolling terrain and blazing descents, where you can ride as fast as you dare.

### Details

Begin by pedaling 2.5 miles across sunny sagebrush flats on the "new and improved" Co-op Creek road (FR 082). This well-maintained dirt and gravel road (tech 2) is part of the Arterial Highway, which connects Spanish Fork Canyon, Strawberry Reservoir, and Mirror Lake Highway. As you pedal this road, you'll wonder if it's being primed for paving. At a steel gate, the road bends left and begins rising at a government-regulation six-percent grade. (Here, the old Sleepy Hollow road on the right and the old Co-op Creek road on the left have been converted to non-motorized trails. They were very rough when they were converted in 1994. Now, after a decade of use, they might be tempting singletracks. Go check them out.) The road rises quickly above the lush creek-side habitat, and you'll gain sweeping views of Strawberry Reservoir, Strawberry Ridge, and the distant Wasatch Range. From the summit (**m6.0**), you'll pick up speed progressively while descending off the mountain.

Stay straight on FR 082 at the junction signed for Willow Creek and Currant Creek, but fork right 2 miles farther to continue on FR 082 (**m10.5**), which is now a lesser-used doubletrack, and brace yourself for a speedy descent to Currant Creek Reservoir (tech 2-3). You'll splash through South Fork Currant Creek and pass pond-filled meadows along the way. Keep an eye out for blue herons nesting in the marshes. When you reach Cur-

Two climbs net you two fast, furious descents.

rant Creek Reservoir (**m14.6**), turn right onto FR 471, and pedal 1.2 miles to the Racetrack Creek road (FR 084). You can stock up on water at the Forest Service campground just around the bend.

The Racetrack Creek road rises without switchbacks, without any breathers, and without mercy for 3 miles. (Be sure to stay left on FR 084 at the junction signed for Alvies Bench, which is a cutoff to the Willow Creek-Currant Creek junction on FR 082, presumably.) Invariably, the steepest sections are also the most technical (tech 3-4). Just past where the road crosses hummocky meadows and levels, turn left at a junction signed for Trout Creek (**m19.4**), and take in the view of Currant Creek Reservoir far below. (If you go straight at this junction, you'll climb into Racetrack Peak's upper basin—burly but cool.) Cross over a small ridge, climb moderately around the head of Layout Canyon, and enjoy some

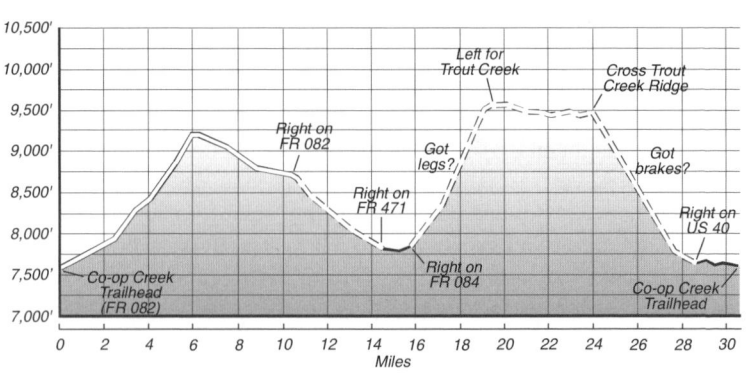

## Racetrack Peak 199

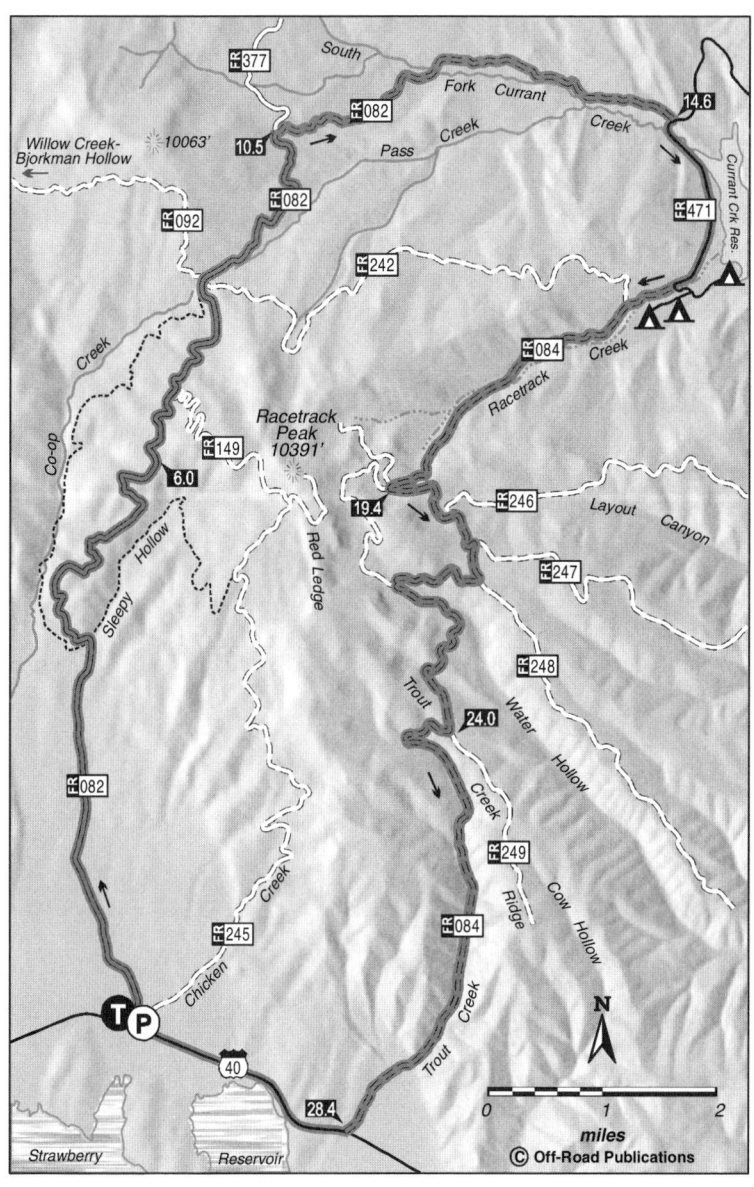

much-deserved cruising on smooth doubletrack. Fork right at the junction for Big Dry Hollow, rocket across open fields, and then fork right at the junction for Water Hollow Ridge.

You'll be tempted to let gravity pull you downhill at breakneck speeds, but the tranquility of these quiet woods beckons for a slower pace. Two short climbs take you to Trout Creek Ridge (**m24.0**). From there, it's all downhill on FR 084. Feather your brakes or you'll instantly reach highway speeds (tech 3). As the canyon widens, the tree-lined road succumbs to sunny sagebrush flats and winds down to US 40 (**m28.4**). Two miles of the highway's soothing pavement take you back to the Co-op Creek trailhead.

### Know Before You Go

- You may encounter vehicles, including motor homes and trailers, on the Co-op Creek road/Arterial Highway (FR 082). Doubletracks are open to vehicles and OHVs.
- Cattle and sheep range through the area, so all surface waters should be avoided or purified.
- There is a developed Forest Service campground at Currant Creek Reservoir where you can stock up on water.
- This loop reaches high elevations, so be prepared for rapidly changing alpine weather.
- Some roads may be impassable when wet.

### Maps & More Information

- USGS 1:24,000: Co-op Creek, Jimmies Point, and Strawberry Reservoir NW, Utah.
- Uinta National Forest (Heber Ranger District): (435) 654-0470.
- Strawberry Visitor Center (at Strawberry Reservoir): (435) 548-2321.

### Trailhead Access

From Heber, drive 24 miles on US 40 toward Strawberry and Duchesne to the Co-op Creek/Arterial Highway (FR 082). It's 1.3 miles past the Strawberry Bay road and the Strawberry Visitor Center. Park and embark from the snowmobile staging area next to the highway.

# 38 Strawberry Narrows Trail

**JUST THE FACTS**

| | |
|---|---|
| **Location:** | 38 miles southeast of Heber |
| **Length:** | 21.4 miles, loop (12 miles, one-way on trail only) |
| **Tread:** | 0.3 mile paved road, 10.7 miles dirt roads; 1.3 miles doubletrack; 9.1 miles singletrack |
| **Physically:** | Strenuous (moderate dirt road climb; short rough, tough climbs on singletrack; moderate if riding trail only) |
| **Technically:** | 2-4+ (good dirt roads; smooth, lumpy, & choppy singletrack) |
| **Gain:** | 2,400 feet (800 feet, one-way on trail only) |
| **In a nutshell:** | FR 109-FR 090-Strawberry Narrows Trail |

## Why Should You Ride This Trail?

Strawberry Narrows Trail has the potential for greatness. Twelve miles of rolling, non-motorized singletrack edge a quiet alpine lake that is lined with pristine timber. As its name suggests, much of the trail follows the "narrows," where a constricted waterway, measuring 5 miles long but at times only 500 feet wide, connects the reservoir's two main bays. Creatures of nature are your constant companions: deer and rodents scamper through the woods, grey herons take flight, and birds of prey swoop down from the skies to pluck their catch from the reservoir. If you're a brave soul, then take a mid-ride plunge in the frigid lake; it's the ultimate refresher during the dog days of summer.

The only downside to the Narrows Trail is that it is underutilized, and begs to be ridden more often. So, give the region's overused trails a break for one weekend, and head out to Strawberry Reservoir. Bring some friends, too. You'll go home happy and the Narrows Trail will thank you.

## Details

Naturally, you can ride the Strawberry Narrows Trail out-and-back from either trailhead. Your best bet is to start from the Aspen Grove trailhead because the trail darts into the woods immediately and follows the Narrows for 8.5 miles to Poison Ridge, which makes for a good turnaround point. From Renegade Point, you must cross nearly 4 miles of sagebrush on lumpy and bumpy tread to reach Poison Ridge and to begin the Narrows section proper. To turn the Narrows Trail into an adventure, however, try the loop version presented here. After the initial hefty climb, you'll cruise effortlessly across rolling highlands and descend at breakneck speeds to Aspen Grove. There, you'll pick up the Narrows Trail and ride along the lake's edge for 10 miles back to the starting point. It's da' kine.

From Big Spring, don't take the road straight up the hollow because it dead ends; instead, take the dirt road north (FR 109), bend right around a switchback, and then chug up the canyon high on its side. In less than 2 miles, the road turns sharply left, the grade levels, and you are treated to a huge view of the Strawberry Reservoir valley and the seemingly impenetrable Wasatch Range to the distant west. Climb one more short hill and culminate the climb at a T-junction (**m3.2**). Although the left fork (FR 090) leads to dispiriting places like Devil's Pass and Stinking Spring, that's the way you want to go.

Roll along the ridge above French Hollow; then click into your high gears, and speed along on smooth dirt (tech 2) for 2.5 miles, contouring around the ridge-top knolls. Your pace will quicken as the road declines more noticeably, and you'll reach highway speeds if you let off the brakes. A steeper straightaway section leads into two big curves where gravel, ruts, and washboards lurk (tech 2-3), so keep your speed at bay and watch your wheels. Connect with pavement and come to a four-way junction. To restock on water or grab some munchies, take the right fork to the Aspen Grove Marina general store and campground; otherwise, take the left fork and ride the dirt road one-half mile to access the Strawberry Narrows Trail, No. 304 (**m11.0**)

Initially, the trail rises moderately over Badger Point; thereafter, it hugs the shoreline. The trail varies from baby-butt smooth to lumpy and bumpy to choppy with scattered rocks (tech 2-3), as it weaves through stands of aspen and fir underlain with lush grasses and prickly thistle. Views are especially good where the trail exits the timber to sloping sage fields. Don't fret if you encounter a few dicey sections (tech 3-4); they're short, and smooth trail will prevail.

About 4 miles out, the path descends gradually for a few tenths of a mile into a small narrow bay, and you might have to walk up a steep rough hill to get over a rocky point on the other side. Thereafter, the trail rises uphill in stair-step fashion, taking you a couple hundred feet above the lake's level to a magnificent viewpoint of the Narrows (**m15.3**). You can see the remainder of your route, as it winds into several bays created by the gooseneck waterway. This is a good lunch spot and turnaround point for intermediate riders who started from the Aspen Grove trailhead.

Continuing on, the trail descends into Broad Hollow on rougher tread (tech 4), so if you're riding out-and-back from Aspen Grove, you'll have

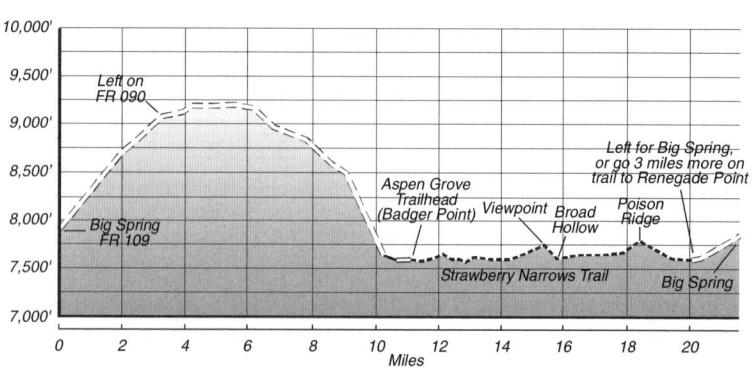

climb this rugged section on the return. Parts of trail over the next couple of miles can have choppy rocks and lumpy tread, and you'll have to contend with several abrupt hills, so persevere. The trail has a smoother flow to it where it passes a sign for Strawberry River and Indian Creek Confluence. When you exit the aspens at Poison Ridge (**m18.6**), you can see Renegade Point across 4 miles of sagebrush flats, but you won't go there. Descend from Poison Ridge and ride near the lake's edge for 1.5

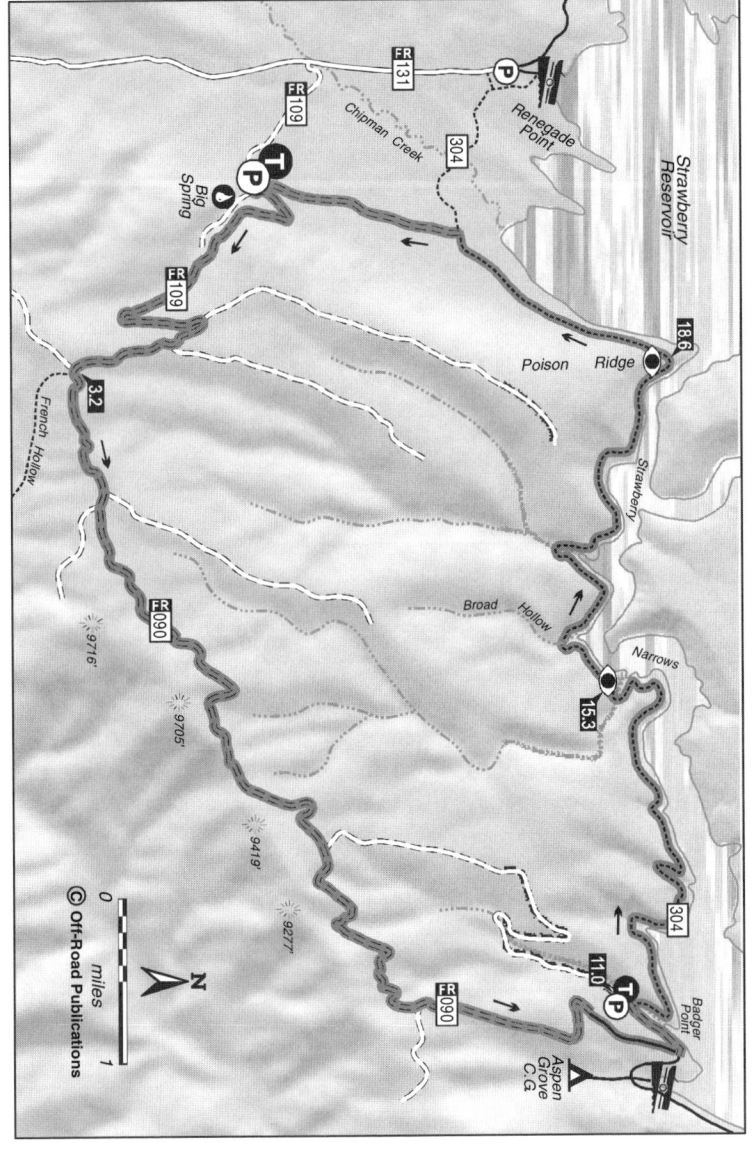

The Strawberry Narrows Trail offers promising singletrack . . .

miles; then fork left at a four-way junction onto a doubletrack signed "Big Spring." Culminate the loop by climbing steadily for 1.3 miles back to where you parked at Big Spring.

If you are playing through to Renegade Point, then go straight at the four-way junction with the Big Spring jeep road and cross the treeless plains edging the reservoir's broad murky bay. Only Chipman Creek's trickling water can offer you relief from the beating sun on a warm midsummer's day. Climb over a hump of sage, descend into a draw, and repeat. Pass a trail forking left (it exits to FR 131 just south of Renegade Point), and bounce along the trail to the Renegade Point trailhead.

### ! Know Before You Go

- The marinas at Renegade Point and at Aspen Grove have outhouses, water taps, and small general stores stocked with basic munchies, drinks, and ice.
- Developed campgrounds are located near the Aspen Grove and Renegade Point trailheads.
- A day-use fee of $4.00 per vehicle is charged if you park at the Renegade Point marina or the Aspen Grove marina. You can park for free at the roadside pullout on FR 131 about one-half mile south of

. . . and great views.

Renegade Point marina or at the Aspen Grove trailhead 0.5 mile down the dirt road from the marina. No fee is charged if you park at Big Spring for the loop ride.

### ? Maps & More Information

- USGS 1:24,000: Strawberry Reservoir NE, Strawberry Reservoir SE, and Strawberry Reservoir SW, Utah.
- Uinta National Forest (Heber Ranger District): (435) 654-0470.

### Trailhead Access

From the junction of US 40 and US 189 in Heber, drive 22.7 miles south on US 40 to the turnoff for Strawberry Reservoir and Visitor Center. To reach the Renegade Point trailhead, take the paved Strawberry Reservoir Road (FR 131) 14 miles to the Renegade Point Day Use Area. To reach Big Springs (suggested parking for the loop), continue past Renegade Point on FR 131 (all-weather dirt and gravel) for 1.3 miles, and turn left onto FR 109 (light-duty dirt road) for Soldier Creek Dam and French Hollow. Go another mile to where the road enters the aspens at Big Spring. Park at your discretion at one of several backcountry campsites.

To reach the Aspen Grove trailhead, continue on US 40 past Strawberry Visitor Center for 11 miles, and then turn right onto FR 090 for Aspen Grove and Soldier Creek Dam. Drive 5.3 miles to the junction for Aspen Grove Campground and boat dock, go straight for 0.5 mile on pavement, and then take a dirt road for 0.5 mile to the trailhead.

# 39 Strawberry Peak

## Just the Facts

**Location:** 20 miles southeast of Heber
**Length:** 16.5 miles, loop
**Tread:** 3 miles all-weather dirt road, 13.5 miles doubletrack
**Physically:** Moderate (gentle and moderately steep hills; some rocky sections; short hike to reach peak)
**Technically:** 2-3+ (hard-packed dirt with some ruts and rocky stretches)
**Gain:** 1,750 feet
**In a nutshell:** FR 503-FR 135-FR 137-FR 046 (Main Canyon Road)

## Why Should U Ride This Trail

*Although Strawberry Peak is indisputably the highest point on Strawberry Ridge, calling it a "peak" is generous because it is barely more than a knoll. Still, this unassuming mount is worth striving for. From its rounded, treeless summit, you'll find an inspiring view east of the backside of the southern Wasatch Range along with its vast but largely uncelebrated hinterlands. In the opposite direction, you'll sight across Strawberry Reservoir to the rolling Uinta Basin and beyond to the distant Uinta Mountains. The panorama gained from Strawberry Peak compliments this peaceful woodland tour, which links together a variety of dirt roads.*

## Details

Head up FR 503, signed "Buck Spring 7.5 miles." The dirt road rises gently for 0.5 mile, bends left at a corral, and crosses Hobble Creek. Do not confuse *this* insignificant rivulet with the blue-ribbon stream of the same name near Springville. Beyond, the road traverses forested hillsides for 3 miles then bends right and rises moderately steeply over rocks and ruts up Point of Pines Canyon (tech 3+). Turn sharply right at the signed junction for Clyde Creek (**m5.4**), and continue climbing up the rocky jeep road toward Buck Spring. You'll reach Strawberry Ridge in 0.5 mile.

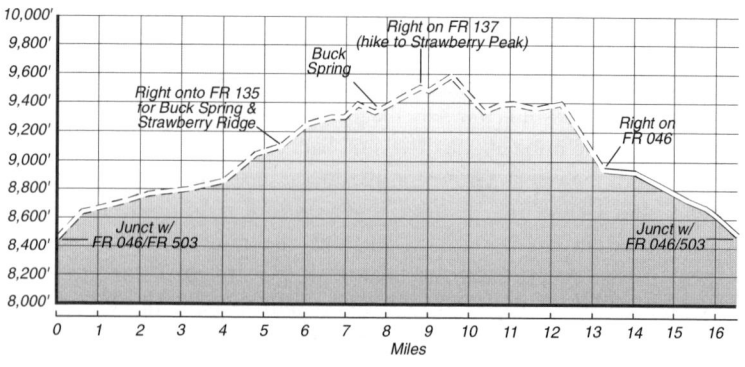

# Strawberry Peak

The Strawberry Ridge road (FR 135) winds through groves of fluttering aspens with crookneck trunks. The road undulates a bit, rises steeply around the flanks of Twin Peaks, and descends to a picturesque alpine meadow surrounding Buck Spring. Stay left and uphill on FR 135, following a sign for Left Fork Hobble Creek; then 1.5 miles farther fork right/north onto FR 137 (now the Strawberry Ridge road) where FR 135 goes

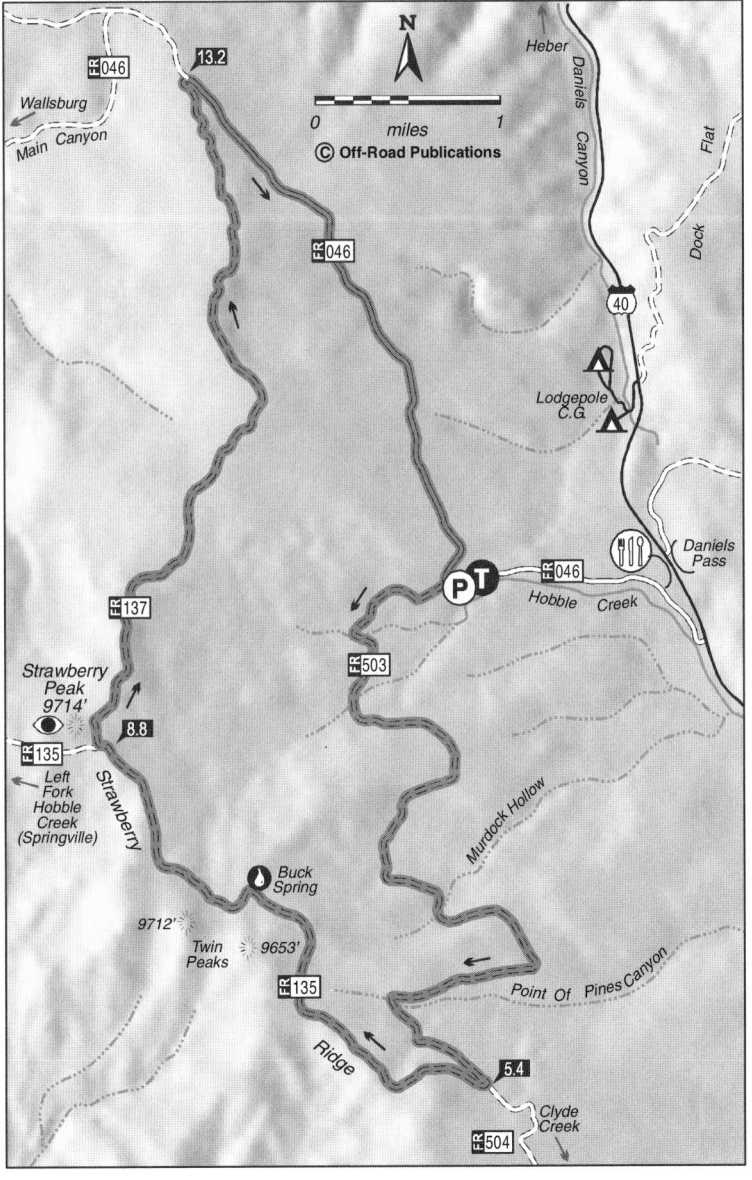

left for Left Fork Hobble Creek (**m8.8**) and at the base of Strawberry Peak. Immediately ahead, you'll come to an overgrown doubletrack that forks left and rises to the summit of Strawberry Peak. If you hike up it—it's too steep and rough to ride—you'll find a circumferential view of north-central Utah, including the Hobble Creek and Diamond Fork basins, the Wasatch Range from Mount Nebo to Mount Timpanogos, Strawberry Reservoir and the Uinta Basin, and the distant Uinta Mountains.

Pedal north of Strawberry Peak up a steep hill, and then roll along the thickly wooded ridge top. After 3 miles, you'll begin a mile-long lumpy and bumpy descent to the junction with Main Canyon Road (FR 046, **m13.2**); turn right/southeast. (The left fork leads to Main Canyon and eventually to Wallsburg, which is a full day's ride from the trailhead). The remaining 3.3 miles undulate gently through sweeping turns. The gravel can be thick, but it won't bog down your knobby tires. Shift to your big chainring and sprint to the finish.

## ! Know Before You Go

- All roads are open to motorized uses, and Main Canyon Road (FR 046) is a backcountry thoroughfare between Daniels Pass and Wallsburg.
- Daniels Summit General Store (convenience store and café) offers munchies, burgers, and even prime rib. Yum!

## ? Maps & More Information

- USGS 1:24,000: Twin Peaks, Utah.
- Uinta National Forest (Heber Ranger District): (435) 654-0470.
- Strawberry Visitor Center: (435) 548-2321.

## Trailhead Access

From Heber, take US 40 for 17.5 miles to Daniels Pass. Go 1 mile farther, and turn right/west on FR 046 for Main Canyon. Park at your discretion 1.5 miles up the road near the junction with FR 503.

## 40
# Bald Knoll-Windy Pass

**JUST THE FACTS**

| | |
|---|---|
| **Location:** | 15 miles southwest of Heber |
| **Length:** | 22 miles, one-way |
| **Tread:** | 13.5 miles singletrack, 4 miles doubletrack, 4.5 miles pavement |
| **Physically:** | Extremely strenuous (steep climbs, rugged descents, big gain, rough tread, remote) |
| **Technically:** | 3-4+ (rock-studded dirt road with shallow creek crossings; narrow, choppy singletrack with steep, rocky ascents and descents) |
| **Gain:** | 3,500 feet |
| **In a nutshell:** | FR 121-GWT (No. 001-No. 058)-South Fork Road-Vivian Park |

Tap into the Great Western Trail on this remote section tucked away on the backside of the Wasatch Range. This is a big ride that ventures from one valley to another and crosses mountaintops along the way. You'll ride along the margins of stream-fed canyons, penetrate alpine forests, and gain extraordinary views from unusual angles of the southern Wasatch Range. This ride will whoop the butt of anyone who underestimates it because the conditions of the trails change yearly depending on how much use and what kind of use they receive, so relish the sweet parts and keep an open mind if things turn sour. Even if they do, this expedition is full of pleasant backcountry surprises, and by the day's end you'll agree that the Great Western Trail is a corridor of diversity.

### Details

Start out on FR 121 with about 3 miles of rock-studded doubletrack (tech 2+), crossing Right Fork Little Hobble Creek several times. Fork right near an old wooden corral in the broad pasture of Little Valley and follow a carsonite post marking the Great Western Trail (GWT) (**m3.1**). Fork right again 1 mile farther onto another doubletrack tagged with GWT markers. (The left fork is the continuation of FR 121.)

Head up the aspen-clad hollow, chasing the GWT markers, and then connect with a singletrack that winds up the narrowing canyon. Climb through aspen groves, gently at first then steeply, to a saddle that separates Bald Knoll from Wallsburg Ridge (**m5.9**). Take the path southward and up a set of switchbacks. Thereafter, the narrow path hugs the steep slopes of Bald Knoll at the 8,200-foot mark and penetrates aspen and fir trees underlain by maples, oaks, and ferns (tech 3-4).

The trail bends south around Bald Knoll and descends gently to a saddle marked with a solitary tree (tech 3-4). Take a deep breath. You'll need all the air your lungs can hold as you tackle the steep, switchbacking climb over the knoll to the west. It's a hike-a-bike, by and large. The path clips the ridge, bends south, and continues rising around a hillside that affords a huge panorama of Provo River's South Fork basin, Wallsburg Ridge, and the distant Wasatch peaks. Lightning Peak and a series of gla-

You'll score some sweet singletack on this section of the GWT, but at a price.

cial cirques, simply named First through Fourth Holes, define the west side of the Provo Peak ridge. A sharp, technical descent takes you to Windy Pass where, not surprisingly, the breeze can reach bothersome levels (**m12.3**).

It's all downhill from here, but don't think you're out of the woods just yet because many sections are rough and require a full repertoire of riding skills (tech 3-4+). The GWT plummets north into the head of Water Hollow, wraps around the sheer flank of Lightning Peak, and angles into upper Shingle Mill Canyon. The alpine forest that was plentiful at higher elevations yields to tenacious oak, maple, and alpine sage at these lower, warmer climes. Turn right onto a dirt road at the Big Springs trailhead (**m17.0**), go around a steel gate, and take the road down to Trefoil Ranch. Cap off the ride by zooming 4.5 miles down the paved road to Vivian Park.

### Know Before You Go

- The GWT from Windy Pass to the Big Springs trailhead is very popular with equestrians and hikers, so expect and respect other trail users. Descend prudently.
- You may encounter motorists between Trefoil Ranch and Vivian Park.
- Vivian Park has water taps, restrooms, and picnic areas. Snows Marina, at the turnoff for Wallsburg, has a small convenience store. Wallsburg has a general store.

### Maps & More Information

- USGS 1:24,000: Bridal Veil Falls, Charleston, and Wallsburg Ridge, Utah.
- Uinta National Forest (Pleasant Grove Ranger Distr.): (801) 785-3563.
- *Mountain Biking Utah's Wasatch Front,* by Gregg Bromka (Off-Road Publications).

### Trailhead Access

First, drive your pick-up vehicle to Vivian Park in Provo Canyon: From Heber, travel southwest on US 189 and around Deer Creek Reservoir. Turn off for Vivian Park/South Fork about 5 miles below the dam. Now shuttle all bikes and bodies to Wallsburg. From Vivian Park, drive up Provo

# Bald Knoll-Windy Pass    211

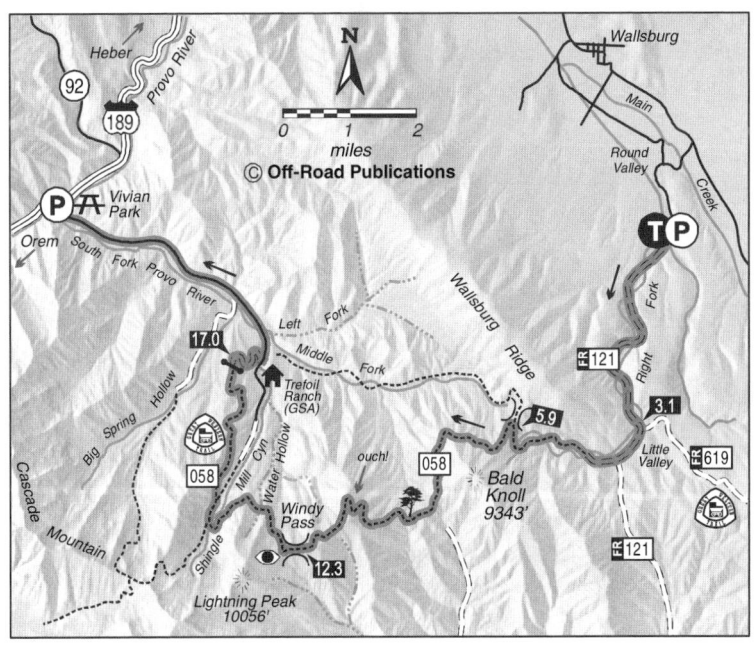

Canyon on US 189, and turn right onto UT 222 for Wallsburg about 2.8 miles east of Deer Creek Reservoir's dam (across from Snows Marina). Pass through Wallsburg (pretty much any road will do), and continue 2 miles on Main Canyon Road. Turn right at a junction for Little Valley Road. Curve around a knoll, and stay left at another junction for Little Valley Road. About 0.5 mile after the pavement turns to dirt, park at your discretion at the edge of a meadow where several jeep roads fork left. Obey all signs restricting travel and parking.

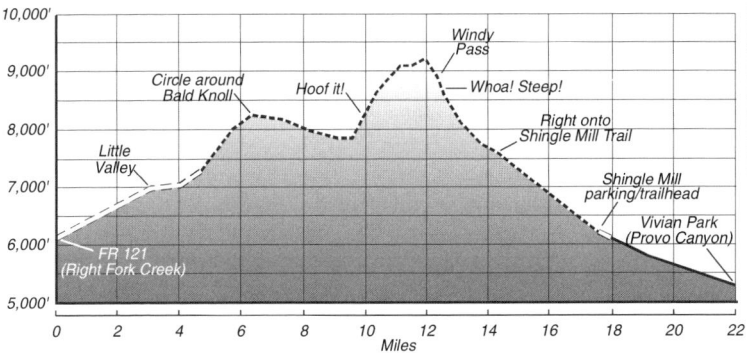

## 41 South Fork Deer Creek Trail

**JUST THE FACTS**

| | |
|---|---|
| **Location:** | Summit of American Fork Canyon, 16 miles west of Heber |
| **Length:** | 6.4 miles, loop |
| **Tread:** | All singletrack |
| **Physically:** | Moderate (long climb on South Fork Deer Creek Trail to Ridge Trail 157; short climbs on Ridge Trail 157) |
| **Technically:** | $2^+$-$3^+$ (multi-use trails w/ some rocky & eroded sections) |
| **Gain:** | 1,150 feet |
| **In a nutshell:** | South Fork Deer Creek-Ridge Trail 157-South Fork Deer Creek |

### Why Should U Ride This Trail?

Go snooping around the summit of American Fork Canyon and you'll uncover a tight-knit web of singletracks going every which way. Much like the trails of Park City, deciphering the code for maximum singletrack enjoyment takes time, effort, trial, error, and a bit of luck. Or you can cut to the chase and just ride the South Fork Deer Creek Trail. You'll start with a solid climb on tight tread that crosses wind-rippled meadows and darts into pristine timber. Ridge Trail 157 takes over and demands more effort from your legs, but each climb brings an equally rewarding descent. The last leg is largely a tribute to gravity: you'll swoop through fragrant conifers, dive into fluttering aspens, and zoom across a grassy meadow to the ride's end. Granted, this loop is short, only 6.4 miles, but it's all on sweet singletrack. Need scenery? Mount Timpanogos is the icon of the southern Wasatch Range for good reason, and you'll be compelled to stop dead in your tracks more than once to snap postcard-perfect photos.

### Details

Which way to ride? Here's the scoop. Counterclockwise, the climb to Ridge Trail 157 is a bit harder, Mount Timpanogos is dead in your sights along the ridge, and you culminate the loop with a beeline descent. Clockwise, the initial climb makes you sweat, but it's steady, Timp is in your periphery along the ridge, and the swooping descent on pine needle-matted tread is a thrill a minute. Ride both ways and decide for yourself, but here's the clockwise version.

From the parking area/campsite off Cascade Springs Drive, pick up South Fork Deer Creek Trail, No. 252, and cross the small footbridge. The climb is moderate at first (tech $2^+$), as you head up a grassy hollow lined with aspens; then the grade steepens, intermittently, as you pass a small mud bog (tech $3^+$). Stay left/straight where a faint pack trail forks right and away from the hollow. A tenth of a mile farther, veer right and climb through the aspens where a faint pack trail forks left and stays in the hollow. A wooden post might mark the latter junction. Cross a dirt road, and then cross the Alpine Loop Highway at the junction with Cascade

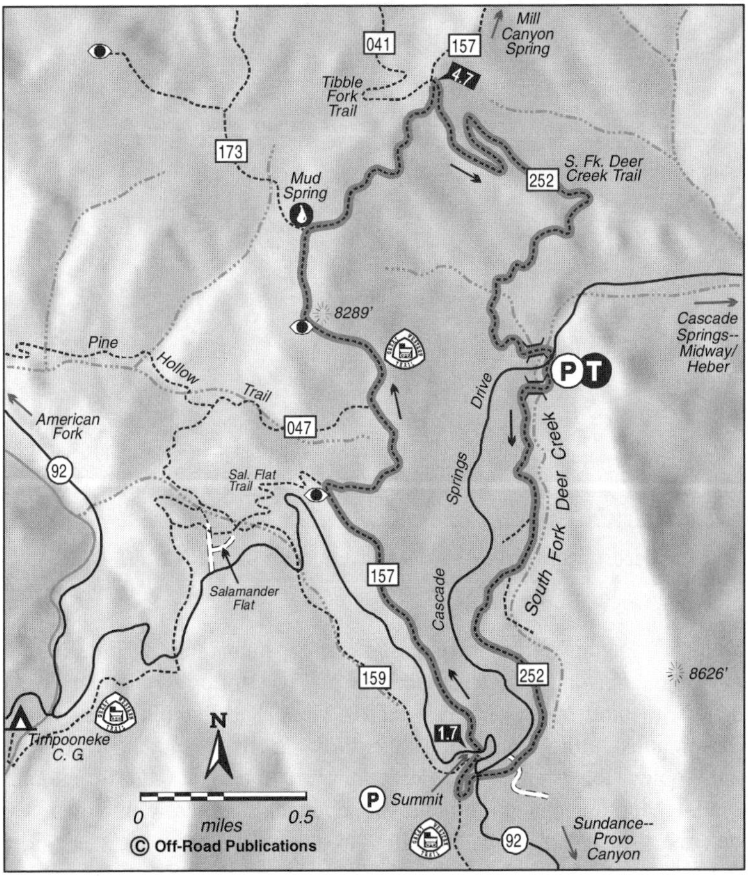

# South Fork Deer Creek Trail 213

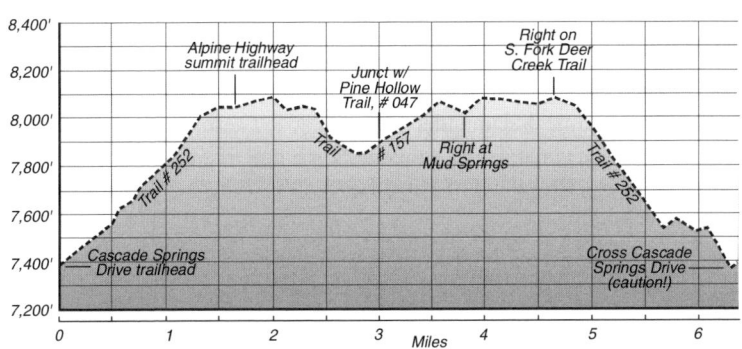

Springs Drive. In 0.1 mile, fork right at the junction with the Aspen Grove Trail, amidst closely spaced aspens and chin-high yarrow, to reach the Alpine Loop Highway summit trailhead (**m1.7**).

Head out Ridge Trail 157, bounce down a couple of quick descents, and climb a few short, rugged hills (tech 3-4). Check out the view of

Singletrack doesn't get much sweeter than on South Fork Deer Creek Trail.

Mount Timpanogos from the junction with Salamander Flat Trail. Round a broad meadow and pass the junction with Pine Hollow Trail; then climb steadily to another inspiring view of Mt. Timp. The Giant Staircase is the conspicuous 2-mile-long trough valley flowing out of Timpanogos Basin, and Wooley Hole is the double-decker cirque to the right. Glide on smooth tread to Mud Springs, go right on 157, and tackle a sharp climb over log water bars (tech $4^+$). The path mellows as it crosses to the ridge's east side and rolls across brushy slopes to the Tibble Fork Trail/South Fork Deer Creek Trail junction (**m4.7**).

Go right on South Fork and freewheel past a scenic viewpoint; then bank down through dense fir trees on a switchbacking course (tech 3). There's a little climb a mile down that requires you to be quick with your shifters; then the trails drops into a meadow and banks down to a footbridge over a creek. Pump up the short ramp and cross Cascade Springs Drive to end the ride. Another lap anyone?

**Option:** Singletrack, singletrack, singletrack!
For tips on tying together other trails in the neighborhood, including Tibble Fork, Mud Spring, Salamander Flat, Great Western, Pine Hollow, and Mill Canyon Springs Trails, consult *Mountain Biking Utah's Wasatch Front*, by Gregg Bromka (Off-Road Publications). It's available just about everywhere.

# South Fork Deer Creek Trail

So many trails, so much fun.

### ! Know Before You Go

- American Fork Canyon/Cascade Springs is a recreation fee area: $3 per vehicle for a three-day pass. You can pay at Cascade Springs.
- These trails are popular with hikers, bikers, and equestrians, and Ridge Trail 157 is open to motorcycles. Be especially cautious of horseback riders because many are on guided tours and might not be skilled at controlling a horse. Ride at prudent speeds, so you can stop safely within the distance you can see down the trail.

### ? Maps & More Information

- USGS 1:24,000: Aspen Grove and Timpanogos Cave, Utah.
- Uinta National Forest (Pleasant Grove Ranger Distr.): (801) 785-3563.
- *Mountain Biking Utah's Wasatch Front*, by Gregg Bromka (Off-Road Publications).

### Trailhead Access

From Heber, drive 3.2 miles west on 100 South (UT 113) to Midway. Turn left onto Center Street (UT 113 continued), drive 2.8 miles, and turn right onto Tate Lane for Soldier Hollow and Cascade Springs. Turn right in a half mile onto Stringtown Road then left onto Cascade Springs Drive. The paved road turns to all-weather dirt and rises 5 miles to a summit; then it descends quickly 0.7 mile to Cascade Springs. Take Cascade Springs Drive (paved again) 4.4 miles to a small backcountry campsite on the left that doubles as the parking area/trailhead for South Fork Deer Creek Trail.

## 42

# Ridge Trail 157 (and a little more)

**JUST THE FACTS**

| | |
|---|---|
| Location: | 16.8 miles west of Heber |
| Length: | 12.3 miles, one-way |
| Tread: | 0.5 mile doubletrack, 11.8 miles singletrack |
| Physically: | Strenuous (intermittent climbs on 157 add up quickly, one very rugged descent, sections of buffed and rough trail) |
| Technically: | 3-4+ (tight singletrack with smooth & choppy tread; descent to Mill Canyon Spring is severely eroded) |
| Gain: | 2,100 feet |
| In a nutshell: | Ridge Trail 157-South Fork Deer Creek |

**WHY SHOULD U RIDE THIS TRAIL**

*Like the Wasatch Crest Trail high above Park City, American Fork Canyon's Ridge Trail 157 is a world-class singletrack that traces the top of the Wasatch Range. The trail requires strong legs and acclimated lungs to tackle numerous high elevation climbs, plus it demands a full repertoire of riding skills to handle the varied trail conditions. The trail itself is top notch—a blend of buffed and rugged singletracks—which is reason enough to ride it. What sets Ridge Trail 157 apart from other alpine trails is the truly superlative scenery. The Alpine Ridge, home to the Lone Peak Wilderness, catches your eye early on. As it fades in the distance midway through the ride, Mount Timpanogos grows increasingly majestic. As solid as these mountains seem, glaciers made easy work of grinding down the volumes of rock, leaving behind deep canyons and hanging valleys separated by sharp peaks, some nearly 12,000 feet tall. So if you're looking for an alpine singletrack with plenty of eye candy, then make a beeline to American Fork Canyon and ride Ridge Trail 157.*

### Details

Head south on Ridge Trail 157/Great Western Trail, signed "Forest Lake and Alpine Loop," and take a deep breath because the first hill is devilishly steep. Ugh! Surf over loose sand and rock down to Sandy Baker Pass (tech 4) and veer right onto Trail 157, which contours through mixed timber (tech 2+-3+). Sweet! As you wrap around the flank of Mill Canyon Peak, a tremendous panorama unfolds with Box Elder Peak overshadowing American Fork Canyon to the west and the Alpine Ridge shaping the northern skyline like an inverted saw blade. An eagle's eye can spot Snowbird Resort's tram summit atop Hidden Peak; more conspicuous is the back of Alta Ski Area's Devil's Castle. Below the trail, an immense swath of bowled down trees conjures up images of Mount Saint Helen's fiery volcanic winds. But here, the results were produced by the fury of winter's avalanches.

Climb steadily on tight tread and through pockets of aspens. During the height of summer, you'll take wildflower "face shots" from the tall blossoms growing alongside the trail. Beyond the junction with Forest

The Alpine Ridge backdrops the first part of Ridge Trail 157.

Lake Trail, the path crosses a talus slope then tilts upward to reach a small ridge (**m2.9**), and you'll have to hike-a-bike briefly. Wham! From the ridge, you're slapped in the face with a shocking view of Mount Timpanogos, and the Alpine Ridge becomes a fleeting memory.

The trail contours past the junction with Holman Trail, No. 039, and passes Rock Spring. Just beyond the junction with East Ridge Trail, No. 038, the trail begins the notoriously nasty descent to Mill Canyon Spring. Years of use and abuse by a variety of trail users has left the path deeply entrenched and filled with rock and rubble (tech 4⁺). Breathe easy at Mill Canyon Spring (**m5.6**), and then head due south on a doubletrack.

A series of rugged ridge-top pulses and quick paint-shaker descents (tech 3-4) take you to the combined junction of Tibble Fork Trail, No. 041, and South Fork Deer Creek Trail, No. 252 (**m7.7,** see "Option"). Thereafter, 157 rolls more smoothly along the subtle ridge top. Bounce down a half-dozen log bars to Mud Spring, veer left/south, and take delight in both the smooth tread and the many scenic views of Mount Timpanogos. A swift descent takes you past the junction with Pine Hollow Trail, No. 047, and curves around a grassy meadow. Don't think you're

**218** Mountain Biking Park City & Beyond

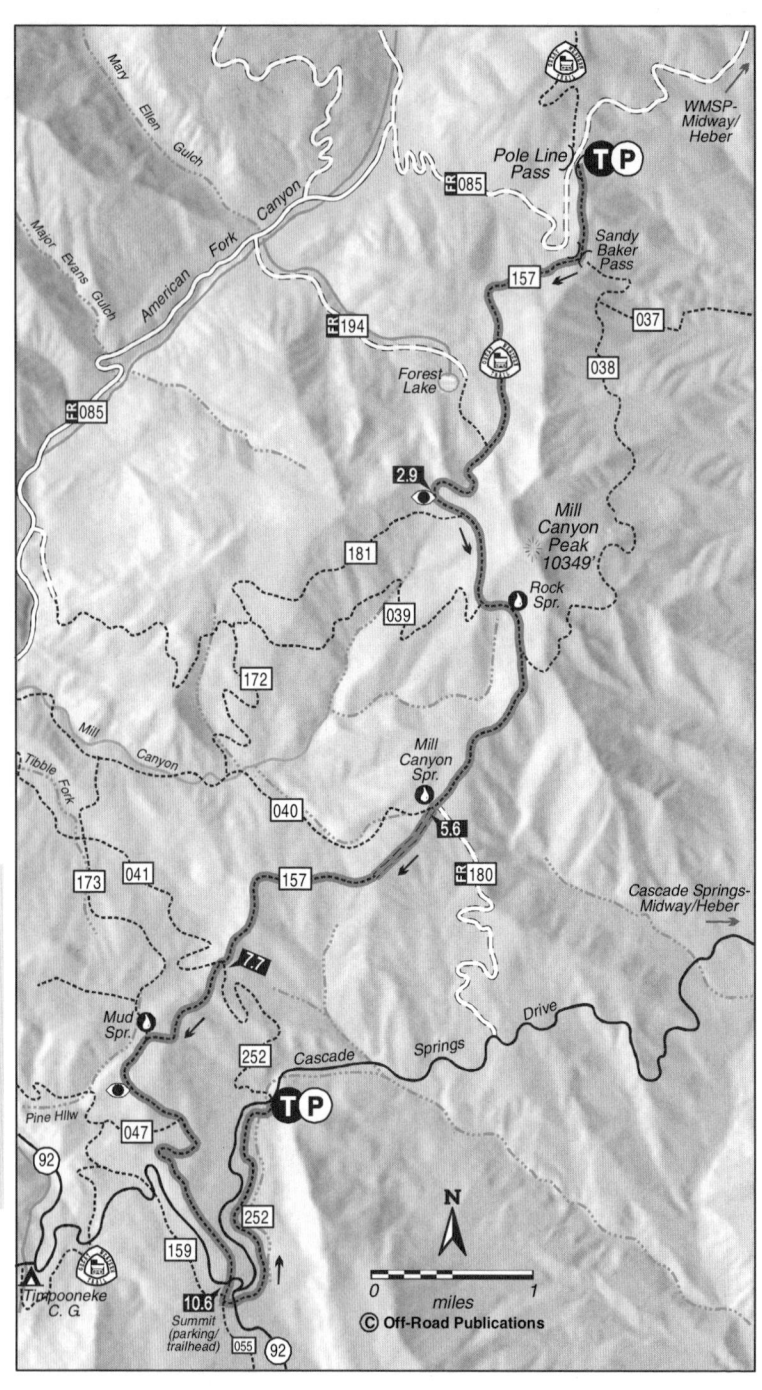

home free just yet because there's a bugger of a climb past the junction with Salamander Flat Trail and another grinder shortly before Ridge Trail 157 ends at the Alpine Loop Highway summit trailhead (**m10.6**).

But wait, there's more. Although Ridge Trail 157, proper, ends at the highway summit, the best part of this ride is right around the corner—the corner of the outhouse, that is. Hop onto Summit-Aspen Grove Trail, No. 055, duck into the aspens and dodge the head-high yarrow, and then fork left onto South Fork Deer Creek Trail, No. 252, after just 0.1 mile. Cross the Alpine Loop Highway at the junction with Cascade Springs Drive and resume on singletrack. Gravity will steer you downhill through groves of aspens and across grassy meadows on nearly 2 miles of blissful singletrack. Your whoops of elation will follow you down the trail and echo in your mind long after the ride's end.

**Option:** South Fork Deer Creek Trail Cutoff
You can eliminate two short burly climbs on Ridge Trail 157 by skipping the last 3 miles of trail and turning off onto South Fork Deer Creek Trail (see **m7.7** above). You'll trade some killer views of Mount Timpanogos for a raging descent. See the chapter "South Fork Deer Creek Trail."

**Option:** Cascade Springs Road Descent
Save gasoline by parking your vehicle at Cascade Springs and ending your ride by descending the paved Cascade Springs Drive. You'll add on about 4.4 miles of smooth downhill pavement punctuated with short gentle climbs. Be alert to motorists.

### ! Know Before You Go

- American Fork Canyon is a recreation fee area: $3 per vehicle for a three-day pass. You can pay at Cascade Springs.
- Snake Creek Road is popular with 4 x 4s and OHVs.
- Ridge Trail 157 is popular with equestrians, so ride cautiously and courteously.
- Sheepherding is common around Pole Line Pass.
- Rock Spring is a reliable water source, but it's only a trickle.

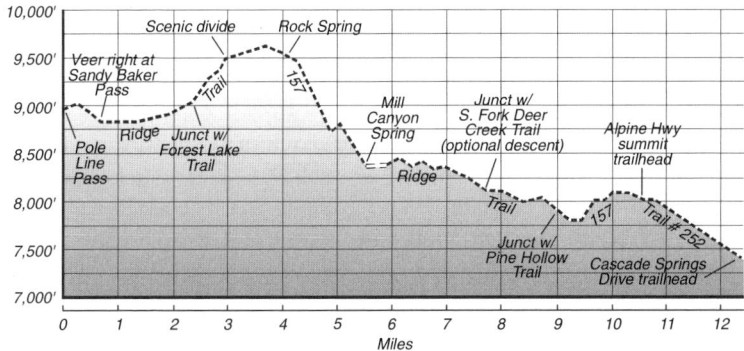

Mount Timpanogos is your constant companion on the second part of Ridge Trail 157.

- Be prepared for rapidly changing alpine weather.

### ? Maps & More Information

- USGS 1:24,000: Aspen Grove, Brighton, Dromedary Peak, and Timpanogos Cave, Utah.
- Uinta National Forest (Pleasant Grove Ranger Dist.): (801) 785-3563.

### Trailhead Access

To set up a shuttle, first drive a vehicle to the ride's end. From Heber, drive 3.2 miles west on 100 South (UT 113) to Midway. Turn left onto Center Street (UT 113 continued), drive 2.8 miles, and turn right onto Tate Lane for Soldier Hollow and Cascade Springs. Turn right after one half mile onto Stringtown Road then left immediately onto Cascade Springs Drive. Pavement turns to an all-weather dirt road, which rises 5 miles to a summit then descends quickly 0.7 mile to Cascade Springs. Take Cascade Springs Drive (paved again) 4.4 miles to a small backcountry campsite on the left that doubles as the parking area/trailhead for South Fork Deer Creek Trail.

To reach the Pole Line Pass trailhead, return to Midway and go left onto Main Street. Follow signs for Wasatch Mountain State Park and go to the Visitor Center; then drive 11.3 miles up Snake Creek Road to Pole Line Pass. Note: The first 3 miles of Snake Creek Road are paved; the remainder is light-duty dirt and rock. The road is suitable for passenger cars when dry but may be rough periodically. Passenger cars are not recommended west of Pole Line Pass; it's too rough.

## 43 Dutch Hollow

**JUST THE FACTS**

**Location:** Wasatch Mountain State Park (5 miles northwest of Heber)
**Length:** Up to 17.5 miles
**Tread:** Mostly singletrack
**Physically:** Easy to strenuous (incremental climbs add up quickly; see trails below)
**Technically:** 2-4+ (blend of smooth-rolling and exacting trails)
**Gain:** Variable
**In a nutshell:** Follow suggested routes, or make it up as you go

**WHY SHOULD U RIDE THIS TRAIL**

Built largely by local mountain bikers with mountain bikers in mind, but under the watchful eye of Wasatch Mountain State Park (WMSP), the Dutch Hollow Trail System now boasts over 17 miles of non-motorized multi-use trails that are designated open to mountain bikes. In the few short years it took to build, evaluate, and designate these trails, WMSP has set a prime example of how government and citizens can work hand in hand to accomplish a common goal. Best of all, most of the singletracks are true-to-nature, hand-built one-laners, not machined-cut swaths. With trails ranging in difficulty from easy to strenuous, Dutch Hollow caters to mountain bikers of all abilities. Scenery is wide sweeping, starting with the agrarian Heber Valley and rising through rolling timbered mountain lands to the formidable treeless peaks of the Wasatch Range. And Dutch Hollow's relatively low elevation makes it ideal for early and late season pedaling.

### Details

Wasatch Mountain State Park has a free brochure of the Dutch Hollow Trail System, which describes in brief each of its 13 trails with color-coded difficulty. Rather than duplicate that data, here are suggestions on how to link together trails for extended tours.

**Dutch Hollow Road** (7.0 miles or more out-and-back; moderately easy to strenuous; tech 2-4): The Dutch Canyon jeep road dissects the trail system and is pretty straightforward. You ride uphill as far as your legs are willing and then return with gravity on your side. The first 1.3 miles (to the top of Dutchman Way Trail) is moderately easy and crosses the creek several times. In spring, the crossings might be deep; by midsummer they nearly dry up. The road steepens up to the Park-Heber Tunnel then steepens more as it continues up the hollow. You'll exhaust your granny gears about 3.2 miles up, where the road angles skyward up the mountain side. The return is all freewheeling, and you might get soaked from the many creek crossings.

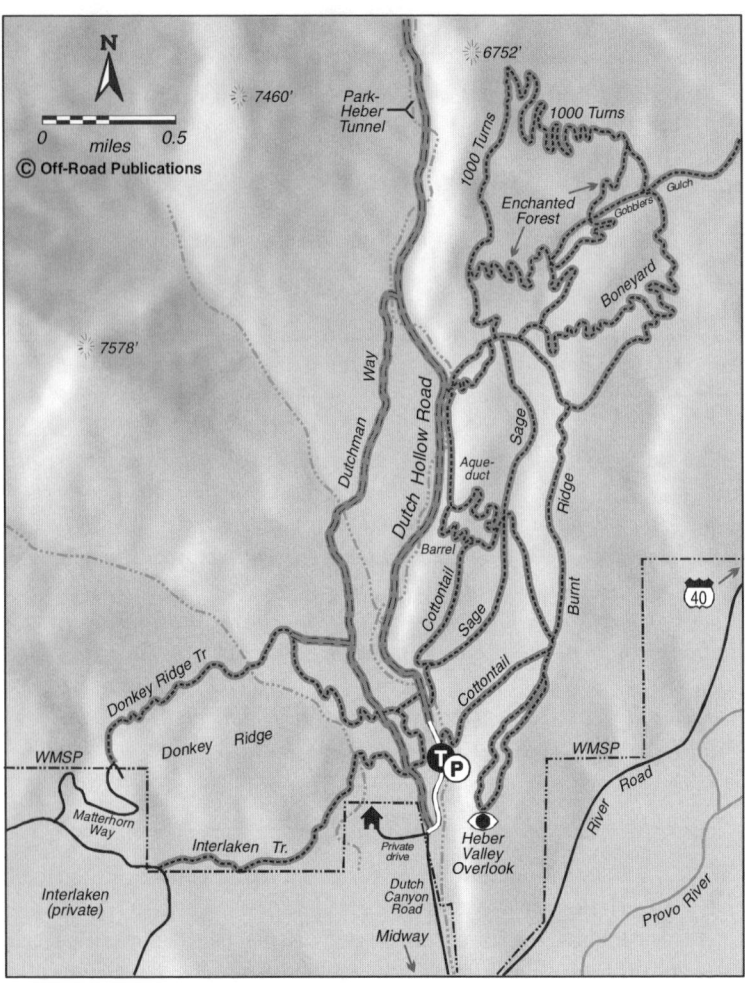

**Cottontail-Heber Valley Overlook** (2.3 miles, easy, tech 2-3): The International Mountain Bike Association (IMBA) lent a hand in designing and building this trail, so you can be assured of biker-friendly tread. The trail starts out next to the outhouse at the parking lot, curves up the hollow, and then angles up to Burnt Ridge. Go right for an easy loop to the Heber Valley Overlook, return to the Burnt Ridge junction, and veer left to continue on Cottontail. The sights of the fertile Heber Valley and majestic Wasatch Range are inspiring. Cross Sage Trail in the hollow, and coast back to the parking area. Use Cottontail as a stepping stone for longer rides on Sage and Burnt Ridge Trails.

**Sage-Aqueduct-Barrel Loop** (2.5 miles, moderate, tech 2-3+): Sage Trail is the main route to Dutch Hollow's advanced upper trails, but you can skip them altogether by looping back to the trailhead on Aqueduct and Barrel Trails. This loop is singletrack the whole way with biker-friendly tread most of the time. The last descent on Barrel Trail has tight turns and rougher conditions.

Enchanted Forest Trail.

Take Sage Trail north from the parking lot, and climb gradually up the broad hollow. As the hollow narrows, the trail steepens to a moderate climb to the T-junction with Enchant-ed Forest. Go left and descend Sage Trail toward Dutch Hollow Road, but fork left onto Aqueduct Trail before you reach the road. Aqueduct Trail follows an old aqueduct line, not surprisingly, along the steep hillside and then enters a low saddle between two knolls. Descend on either Aqueduct or Barrel Trails to Cottontail Trail and take Cottontail back to the trailhead. Barrel Trail was build to mimic Deer Crest's Spin Cycle Trail, with high-banked turns swooping down a steep gully. Aqueduct Trail takes a more mellow and roundabout approach.

**Sage-Dutchman Way Loop** (3.1 miles, moderately easy, tech 3): If the black diamond singletracks named Boneyard and 1,000 Turns sound spooky, then you'll enjoy this mellow loop, which is rated "green/easy" on the Dutch Hollow trail map. Start out by chugging 1 mile up Sage Trail, which gets moderately steep near the top (tech 3). Go left at the T-junction with Enchanted Forest Trail, and descend Sage Trail to Dutch Hollow Road. Go right and climb the road for 0.3 mile to the upper Dutchman Way Trail junction on the left.

Although Dutchman Way is technically a doubletrack, it rides like "parallel singletracks." The trail is smooth dirt and sand with scattered rocks, and it descends gradually across a sloping field of sage and brush (tech 2-3). Don't let your speed get away from you because some turns are sharp and approach quickly. Also, the trail is popular with equestrians, so you need to be able to slow down at a moment's notice. Pass trail junctions with Donkey Ridge and Interlaken Trails, both forking right, and exit the trail to paved Dutch Canyon Road. Go left, and take the road back to the parking area.

**Interlaken-Donkey Ridge Trails** (1.1-1.4 miles one-way, moderately easy-moderately strenuous, tech $2^+$-$3^+$): Add these trails to the Sage-Dutchman Way loop, and score some sweet singletrack. Interlaken Trail rolls across grass and sage fields and through mixed timber on the south flank of Donkey Ridge. The singletrack is tight and smooth, but there are enough tricky bits to keep things spiced up. When you intersect the paved Interlaken Road (private), turn around and glide back to Dutchman Way.

Donkey Ridge Trail goes around the north side of it's namesake knoll and rises more steeply than Interlaken, so it's geared for bikers who like to climb. After rolling up the sagebrush hill initially, the trail crosses a gully and rises sharply to the trail's end at Matterhorn Way (private). Turn around and descend like wind-fanned wildfire back to Dutchman Way.

**Boneyard-Enchanted Forest-1000 Turns Loop** (4.6 miles, strenuous, tech 4+): This figure-eight loop packs a lot of action in 4.6 miles because it follows Dutch Hollow's most difficult trails. These trails were hand built by local mountain bikers who like their trails tight, turny, and technical. You'll need honed skills and strong legs to make it around the loop without "dabbing," or putting a foot down.

Start out by climbing 1 mile up Sage Trail to the T-junction. Begin the first loop by going right then immediately left onto Boneyard Trail (singletrack), which darts into the oak and maple. Like a champion boxer, you'll bob-and-dodge through the tenacious brush, rapidly shifting both your gears and body position to adjust to the ever-changing terrain and to round the hairpin turns (tech 4). As Boneyard descends northward off the knoll, the trail opens to wider turns and faster straights. Come to a 4-way junction at the bottom of Gobblers Gulch, and fork left to climb the hollow. (Straight ahead is 1000 Turns, which you'll get to later.) Climbing the hollow is a low-gear grind with occassional ruts and gravel (tech 3). Ignore two trails forking right: the first cuts over to 1000 Turns, the second is Enchanted Forest, which you'll descend in short order. As you near the top, fork left to climb more gradually out of the hollow and to return to the T-junction with Sage Trail.

For the second and harder loop, go right onto Enchanted Forest and traverse through the timber. Fork right at the junction with 1000 Turns, and descend the twisted trail into Gobblers Gulch, which you just climbed (tech 3-4). At the familiar 4-way junction at the bottom, turn left, take a deep breath, and climb 1000 Turns. Granted, the turns are a tad shy of 1000 in number, but there is nary a straightaway either. The turns are tight and they require bursts of power coupled with delicate balance to clean them (tech 4+). Sometimes you can cheat by pushing off a trail-side tree when you start to teeter. Top out, fork right on Enchanted Forest, and return to the top of Sage Trail. You decide how to return to the trailhead.

**The Full Monty** (17 miles, moderately strenuous, tech 2-5): Make your drive to Dutch Hollow worth while by linking together nearly every trail in the system. You'll ride 17 miles on almost all singletracks and climb nearly 2,000 feet. You'll go home happy—and tired.

Start out on Cottontail Trail with a gentle warmup to the Heber Valley Overlook. Skip the climb up Burnt Ridge (rocky doubletrack), but climb the upper half of Sage Trail to the T-junction. Go right and follow the Boneyard-Enchanted Forest-1000 Turns loop described above. Upon returning to the T-junction at the top of Sage Trail, go right and descend to Dutch Hollow Road. Climb the road 0.3 mile, and fork left on Dutchman Way for a fast descent on the sandy and rocky doubletrack. Climb Donkey Ridge Trail and return then ride out-and-back on Interlaken Trail. Upon returning to Dutchman Way, go straight across and connect with a short trail that returns you to the parking area. Now that's a ride.

### Know Before You Go

- All Dutch Hollow trails are open to hikers, equestrians, and mountain bikers, so ride cautiously and courteously. Your actions will dictate future access privileges and trail developments. Other trail users have the right-of-way, as well as those going uphill. Be especially cautious when encountering horses. Step off the trail and let them pass.
- Dutch Hollow Road is open to street legal vehicles.
- The parking area/trailhead has an outhouse but no water tap.
- These trails have little shade and can be deathly hot at midday during midsummer when temperatures can reach nearly 100 degrees. Conversely, Dutch Hollow is a great choice for spring and fall.
- The Dutch Hollow area is open to hunting. Check with the Utah Division of Wildlife Resources for dates, (801) 538-4700, www.wildlife.utah.gov, or call Wasatch Mountain State Park: (435) 654-1791.
- Camping and fires are prohibited.
- Dogs must be leashed on Dutch Hollow Trails and throughout Wasatch Mountain State Park.

### Maps & More Information

- USGS 1:24,000: Heber City, Utah (trails are not shown).
- "Dutch Hollow Trails" (brochure) from Wasatch Mountain State Park: (435) 654-1791.

### Trailhead Access

From Heber, drive 2.8 miles west on UT 113 (100 South) to Midway, and turn right onto River Road. Take River Road 1.8 miles north then east to Dutch Canyon Road. Go 0.4 mile, and fork right on a dirt road, signed "WMSP," which accesses the trailhead/parking area.

From Park City, take UT 248 (Kearns Boulevard) to US 40. Drive 9.2 miles south on US 40, and turn right onto River Road, signed as "Midway, Wasatch Mountain State Park." After 2.3 miles, turn right on Dutch Canyon Road. Go 0.4 mile, and fork right on a dirt road, signed "WMSP," which accesses the trailhead/parking area.

# APPENDIX

# Sources of Additional Information

## Federal Government

### Uinta National Forest

Supervisor's Office
88 West 100 North
Provo, UT 84603
(801) 377-5780
www.fs.fed.us/r4/uinta/

Pleasant Grove Ranger District
390 North 100 East
Pleasant Grove UT 84062
(801) 785-3563

Heber Ranger District
2460 South Highway 40
P.O. Box 190
Heber City, UT 84032
(435) 654-0470

### Wasatch-Cache Nat'l Forest

Supervisor's Office
8236 Federal Building
125 S State St
S LC UT 84138 (801) 524-3900
www.fs.fed.us/r4/wcnf/

Kamas Ranger District
50 East Center St
Kamas UT 84036
(435) 783-4338

Public Lands Info. Center
c/o R.E.I.--Recreational Equipment Incorporated
3285 East and 3300 South
Salt Lake City, UT 84109
(801) 466-6411

## State Government

Utah Dept. of Natural Resources
1594 W North Temple
SLC UT 84114
(801) 538-7200
www.nr.utah.gov

Division of Parks & Recreation
(801) 538-7220
www.stateparks.utah.gov/

Wasatch Mountain State Park
PO Box 10
Midway, UT 84049
(435) 654-1791

Utah Geological Survey
Natural Resources Map and Bookstore
1594 W North Temple
Salt Lake City UT 84114
(801) 537-3300
www.mapstore.utah.gov/

## Local Government

Mountainlands Association of Governments
2545 N Provo Canyon Rd.
Provo, UT 84604
(801) 229-3848

Park City Municipal Corporation
P.O. Box 1480
Park City, Utah 84060
(435) 615-5000
www.parkcity.org

## Ski Areas

Deer Valley Resort
P.O. Box 1525
Park City, UT 84060
(435) 649-1000
1-800-424-DEER (3337)
www.deervalley.com

Park City Mountain Resort
P.O. Box 39
1310 Lowell Avenue
Park City, UT 84060
(435) 649-8111
1-800-222-7275
www.parkcitymountain.com/

The Canyons Resort
4000 Canyons Resort Drive
Park City UT 84098
(435) 649-5400
Adventure Desk: (435) 649-9619
www.thecanyons.com/

Deer Crest
P.O. Box 2129
Park City, UT 84060
(435) 655-8215

## Trail Organizations

International Mountain Bike Association (IMBA)
P.O. Box 7578
Boulder, CO. 80306
(303) 545-9011
1-888-442-4622
www.imba.com

Leave No Trace
www.lnt.org

Tread Lightly
298 24th Street Suite 325
Ogden UT 84401
1-800-966-9900
www.treadlightly.org

Mountain Trails Foundation
P.O. Box 754
Park City UT 84060
(435) 649-6839
www.mountaintrails.org/

Synderville Basin Special Recreation District
5705 Trailside Drive
P.O. Box 980127
Park City, UT 84098
Phone: (435) 649-1564
Fax: (435) 649-1567
www.basinrecreation.com

Historic Union Pacific Rail Trail State Park
c/o Mountain Trails Foundation
P.O. Box 754
Park City, Utah 84060
(435) 649-6839

The Endurance 100
http://www.thee100.com/

### Visitor Information

Park City Chamber of Commerce and Visitors Bureau
http://www.parkcityinfo.com/
P.O. Box 1630
Park City, UT 84060
(800) 453-1360
(435) 649-6100

Walk-in locations:
Park City Visitor Information Center
(435) 658-4541
750 Kearns Blvd
Open 9 a.m.-6 p.m., seven days a week

Park City Historic Museum
(435) 615-9559
528 Main Street
Open 10 a.m.-7 p.m. Monday-Saturday, and noon-6 p.m. on Sunday. Hours may vary during spring and fall

Heber Valley Chamber of Commerce & Visitor Center
475 North Main
Heber City, UT 84032
(435) 654-3666
www.hebervalleycc.org/

Park City Magazine
www.parkcitymagazine.com/

www.parkcity.com (Sponsored by Park City Magazine)

Official website for the state of Utah:
www.utah.gov

Utah Office of Tourism
Council Hall/Capitol Hill
300 North State
Salt Lake City, UT 84114
801-538-1900
www.travel.utah.gov

### Bicycling Sources

Cole Sport
1615 Park Ave.
Park City UT 84098
(435) 649-4806
www.colesport.com

Jans Mountain Recreation Experts
1600 Park Ave.
Park City UT 84060
(435) 649-4949
www.jans.com

White Pine Touring
1790 Bonanza Dr.
Park City UT 84060
(435) 649-8710
www.whitepinetouring.com

Summit Cycles and Snow
1571 W Redstone Center Dr.
Park City UT 84098
(435) 575-0355

Canyon Mountain Sports
4000 The Canyons Resort Dr.
Park City UT 84098
(435) 615-3440

Pearl Izumi
Tanger Outlet Stores
(435) 615-7800
www.pearlizumi.com

## About the Author

"Everyday's a holiday," says author Gregg Bromka when he's mountain biking in Utah's Wasatch Range. "Why go anywhere else when the trails are this good?"

What started as a hobby for Gregg in 1988, with the first version of this Wasatch guidebook, has evolved into an obsession to scout out mountain biking trails throughout Utah. His pursuit to share his experiences has lead to more than a half-dozen guidebooks over the years, with additional projects in the making. Through his efforts, may you discover the joy of off-road bicycling in Utah.